# SOCIAL NETWORK ANALYSIS

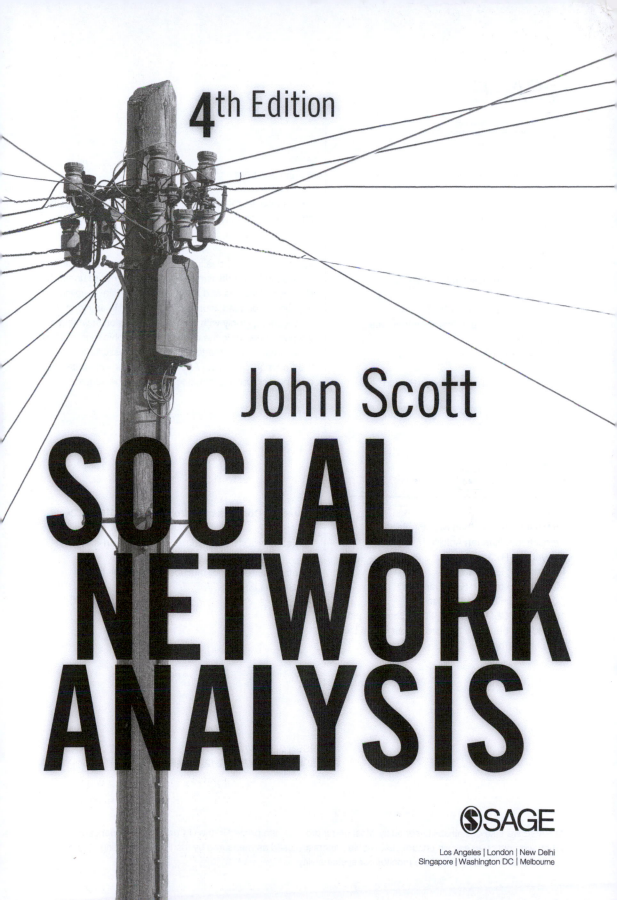

# 4th Edition

## John Scott

# SOCIAL NETWORK ANALYSIS

**$SAGE**

Los Angeles | London | New Delhi
Singapore | Washington DC | Melbourne

Los Angeles | London | New Delhi
Singapore | Washington DC | Melbourne

SAGE Publications Ltd
1 Oliver's Yard
55 City Road
London EC1Y 1SP

SAGE Publications Inc.
2455 Teller Road
Thousand Oaks, California 91320

SAGE Publications India Pvt Ltd
B 1/I 1 Mohan Cooperative Industrial Area
Mathura Road
New Delhi 110 044

SAGE Publications Asia-Pacific Pte Ltd
3 Church Street
#10-04 Samsung Hub
Singapore 049483

MIX
Paper from
responsible sources
FSC® C011748
FSC
www.fsc.org

Editor: Mila Steele
Editorial assistant: John Nightingale
Production editor: Ian Antcliff
Copyeditor: Richard Leigh
Proofreader: Emily Ayers
Marketing manager: Sally Ransom
Cover design: Shaun Mercler
Typeset by: C&M Digitals (P) Ltd, Chennai, India
Printed and bound by Ashford Colour Press Ltd,
Gosport, Hampshire

© John Scott 2017

First published 1991. Second edition 2000; reprinted 2001,
2003, 2004, 2005 (twice), 2006, 2007 (twice), 2009 (twice)
This edition 2017

**Library of Congress Control Number: 2016947736**

**British Library Cataloguing in Publication data**

A catalogue record for this book is available from
the British Library

ISBN 978-1-4739-5211-9
ISBN 978-1-4739-5212-6 (pbk)

# Contents

# List of Figures

# About the Author

John Scott was formerly Professor of Sociology and Pro Vice-Chancellor for Research at Plymouth University and was previously Professor of Sociology at Essex University and Leicester University. He is Honorary Professor at Copenhagen University, Essex University and Exeter University. He is a Fellow of the British Academy and a Fellow of the Academy of Learned Societies in the Social Sciences. An active member of the British Sociological Association, he has held the posts of Secretary, Treasurer, Chairperson and President and was awarded the 2014 Distinguished Service to Sociology Award. In 2013 he was awarded a CBE for services to social science. His most recent publications are *Conceptualising the Social World* (Cambridge University Press, 2011), *The Sage Handbook of Social Network Analysis* (edited with Peter Carrington, Sage, 2011), *Envisioning Sociology. Victor Branford, Patrick Geddes, and the Quest for Social Reconstruction* (with Ray Bromley, SUNY Press, 2013), and *The Palgrave Handbook of Sociology in Britain* (edited with John Holmwood, Palgrave, 2014).

# Preface to the Fourth Edition

This book was first published in 1991, appeared in a second edition in 2000, and a third edition in 2013. Advances in social network analysis have been quite rapid and successive editions have retained the basic shape and argument while incorporating the most important advances. In the second edition I was able to take especial account of advances in network visualisation, and in the third edition I added an account of approaches to network dynamics and a more extensive coverage of software. My aim has always been to simplify the techniques of social network analysis in order to make them accessible to those with a limited mathematical background. I hope, however, that I have done this without distorting the methods or over-simplifying. The book has been extensively used in teaching, and for this edition I have taken the opportunity to increase its usefulness to students. I have made some of the sub-headings rather more friendly and have included a short summary at the head of each chapter. I have also included a practical exercise at the end of each main chapter so that students can review and consolidate the key issues addressed in the chapters.

As with previous editions, I am grateful to a number of colleagues, correspondents and anonymous reviewers for corrections and suggestions that have helped to improve the book.

John Scott

# ONE

## What is Social Network Analysis?

he idea of the social network has become commonplace since the recent rapid development of 'social networking' websites and the growth of social media. Facebook, Twitter, LinkedIn, and similar websites encourage their users to build up lists of 'friends', 'followers' and 'contacts' that can grow through indirect connections to others. These sites attempt, in different ways, to take seriously the old adage that 'it is not *what* you know but *who* you know': a network of connections can provide help, support, opportunities, and even a sense of well-being that would not otherwise be possible. These social media develop the established business technique of 'networking', of meeting and greeting influential others at meetings, seminars and conferences.

In sociology, the idea of a social network has a far longer history and a much broader meaning. Social networks include digital and online networks but also include such networks as face-to-face relationships, political associations and connections, economic transactions among business enterprises, and geopolitical relations among nation states and international agencies. Over the years, sociologists have devised a variety of ways of examining and interpreting relationships of all kinds and so of subjecting them to systematic forms of analysis. What has come to be called *social network analysis* is not a practical guide to making friends or building business contacts, though it may be able to help in these activities. Rather, it comprises a broad approach to sociological analysis and a set of methodological techniques that aim to describe and explore the patterns apparent in the social relationships that individuals and groups form with each other. This reference to 'patterns' suggests that social network analysts are particularly interested in the construction of pictures and diagrams that disclose the patterns that are not generally apparent to human observers. This is, indeed, true, but social network analysis seeks to go beyond the visualisation of social relations to an examination of their structural properties and their implications for social action.

Social network analysis developed first in a relatively non-technical form from the structural concerns of sociologists and anthropologists who explored the 'interweaving' and 'interlocking' relations through which social actions are organised through using such textile-based metaphors as the 'fabric' and 'web' of social life. From the 1930s to the 1970s, an increasing number of these and other social scientists began to take these metaphors more seriously and began to use mathematics to investigate the 'density', 'connectedness' and 'texture' of social networks. Groups of specialists began to concern themselves with devising more systematic translations of the key ideas involved in the metaphor. From the early 1970s, an avalanche of technical work and specialist applications appeared, and it is from these writings that the key concepts of social network analysis have emerged. The various techniques developed have gradually been incorporated into the mainstream of data analysis and a wider sphere of applications.[1]

This development of techniques has encouraged many social researchers to seek the advantages of using social network analysis. However, when they turn to the technical literature they find that it is, indeed, highly 'technical'. Many who have seen the potential offered by network analysis have found it difficult to come to grips with the highly technical and mathematical language that necessarily characterises much of the discussion in the technical literature. Practical researchers rarely have the time or inclination to grapple with texts and sources that have, by and large, been produced by highly numerate specialists with a strong mathematical and methodological background. Those without a good mathematical competence find this literature especially daunting. Ostensibly introductory texts written by methodological specialists can often fail to adequately convey the possibilities that can be realised through the use of social network analysis.

I am not a specialist with any mathematical training, but a researcher who came to social network analysis because of the particular needs of data handling I had in a research project that I was undertaking on corporate power. Over the years I, too, have struggled to achieve a degree of understanding of what is involved in the principal measures of network structure and dynamics. I have attempted in this book to translate that mathematics into a simpler language – I hope without over-simplification – and to assess the relevance of particular mathematical models and measures for specific research needs. My aim in the book, therefore, is to draw on this experience and to present a systematic summary of these measures together with some illustrations of their uses. I have not attempted to present a comprehensive treatise on structural analysis in sociology (for these see Berkowitz, 1982; Crossley, 2010), nor have I tried to review the large number of applications of social network analysis that have been published (see, for example, Wellman and Berkowitz, 1988). Many powerful applications have appeared in the important series 'Structural Analysis in the Social Sciences' edited by Mark Granovetter (see, for example, Mizruchi and Schwartz, 1987; Schweizer and White, 1998; Ansell, 2001; Ikegami, 2005). My aim has been to identify the key concepts used in assessing network structure and to translate the mathematical discussions of these ideas into more comprehensible terms.

It is of the utmost importance that researchers *understand* the concepts that they use. There are, for example, a large number of different definitions of what constitutes a 'clique' and the various ideas related to it, and a researcher cannot simply take a computer program off the shelf and assume that the way in which it operationalises the clique concept will correspond with the idea that she or he has in mind. It is for this reason that I emphasise, throughout the book, that the choice of measures and decisions on their application to particular topics are matters that always require the *informed judgement* of the practising researcher. These choices and decisions involve theoretical and empirical questions that cannot be avoided by a reliance on mathematical measures that are only partly, if at all, understood. Only if the researcher has a clear understanding of the logic of a particular measure can he or she make an informed *sociological* judgement about its relevance for a particular piece of research.

# THE DATA USED IN SOCIAL NETWORK ANALYSIS

A first task must be to define the kinds of data for which social network analysis can most appropriately be used. Readers who are interested in applying it in their research will, undoubtedly, have some ideas about this already: it seems to be particularly useful for investigations of kinship patterns, community structure, interlocking directorships and so forth. What is essential is that the common features of the data used in these studies are clearly understood. The central assumption made here is that social network analysis is appropriate for 'relational data', and that techniques developed for the analysis of other types of data are likely to be of only limited value for research on social networks.

All social science data are rooted in cultural values and symbols. Unlike the physical data of the natural sciences, social science data are constituted through meanings, motives, definitions and typifications. As is well known, this means that the production of social science data necessarily involves a process of interpretation. Through such processes of interpretation, social scientists have formulated distinct types of data, for each of which distinct methods of analysis are appropriate.

The principal types of data used in social science are attribute data and relational data.[2] Attribute data are those that relate to the attitudes, opinions and behaviour of agents, in so far as these are regarded as the properties, qualities or characteristics that belong to them as individuals or groups. The items collected through surveys and interviews, for example, are often regarded simply as attributes of particular individuals that can be quantified and analysed through many of the available statistical procedures. The methods most appropriate for attribute data are those of variable and multivariate analysis, whereby attributes are measured as values of particular variables such as income, occupation and education.

Relational data, on the other hand, concern the contacts, ties and connections, and the group attachments and meetings that relate one agent to another and that cannot be reduced to the properties of the individual agents themselves. Relations are not the properties of agents, but of the relational systems of agents built up from connected pairs of interacting agents. The methods appropriate for relational data are those of network analysis, in which the relations are treated as expressing the linkages that run between agents. Relational data consist of agents as 'cases' together with the connections and affiliations that comprise their social relations. While it is, of course, possible to undertake quantitative and statistical counts of relations, and to investigate the statistical significance of relational patterns, network analysis comprises a body of qualitative measures for describing network structure and development.

Attribute and relational data are not the only types of data used in the social sciences, although they are the most widely discussed in texts on research methods. A third type comprises what can be called 'ideational' data, which directly describe the meanings, motives, definitions and typifications involved in actions. Techniques for the analysis of ideational data are less well developed than those for attribute and relational data, despite their centrality to the social sciences. Typological analysis of the kind outlined by Weber (1920–21), together with various forms of discourse analysis, is the most fruitful approach here, but these methods are in need of further development (see Layder, 1992).[3] Recent work in social network analysis has begun to explore the ways in which cultural meanings are discursively involved in the constitution of social relations and help to shape the networks into which they are formed (Emirbayer and Goodwin, 1994; White, 2008; Mische, 2003, 2011).

Although there are distinct types of data (as set out in Figure 1.1), each with their own appropriate methods of analysis, there is nothing specific about the methods of data collection and sampling that can be used to produce them. There is, for example, nothing significant that distinguishes methods for the collection of attribute data from those for the collection of relational data. The types of question used in a social survey may differ, for example, but the principles of survey construction and analysis are the same. The three types of data are often collected alongside one another as integral aspects of the same investigation. A study of political attitudes, for example, may seek to link these to group memberships and community attachments; or an investigation of interlocking directorships may seek to link these to the size and profitability of the companies involved. In either case, questionnaires, interviews, participant observation or documentary sources can be consulted in order to generate the data. This combination of approaches has been much discussed in recent literature on mixed methods or multi-methods research (Creswell, 1994; Creswell and Plano, 2007). While mixed methods are nothing new in social research, they have recently been given a more comprehensive rationale as a systematic research strategy. The aim is to combine the strengths – and so minimise the weaknesses – of quantitative and qualitative methods, seeing the two methodologies as complementary and as allowing a more objective and comprehensive triangulation on relational data. Their utilisation in social network analysis has recently been reviewed in Hollstein and Dominguez (2012).

Studies of friendship, for example, have tended to follow the lead of a pioneering study carried out by Moreno (1934), who used questionnaires to investigate friendship choices among selected children. In such studies, researchers simply ask respondents to identify their friends, by asking such questions as 'Please name the friends that you see most often' or 'Please name your four closest friends'. Methodological problems do, of course, arise with this kind of research: an unlimited choice question has sometimes been found to be difficult for respondents to answer; some people may not feel that they have four friends to name; and many people find an open question both time-consuming and tedious.[4] An alternative approach has been to use the roster choice method, in which respondents are asked 'Which of the following people would you regard as a friend?' This question requires considerable knowledge and preparation on the part of the researcher, who must compile a list with which respondents can be presented, but it has the advantage that it can be adapted by asking respondents to rank or to rate their affiliations, so indicating their intensity or significance. In both cases, however, these methodological problems of knowledge and respondent co-operation are exactly the same as those that arise in collecting information on attitudes and opinions. I will discuss these issues of data collection more fully in Chapter 3.

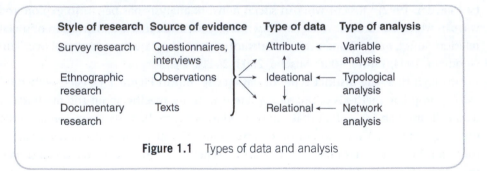

**Figure 1.1** Types of data and analysis

Relational data are central to the principal concerns of the sociological tradition, with its emphasis upon investigating the structure of social action. Structures are built from relations, and the structural concerns of sociology can be pursued through the collection and analysis of relational data. Paradoxically, most of the existing texts on research methods and methods of data collection give little attention to relational data, concentrating instead on the use of variable analysis for the investigation of attribute data. The formal, mathematical techniques of social network analysis, the methods that are specifically geared to relational data, have developed and have been discussed outside the mainstream of research methods. While they have made possible a number of spectacular breakthroughs in structural analysis, they have been largely inaccessible to many of those who would most wish to use them.

## IS THERE A NETWORK THEORY?

The growth of social network analysis has led many to see it as a new theoretical paradigm rather than simply a collection of techniques. Barnes and Harary (1983), for example, have argued that it is possible to advance from the use of formal concepts to the use of formal theory. They argue that the promise of social network analysis can be realised only if researchers move beyond the use of formal concepts for purely descriptive purposes (see also Granovetter, 1979). Mathematics consists of theorems that specify the determinate logical links between formal concepts. Barnes and Harary argue that if the formal concepts prove to be useful ways of organising relational data, then the theorems too should be applicable to those data. The application of theorems drawn from formal mathematics, then, 'reveals real world implications of the model that might otherwise have not been noticed or utilized by the designer of the model' (Barnes and Harary, 1983: 239).

Some have gone even further, seeing social network analysis as constituting a particular theoretical paradigm. There is, however, little agreement as to the basis of this theoretical approach. Most typically, social network analysis has been seen as rooted in a form of exchange theory (Emerson, 1962, 1964; Cook, 1977, 1982; Cook and Whitmeyer, 1992; Willer, 1999). This is sometimes seen as involving a wider 'transactionalist' approach (Bailey, 1969; Boissevain, 1974) or rational choice theory (Lin, 1982; see also Banck, 1973, and van Poucke, 1979). From this point of view, the making and breaking of social relations are seen as the rational decisions made by reflective agents acting according to their self-interest. This seems, to many, to be a plausible interpretation of the emphasis placed by network analysts on 'transactions' and the flow of resources. This argument is, however, too restrictive. While human actors may indeed act rationally, they do not act exclusively in terms of self-interest and may co-operate for a whole variety of reasons.

Social network analysis has also recently been linked with one particular substantive theory: the theory of social capital, first outlined in a systematic way by Putnam (2000). According to this point of view, social networks are a particular form of social capital that individuals can employ to enhance their advantages and opportunities. This has generated some powerful applications of social network analysis (Lin, 2001; Burt, 2005; Lin and Erikson, 2008), and it has, perhaps, been stimulated by the already noted growth of 'social networking' websites such as Facebook, MySpace and Twitter, through which people can build up networks of contacts and can come to regard their 'friends' as a source of social capital. Such a limitation of social network analysis is too restrictive. Social networks *are* relevant as sources of social capital, but they are more than this – they may, for example, be networks of economic transactions and political conflicts as well. Similarly, the 'social networks' built up through friendship and contact websites are simply one form of the myriad social connections in which individuals are engaged. Social network analysis must be seen as a comprehensive and all-encompassing approach to the relational features of social structures.

The actor-network theory derived from the work of Latour (2005) has sometimes been seen as a theoretical approach specific to the analysis of social networks. For these theorists, 'actors' are not to be equated with human individuals or even groups but are to be seen as constituted by the relations that connect individuals to material objects, other people, cultural meanings and environmental conditions. It is these 'networks' that act: people-in-cars are actors in traffic systems, people-with-armaments act in warfare, people-with-implements carry out medical operations, and so on. In each case, the particular form of action is incomprehensible without an awareness of the 'network' that acts. Important as these insights are, they do not incorporate ideas from social network analysis, and the approach of social network analysis continues to offer possibilities for investigating the social networks formed by the actor-networks.

The work of Manuel Castells (2000) has popularised the idea of a 'network society'. He has set out a view of the global structure of economic, political and cultural relations as a network and he has highlighted the need to examine the processes through which global integration has been achieved and its implications for business enterprises, nation states and social movements. Castells has rejected social network analysis as a tool of analysis, regarding it as a body of formal 'theory' that is too abstract to be useful in studying the global political economy. However, I have shown that social network analysis is not a specific body of theory but a collection of theoretically informed methods. As such, it has great potential for investigating the network society. In fact, powerful analyses of the world system have been undertaken using just these methods (see Maoz, 2011).

The relation between theory and method in social network analysis is best understood on the basis of the arguments of Emirbayer and his colleagues (Emirbayer, 1997; Emirbayer and Goodwin, 1994; see also Berkowitz, 1982), who see social network analysis as a specific implementation of the relational orientation to sociological explanation. This incorporates an awareness of the subjective meanings that define social relations and so is closely linked to cultural theories (see White, 1992a, 1993, 2008, and the discussion in Brint, 1992, and White, 1992b; see also Crossley, 2010, and Scott, 2011b: Ch. 6). Other writers have recently developed alternative, but complementary, conceptualisations of relational sociology that see it as implemented through social network analysis (Powell and Dépelteau, 2013a, 2013b). As such, a number of relational theories are compatible with the techniques of social network analysis: not only exchange theory but also structural functionalism, structuralism and many forms of Marxism. Social network analysis provides a vocabulary and set of measures for relational analysis but it does not imply the acceptance of any one particular theory of social structure (but see Borgatti and Lopez-Kidwell, 2011).

## AN OVERVIEW

This book is a guide or handbook for social network analysis, and not a text to be read through at one sitting. I have tried to confine subsidiary points and abstruse technicalities to footnotes, but a certain amount of complexity necessarily remains in the main text. I hope that this is at an absolute minimum. The newcomer to social network analysis is advised to read Chapters 2–4 and then to skim through the remainder of the book, coming back to points of difficulty later. Those readers with more familiarity with social network analysis may prefer to reverse this procedure, scanning Chapters 2–4 and then giving greater attention to a thorough review of Chapters 5–10. The chapters are best read in detail whenever a particular technique is to be used in a specific investigation. Although later chapters depend upon arguments raised in earlier chapters, each can be treated as a reference source to return to when attempting to use a particular technique.

Chapter 2 discusses the history of social network analysis, looking at its origins in early sociology and the social psychology of small groups and its subsequent development in sociological and social anthropological studies of factories and communities, and moving on to the advanced work undertaken by sociologists at Harvard University in the 1970s and physicists since the 1990s. The chapter shows how key theoretical ideas emerged within the various traditions of research and that the corpus of models and measures available today is the outcome of an accumulation of independently developed ideas that have come together since crucial work carried out from the 1970s.

In Chapter 3, I look at some of the issues that arise in data collection for social network analysis. I look at issues in defining the boundaries of social networks, in selecting and sampling relations for study, and in formulating questions and observational protocols for compiling relational data. In Chapter 4 I turn to the questions of how relational data are to be organised in databases that allow a ready analysis of their structural properties. I introduce matrices and sociograms as easy and intuitive ways of modelling relational data and I survey the leading computer programs that help in the analysis of social networks.

Chapter 5 introduces the basic building blocks of social networks. It starts with a consideration of the fundamental sociometric idea of representing a network as a 'graph' of 'points' and 'lines', and it shows how these can be used to develop concepts such as 'distance', 'direction' and 'density'. I also look at the relationship between the analysis of 'egocentric' networks focused on particular individuals and whole networks with global properties. In Chapter 6, I look at how issues of popularity, brokerage, mediation and exclusion can be explored through the 'centrality' of points and the 'centralisation' of whole networks, building on the argument of Chapter 5 to show how it is possible to move from local, 'egocentric' measures to global, 'socio-centric' ones. Chapter 7 turns to the investigation of groups, factions and social divisions, introducing the concepts of 'cliques' and 'circles' as the subgroups into which networks are divided. In Chapter 8 there is a shift of focus to the question of structural locations and class positions, utilising concepts of 'blocks' and their articulation into more complex 'topological' structures. Chapter 9 is concerned with the change and development of networks over time, using recent work on network dynamics. The chapter also considers recent studies of statistical approaches to explaining network dynamics and testing alternative hypotheses about network structure and change. Finally, Chapter 10 returns to the pictorial representation and modelling of social networks, showing how formal approaches to the display of relational data move beyond simple network diagrams to the production of multi-dimensional 'maps' of social structures and a variety of graphical methods for the visual display of network structure.

Most chapters conclude with a consideration of the application of the measures discussed in particular empirical studies. The investigations that are reviewed cover such areas as kinship, community structure, corporate interlocks and elite power. The aim of these illustrations from leading researchers is to give a glimpse of the potential offered by social network analysis. In Chapters 3–10 these are complemented by exercises in which readers are invited to engage with the concepts through devising and undertaking studies of their own.

## ———— FURTHER READING ————

Scott, J. (2012) *What is Social Network Analysis?* London: Bloomsbury Publishing.

Aims to give an introduction to the area that assumes no prior knowledge.

Scott, J. and Carrington, P. (eds) (2011) *The Sage Handbook of Social Network Analysis*. London: Sage Publications.

A comprehensive reference book that provides introductory chapters and more advanced discussions that you will want to come back to throughout your studies.

# TWO

## The History of Social Network Analysis

This chapter provides:

- A rapid overview of the ways in which social network analysis has developed in sociology, social anthropology and social psychology
- Some of the key ideas and those who originated them
- A discussion of how developments in analysis have been influenced by developments in mathematics and computing

A number of diverse strands have shaped the development of present-day social network analysis. These strands have intersected with one another in a complex and fascinating history, sometimes fusing and at other times diverging onto their separate paths.[1] A clear lineage for the mainstream of social network analysis can, nevertheless, be constructed from this complex history. In this lineage there are three main traditions: the sociometric analysts, who worked on small groups and produced many technical advances using the methods of graph theory; the researchers of the 1930s, who explored patterns of interpersonal relations and the formation of 'cliques'; and the social anthropologists, who built on both of these strands to investigate the structure of 'community' relations in tribal and village societies. These traditions were eventually brought together in the 1960s and 1970s, when contemporary social network analysis was forged (Figure 2.1).

The founders of sociology saw societies as social organisms or systems with 'structures' of institutions and relations. Few of them, however, explored social structure in any detail. It was principally among German theorists such as Simmel, Vierkandt and von Wiese that social structure began to be conceptualised through the metaphor of the 'web' or 'network'. This concept was introduced as a way of emphasising the openness and flexibility of social structure, which was seen as the constantly shifting outcome of the 'interweaving' actions of individuals and groups. The metaphors of weaving, fabric, web and network came to be employed more widely during the 1920s and 1930s and provided a distinctive way of approaching the study of social relations.

A group of German émigrés influenced by Wolfgang Köhler's 'gestalt' theory were working in the United States on cognitive and social psychology during the 1930s. Their work on webs of relations led to a considerable amount of research on the problems of sociometry and 'group dynamics'. Using laboratory methods or laboratory-like case studies, they explored group structure and its influence on the flow of information and ideas through groups. At around the same time, anthropologists and sociologists at Harvard University were developing some of the ideas of the British social anthropologist Radcliffe-Brown. They produced important factory and community studies that documented the importance of informal, interpersonal relations in social systems. In Britain, principally at Manchester University, a parallel line of development from the work of Radcliffe-Brown emphasised the analysis of conflict and contradiction and applied these ideas in studies of African tribal societies and, a little later, in rural and small-town Britain.

Building on the earlier traditions, they made considerable advances in combining mathematics with substantive social theory. Not until well into the 1960s, however, did the final breakthrough to a well-developed methodology of social network analysis occur. It was at Harvard that Harrison White began to extend his investigations of the mathematical basis of social structure, forging together some of the key insights of his North American predecessors and creating a unique synthesis that was developed and enlarged by the students he trained. As these students moved through their careers to departments across the world, the arguments of White and the work of the British

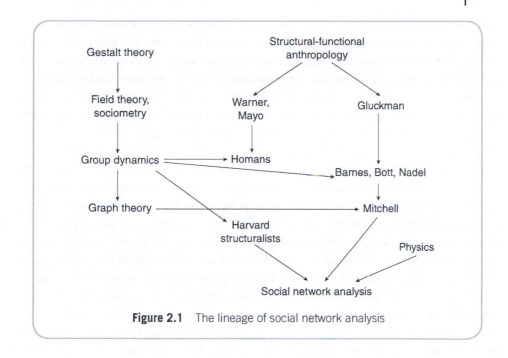

**Figure 2.1**   The lineage of social network analysis

researchers were united into a complex but increasingly coherent framework of social network analysis.

Most recently, a number of physicists have begun to explore networks of all kinds and to apply their work to social phenomena. Ignoring or unaware of the earlier work in social psychology, social anthropology and sociology, they rediscovered a number of key ideas but, along the way, they introduced some novel ideas on network dynamics.

In this chapter, I provide a brief outline of the main traditions of social network analysis and the leading innovations of the Harrison White group at Harvard. I will then summarise the recent work of the social physicists. This review will highlight the continuing topics of debate in social network analysis, and I show how these are rooted in the central substantive concerns of sociology.

# THE SOCIOGRAM AND SOCIOMETRY

The gestalt tradition in psychology, associated principally with the work of Wolfgang Köhler (see Köhler, 1925), stresses the organised patterns through which thoughts and perceptions are structured. These organised patterns are regarded as 'wholes' or systems with properties distinct from those of their 'parts' and that, furthermore, *determine* the nature of those parts. The individual objects that people perceive, for example, are seen in particular ways because they are, literally, preconceived within the complex and organised conceptual schemes of the human mind. The objects of the world are not perceived independent of these mental schemes but are, in a fundamental sense, constituted by them. Social psychology in this research tradition has stressed the social determination of these conceptual schemes and has, therefore, emphasised the influence of group organisation and its associated social climate on individual perceptions.

Many of the leading gestalt theorists fled from Nazi Germany during the 1930s and settled in the United States, where Kurt Lewin, Jacob Moreno (who had migrated there in 1925) and Fritz Heider became prominent, though rather different, exponents of a gestalt-influenced social psychology. Lewin established a research centre at the Massachusetts Institute of Technology, later moving it to Michigan, and this centre became the focus of research on social perception and group structure in the approach called 'group dynamics'. Moreno, on the other hand, explored the possibility of using psychotherapeutic methods to uncover the structure of friendship choices. Using experimentation, controlled observation and questionnaires, he and his colleagues aimed to explore the ways in which people's group relations serve as both limitations and opportunities for their actions and, therefore, for their personal psychological development. Although the word 'sociometric' is particularly associated with Moreno, it is an apt description of the general style of research that arose from the gestalt tradition.

Moreno's work was firmly rooted in a therapeutic orientation towards interpersonal relations, reflecting his early medical training and psychiatric practice in Vienna. His aim, elaborated in a major book (Moreno, 1934; see also Bott, 1928) and in the founding of a journal (*Sociometry*, founded in 1937), was to investigate how psychological well-being is related to the structural features of what he termed 'social configurations' (Moreno and Jennings, 1938). These configurations are the results of the concrete patterns of interpersonal choice, attraction, repulsion, friendship, and other relations in which people are involved, and they are the basis upon which large-scale 'social aggregates', such as the economy and the state, are sustained and reproduced over time. Moreno's concern for the relationship between small-scale interpersonal configurations and large-scale social aggregates is a very clear expression of some of the leading ideas of classical German sociology, most notably those developed in the works of Weber, Tönnies and Simmel. Indeed, the latter's so-called formal sociology directly anticipated many sociometric concerns (Simmel, 1908; Aron, 1964).

Moreno's chief innovation was to devise the 'sociogram' as a way of representing the formal properties of social configurations.[2] These could, he held, be represented in diagrams analogous to those of spatial geometry, with individuals represented by 'points' and their social relationships to one another by 'lines'. This idea is now so well established and taken for granted that its novelty in the 1930s is difficult to appreciate. Before Moreno, none of those who had written of 'webs' of connection, the 'social fabric' and, on occasion, of 'networks' of relations, had attempted to systematise this metaphor into an analytical diagram.

For Moreno, social configurations had definite and discernible structures, and the mapping of these structures into a sociogram allowed a researcher to visualise the channels through which, for example, information could flow from one person to another and one

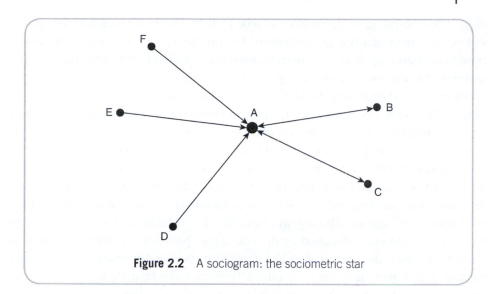

**Figure 2.2** A sociogram: the sociometric star

individual could influence another. Moreno argued that the construction of sociograms allowed researchers to identify leaders and isolated individuals, to uncover asymmetry and reciprocity, and to map chains of connection. One of his principal sociometric concepts was that of the sociometric 'star': the recipient of numerous and frequent choices from others who, therefore, holds a position of great popularity and leadership. For Moreno, the concept of the star pointed to an easily visualised picture of the relations among group members. In Figure 2.2, for example, person A is the recipient of friendship choices from all the other members of a group, yet A gives reciprocal friendship choices only to persons B and C. A is, therefore, the star of attraction within the group. This work had some influence on community research (Lundberg, 1936; Lundberg and Steele, 1938) and became an important area of research in the sociology of education (Jennings, 1948; Evans, 1962).

Lewin's early work on group behaviour was published in a book in which he outlined his view that group behaviour is to be seen as determined by the field of social forces in which the group is located (Lewin, 1936). A social group, he argued, exists in a field: a social 'space' that comprises the group together with its surrounding environment. But the environment of the group is not seen as something purely external to and independent of the group. The environment that really matters to group members is the perceived environment. The perceived environment is what writers in the symbolic interactionist tradition have called the 'definition of the situation', and its social meaning is actively constructed by group members on the basis of their perceptions and experiences of the contexts in which they act. The group and its environment are, therefore, elements within a single field of relations. The structural properties of this social space, Lewin argued, can be analysed through the mathematical techniques of topology and set theory (Lewin, 1951). The aim of 'field theory' is to explore, in mathematical terms, the interdependence between group and environment in a system of relations (Martin, 2003), a view that brought Lewin close to later developments in general system theory. (See Buckley, 1967, for an application of this framework to sociology.)

In a topological approach, the social field is seen as comprising points connected by 'paths'. The points, as in a sociogram, represent individual persons, their goals, or their actions, while the paths represent the interactional or causal sequences that connect them. The field model, therefore, describes causal and interactional interdependencies in social configurations. The paths that run between points tie them together, and the pattern of paths divides a field into a number of discrete 'regions'. Each region is separated from the others by the absence of paths between them: paths run within but not between the regions. The opportunities that individuals have to move about in their social world are determined by the boundaries between the different regions of the field in which they are located. The constraints imposed by these boundaries are the 'forces' that determine group behaviour. The total social field, therefore, is a field of forces acting on group members and shaping their actions and experiences.

## BALANCE AND GROUP DYNAMICS

A further strand of cognitive psychology that made a major contribution to the development of social network analysis was the work of Heider. His initial research had been into the social psychology of attitudes and perception, and he was especially concerned with how a person's various attitudes towards others are brought into a state of 'balance'. The different attitudes taken by an individual are unbalanced in his or her mind when they produce a state of psychological tension. Psychological balance, therefore, depends on the holding of attitudes that do not contradict one another. Heider's particular concern was with interpersonal balance, that is, with the congruence (or lack of congruence) among attitudes to other people. He was concerned, for example, with how a person who is emotionally close to two other people might respond to any perceived conflict or hostility between them. In such a situation, there is an imbalance in the whole field of attitudes held by the individuals. Heider (1946) held that attitudes can be seen, at their simplest, as positive or negative. 'Balance' exists among a set of attitudes when they are similar to one another in their sign: all positive or all negative. If person A likes person B, and person B likes person C, a state of balance exists only if A also likes C, as all the attitudes are then 'positive'. It is important to note that Heider, like Lewin, adopted an explicitly phenomenological stance that relates to the way in which the world is perceived from the standpoint of a focal individual. From this point of view, the important thing is not the actual relation between B and C, but A's perception (accurate or otherwise) of this relationship: 'balance' refers to a psychological state and not to any actually existing relations in a social group.

While field theory itself, as a theoretical framework for social analysis, seemed to prove an intellectual dead-end, Lewin's advocacy of mathematical models of group relations was a fruitful foundation for later work. Of particular importance in building on the insights of Lewin was Dorwin Cartwright, who, together with the mathematician Frank Harary, pioneered the application of a mathematical approach called graph theory to group behaviour (Cartwright and Zander, 1953; Harary and Norman, 1953; see also Bavelas, 1950, and Festinger et al., 1950). Graph theory had first been formulated by König (1936) but, like many works published in Germany in the 1930s, it had little immediate impact on the wider intellectual world. Its significance for the mainstream of intellectual effort was appreciated only in 1950, when his book was republished in the United States and its ideas were developed in the work of Harary and Norman (1953). These mathematical ideas made possible a crucial breakthrough in a theory of what came to be called 'group dynamics'.

This breakthrough consisted of moving from the concept of cognitive balance in individual minds to that of interpersonal balance in social groups. Newcomb (1953) was one of the first researchers to move in this direction, arguing that there is a tendency for two people who are close to one another to each adopt similar attitudes towards third parties or events. Researchers could, therefore, build models of the systematic interdependence between the attitudes held by different individuals within a group. This claim was generalised in the theoretical framework outlined by Cartwright and Harary (1956). In the hands of these writers, the insights of Lewin, Moreno and Heider were brought together in a novel and more powerful synthesis. (See also Harary et al., 1965, which was under preparation from the mid-1950s.) The attempt to apply mathematics to the structure of group relations was not, of course, a new idea – as well as the work of Lewin there were other early contributions, using different mathematical models, at the end of the 1940s (for example, Bavelas, 1948; Festinger, 1949). Building on Lewin's work, however, Cartwright, Zander and Harary evolved powerful models of group cohesion, social pressure, co-operation, power and leadership.

Cartwright and Harary (1956) took up Moreno's idea of representing groups as collections of points connected by lines and treated the resulting sociogram as a 'graph'. The network of actual interpersonal relations among group members could be analysed, they argued, by using the mathematical ideas of graph theory. Graph theory has nothing to do with the graphs of variables familiar to many people from school mathematics. Instead, a graph is simply a set of lines connecting points, and graph theory consists of a body of mathematical axioms and formulae that describe the properties of the patterns formed by the lines. In the work of Cartwright and Harary, the points in a graph represent individuals and the lines show their relations with one another. The lines in a graph can be given signs (+ or –) to indicate whether they refer to 'positive' or 'negative' relations, and they can be given arrow heads to indicate the 'direction' of the relationships. The direction attached to a line is a way of distinguishing, for example, person A's orientation to person B from B's orientation to A: person A may direct a positive relation to B (he likes B), while person B may direct a negative relation to A (she hates A). Moreno's sociograms (Figure 2.2) are examples of 'directed' graphs. This construction of signed and directed graphs allowed Cartwright and Harary to analyse group structure from the standpoint of each of its members simultaneously, and not simply from the standpoint of a particular focal individual. It was, therefore, a major move forward in a strictly sociological direction.

The fundamental argument of Cartwright and Harary can most easily be understood by considering undirected graphs. In an undirected graph, the relation of A to B is assumed to be identical with the relation of B to A. This can occur, for example, because their attitudes are perfectly reciprocated or because they have a common involvement in the same activity. For this reason, the line between any two points can be studied without considering its direction. In an undirected graph, 'balance' describes simply the particular pattern of signs attached to the lines that make up the graph. In Figure 2.3, for example, three different graphs of relations among three actors are shown. In graph (i), A and B have a positive relationship to one another and the whole graph is balanced because of the existence of positive relations between A and C and between B and C. In graph (ii), however, a negative relation between A and C puts a strain on the positive relation between A and B, because of the positive relation that exists between B and C: the graph is unbalanced. Put simply: if my friend likes someone to whom I am antagonistic, there is likely to be a strain in the relation between us. I might be expected to respond to this by persuading my friend to give up his or her liking of the third party, by altering my own relation to that person, or by breaking the relationship with my friend. Each participant in an unbalanced network

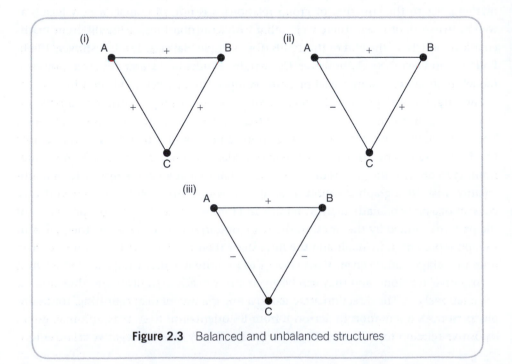

**Figure 2.3** Balanced and unbalanced structures

will be under a similar strain and so will be attempting to resolve the tensions that they experience.[3] Group relations are, therefore, in a dynamic flux, with the final balanced outcome – if it is ever achieved – resulting from the actions and compromises of all the participants involved. Responses aimed at restoring balance to the group can be mapped in new graphs with different signs attached to the various lines. Graph (iii), for example, represents the situation where A successfully persuades B to dislike C, and so restores balance.

Cartwright and Harary argued that complex social structures can be seen as built from simple structures. More particularly, they are composed of overlapping 'triads' such as those depicted in Figure 2.3. Simple triadic structures are the building blocks of larger social structures, and the properties of complex networks of social relations can, they argue, be derived from an analysis of these building blocks (see Hage and Harary, 1983, 1991). In the simplest case, for example, a whole network is balanced when all of its constituent triads are balanced.[4] While the idea of a balanced triad is, perhaps, fairly clear and comprehensible, the idea that a large and complex network is 'balanced' is less so. Indeed, the claim might seem to be neither an interesting nor a useful piece of information. This would, however, be an erroneous conclusion to draw. A very important finding, which has been derived from the work of Cartwright and Harary, is that any balanced graph, no matter how large or complex, can be divided into two subgroups with rather interesting properties: the relations within each of these subgroups will be positive, while those between the subgroups will be negative. Thus, a balanced social network, defined, for example, by relations of solidarity, will consist of two cohesive subgroupings between which there is conflict and antagonism.

In the simple case where all the relations in a network are positive, one of these subgroups will be an empty or null set: all points will fall into a single group.[5] This will not be the case in more complex balanced structures, and a division into subgroups might highlight important structural features of the network. So, the identification of a network as balanced or unbalanced is merely a first step in the move towards its 'decomposition' into its constituent subgroups. Much of the mathematical work concerned with the analysis of balance has centred on the attempt to discover such decomposition techniques. The successful decomposition of a balanced network would allow researchers to derive an understanding of network structure simply from information about the relations between individuals. This discovery has enormous implications for the understanding of group structure, and James Davis (1967, 1968) has been a leading figure in the attempt to discover the conditions under which it might be possible to move towards more realistic decomposition techniques that would allow researchers to identify the existence of more than two subgroups within a network. Recent developments in the analysis of balance have been discussed in Antal et al. (2006).[6]

The concept of balance has been especially influential in experimental studies of group co-operation and leadership and has resulted in one classic study of small group behaviour in a natural setting (Festinger et al., 1959). Many of the ideas that emerged from the sociometric tradition of small group research were, however, taken up by researchers with an interest in general system theory and in the mathematical aspects of cybernetics and rational action. Indeed, the first applications of sociometric ideas to large-scale social systems were initiated by just such researchers. These studies explored the spread of disease from one person to another through chains of contacts, aiming at the derivation of predictive epidemiological models of contagion. A leading figure in this work was Rapoport, who elaborated on the formal implications of the empirical studies (Rapoport, 1952, 1958) and helped to stimulate an interest in applying similar ideas to the transmission of ideas and innovations. Although such work had been undertaken before, along with investigations of the spread of rumour and gossip, the 1960s saw the first major works of this kind to use network concepts (Fararo and Sunshine, 1964; Coleman et al., 1966; see also Rogers, 1962).

## INFORMAL ORGANISATION AND COMMUNITY RELATIONS

Theoretical work in the sociometric tradition, I have argued, involved a considerable effort to uncover ways of decomposing networks into their constituent subgroups. This has also been a feature of the research tradition that developed at Harvard University during the 1930s and 1940s. In this line of work, the investigation of 'informal relations' in large-scale systems led to the empirical discovery that these systems did, in fact, contain cohesive subgroupings. The task that the researchers then faced, and only partly solved, was to discover techniques that could disclose the subgroup structure of any social system for which relational data are available.

Radcliffe-Brown and, through him, Durkheim, were the major influences on this tradition of research. Radcliffe-Brown's ideas had been especially influential among anthropologists in Australia, where he had taught for a number of years. His influence was particularly strong in the work of W. Lloyd Warner, who moved to Harvard in 1929 to work with the Australian psychologist Elton Mayo. The two men worked together in a series of closely related investigations of factory and community life in America, seeing these investigations as applications of the structural concerns of Radcliffe-Brown.

Mayo had moved to Harvard in 1926 in order to take on a leading role in the newly developed research programme of its business school. His principal contact with sociological ideas was through the dominating influence of the biologist Lawrence Henderson, who actively promoted the sociological ideas of Pareto among his Harvard colleagues. Henderson held that this was the only appropriate basis for a truly scientific sociology and that it was, furthermore, the only viable political bulwark against revolutionary Marxism. Mayo's psychological concern for individual motivation was complemented by a growing awareness of what Pareto termed the 'non-rational' components of action. Economic action, for Mayo, was not a purely rational form of action, but was structured also by non-rational sentiments such as those of group solidarity. Pareto was also the great exponent of elite theory, and Mayo saw that a managerial elite that recognised this influence of group relations on economic motivation could most successfully control worker behaviour. Warner's contribution to the Harvard research programme, as befitted a trained field worker, showed a greater concern for detailed investigations of the actual patterns of group behaviour found in particular social settings. To Mayo's theoretical and applied concerns, Warner brought an empirical dimension. Despite these differences – or, perhaps, because of them – the work that the two began at Harvard was crucially important in the development of social network analysis. Their careers overlapped there for only six years, but their research proved massively influential. The major projects that they and their colleagues undertook were investigations of the Hawthorne electrical factory in Chicago and a study of the New England community of 'Yankee City'.

The Hawthorne studies have become classics of social investigation, and they need little mention here (see the useful discussion in Rose, 1975). Briefly, a series of studies of worker efficiency had been undertaken during the 1920s by managers in the Hawthorne works of the Western Electric Company in Chicago. These managers were attempting to discover how alterations in the physical conditions of work (heating, lighting, rest periods, and so on) affected productivity, and they discovered, to their considerable surprise, that productivity increased almost regardless of the particular changes that were made. In an attempt to understand these paradoxical results, the managers called on Mayo and his Harvard team for some guidance in restructuring the research programme. Mayo concluded that the crucial factor responsible for increased productivity had been the very fact of participation in the research project: the workers were pleased that their managers were taking an interest in them, and their sense of involvement and integration into the life of the factory motivated them to greater efforts.

With the advice of Warner, the Hawthorne investigators began an anthropological study, observing workgroup behaviour in a natural setting within the factory. The scene of their observations was the bank wiring room, and the team approached their research in the factory in the same way that a social anthropologist would carry out fieldwork in a village in an alien society. They recorded all that they could observe of group behaviour, aiming to construct a full anthropological account. The particular importance of the Hawthorne studies in the development of social network analysis lies in their use of sociograms to report on group structure. Just as the kinship structure of a village community might be illustrated by a genealogical diagram, the Hawthorne team constructed sociograms to illustrate the structure of informal relations within the workgroup.

The principal report on the Hawthorne studies (Roethlisberger and Dickson, 1939: 500ff.) includes various sociograms constructed by the research team.[7] They saw these as reflecting the 'informal organisation' of the bank wiring room, as opposed to the formal organisation that was depicted in the managerial organisation chart. Sociograms were constructed to show each of a number of aspects of group behaviour: involvement in games, controversy over the opening of windows, job trading, helping, and friendships and antagonisms. The Hawthorne study was the first major investigation to use sociograms to describe the actual relations observed in real situations. In their diagrams, people are represented by circles and their relationships by arrows. The similarity of these diagrams to the sociograms subsequently developed by the group dynamics researchers is obvious, but the researchers give no indication of how they hit upon the idea of such diagrams. There is, for example, no discussion of the evolving work of Moreno. It will be seen from Figure 2.4, however, that the diagrams resemble not only the formal organisation charts used by managers, but also the electrical wiring diagrams that would have been a very familiar feature of the plant. It must be assumed that the influence of Warner encouraged the researchers to adapt conventional anthropological kinship diagrams by drawing on these other influences of the organisational setting.

In drawing the sociograms of the bank wiring group, certain general conventions were followed, but these were artistic rather than sociological. The precise location of each circle on the page was decided by the researcher, the principal constraint being simply that the members of any subgroup identified by the observers should be drawn as close to one another as possible. Apart from this, purely artistic principles of clarity and simplicity governed the design: the number of lines that cross one another, for example, should be as small as possible, and the lines should not vary too much in length. The subgroups identified by the researchers – they called them 'cliques' – were those that the workers themselves recognised as important elements in their situation. Much as any anthropologist might use 'native' categories and concepts as pointers to the structural features of group life, the workers' own terms were taken as indicators of the existence of 'cliques'. 'The group in front' and 'the group in back' were identified from observations of group behaviour and from group vocabulary as the two subgroups within the bank wiring group. There was no attempt to use the sociograms themselves to identify sociometrically defined 'cliques'; the socially perceived subgroups were simply mapped onto the sociograms.[8] Having plotted group structure

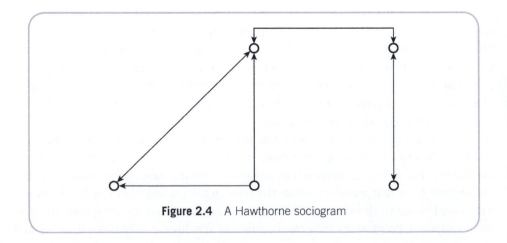

**Figure 2.4**  A Hawthorne sociogram

in this way, however, the researchers made little further use of the diagrams. They appear to lack any theoretical understanding of how social networks might shape the behaviour of individuals.

Warner, meanwhile, had begun a study of the small New England city of Newburyport, to which he gave the pseudonym 'Yankee City'. His fieldwork was carried out between 1930 and 1935, and the research was conceived as a full-blown anthropological study of a modern, urban community. As such, it combined observation with the use of interviews and historical documents. The end of the main phase of fieldwork, however, coincided with a growing antagonism between Warner and Mayo, and Warner left Harvard for Chicago University, where his mentor Radcliffe-Brown was already a visiting professor. Warner and Radcliffe-Brown had two years together at Chicago, a period when the analysis of the fieldwork material from Yankee City would have been at its most intense. Warner spent the rest of his career at Chicago, and it was from there that he supervised and sponsored a number of related studies, most importantly that of 'Old City' in the Deep South.[9]

Warner's own early work had used the methods and ideas of Durkheim and Radcliffe-Brown in the traditional manner to study an Australian tribe, and it was through his contact with Mayo that he first formulated the idea of applying anthropological methods to the study of a modern urban community. Warner had originally intended to study the district of Chicago in which the Hawthorne works were located, but the work of the Chicago school of sociologists (Park et al., 1925) forced him to conclude that the district was 'disorganised' and so would not be amenable to anthropological investigation. Warner felt that only in New England and in parts of the southern states would he find the kind of established and integrated communities that he wished to study.

Warner's work shows a rich variety of theoretical influences. While the influence of Radcliffe-Brown was uppermost, he allied this with an organismic, system model of society which undoubtedly shows the influence of Henderson's interpretation of Pareto. This led Warner to emphasise such factors as stability, cohesion and integration in the structuring of communities. But he also drew on Simmel's ideas of reciprocal relations and of the influence of numbers on group life. It was, I have suggested, Simmel (1908) who pioneered the analysis of dyads and triads as the building blocks of social life. Following the terminology of Simmel and other German sociologists, also adopted by Moreno, Warner talked of social configurations, holding that the social organisation of a community consists of a web of relations through which people interact with one another.

The social configuration that comprises a modern community, argued Warner, consists of various types of subgroup, such as the family, the church, classes and associations. Alongside these is also to be found the type of subgroup that he termed the 'clique': an informal association of people among whom there is a degree of group feeling and intimacy and in which certain group norms of behaviour have been established (Warner and Lunt, 1941: 32). A clique is 'an intimate non-kin group, membership in which may vary in numbers from two to thirty or more people' (Warner and

Lunt, 1941: 110).[10] For Warner, therefore, the clique has the same social significance in community studies as the informal group had in the Hawthorne factory studies. The concept describes a particular configuration of informal interpersonal relations.

The Yankee City researchers claimed that a large number of these cliques could be identified in the city. The major cliques were the groups that many Yankee City respondents referred to by such terms as 'our crowd', 'our circle', and so on. Having discovered the existence of these cliques from the comments of those they studied, Warner and his associates claimed that they were second in importance only to the family in placing people in society. People are integrated into communities through 'informal' and 'personal' relations of family and clique membership, not simply through the 'formal' relations of the economy and political system. Any person may be a member of several different cliques, and 'such overlapping in clique membership spreads out into a network of interrelations which integrate almost the entire population of a community in a single vast system of clique relations' (Warner and Lunt, 1941: 111). This is undoubtedly one of the earliest, if not the earliest use of network terminology to describe the structuring of whole societies into subgroups.

The Yankee City reports used various diagrams to model such things as class structure and family organisation, and it is hardly surprising that the researchers also constructed clique diagrams. To represent this social structure they drew cliques as a series of intersecting circles in a Venn diagram (Warner and Lunt, 1941: 113), but they did not advance to any formal, structural analyses of these diagrams. In the second volume of the Yankee City report, however, there was an attempt to undertake what would now be termed a 'positional analysis' (Warner and Lunt, 1942: 52, Figure 10). They presented a series of tables that show the numbers of people occupying each of a number of structurally defined positions. Figure 2.5 shows the format of one of these diagrams. Having identified six classes and 31 types of clique in Yankee City, Warner and Lunt cross-classified class and clique membership. Each type of clique was defined by the predominant class composition of its overall membership, and the cells of the table show the numbers of people in each class who were members of each of the 31 types of clique.[11] From among the large number of possible combinations – 6 times 31, or 186 – they argued that only 73 positions actually occurred. All the remaining cells in the table were empty. By constructing similar tables for class against each of a number of other social groupings (types of formal association, types of family, etc.), they were able to combine the tables together, stacking them one on top of another, and identified 89 structural positions in the overall, combined network.[12] The particular procedure they employed was rather cumbersome, and it is unnecessary to go further into its outmoded operation, but the Yankee City work remains interesting for its attempt to pioneer such methods of formal structural analysis.

Colleagues of Warner began an investigation of 'Old City', in the South (actually Natchez, Mississippi), during 1936, and in this research they further explored the idea of the 'clique' (Davis et al., 1941). In looking at 'colored society' in Old City, they followed Warner's method of seeing cliques as intersecting circles, mapping the

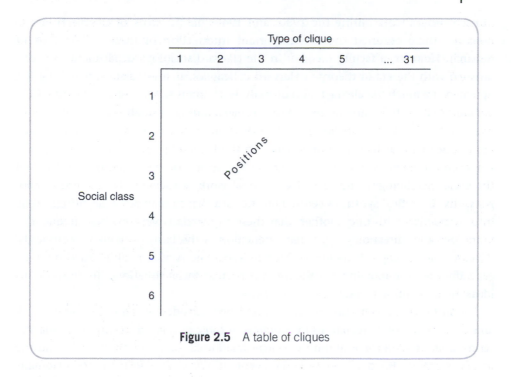

**Figure 2.5**   A table of cliques

overlapping memberships of the most active cliques in a space defined by class and age (Davis et al., 1941: 213, Figure 12). They referred to 'social space' and its 'two dimensions', but there is no explicit mention of any of the work of Lewin on topological field models. The major innovation of this study was its attempt to explore the internal structure of cliques. The researchers argued that a clique could be seen as comprising three layers: a 'core' of those who participate together most often and most intimately; a 'primary circle' of those who participate jointly with core members on some occasions but never as a group by themselves; and a 'secondary circle' of those who participate only infrequently and so are 'almost non-members'. On the basis of their investigation of 60 cliques, using similar techniques to those of the Yankee City researchers, they suggested a number of structural hypotheses about the connections between cliques. They argued, for example, that peripheral, lower-class members of a clique might be able to contact higher-class members of another clique only through the higher-class core members of their own clique.

## MATRICES AND CLIQUES

The ideas that emerged in the Hawthorne, Yankee City and Old City research developed in parallel with those of the sociometric tradition of small group research, but there is no evidence that the leading figures in the two traditions were even aware of each other's work during the 1930s and 1940s. In the work of George Homans, however, there occurred the first important intersection of these two strands of research. Homans, a faculty member in the Harvard sociology department, was dissatisfied with the grand theory of Harvard colleagues such as Parsons, which he felt operated at a much too abstract level of analysis. Homans felt that social theory had to be built up from the foundations of a firm understanding of small-scale social interaction. To this end, he began, during the late 1940s, to try to synthesise the mass of small group research that had been undertaken in the United States. He aimed at nothing less than a theoretical synthesis of this work, drawing on the experimental work of the social psychologists and the observational work of sociologists and anthropologists. His theoretical synthesis centred on the idea that human activities bring people into interaction with one another, that these interactions vary in their 'frequency', 'duration' and 'direction',[13] and that interaction is the basis on which 'sentiments' develop among people. Homans saw Moreno's sociometry as providing a methodological framework for applying this theory to particular social situations. To illustrate his ideas, he re-examined a number of earlier studies.

One section of the Old City report has achieved considerable fame among network analysts because of its reanalysis by Homans. A table of relations is, in mathematical terms, a matrix and Davis and his colleagues had used matrix methods to look at the involvement of 18 women in 14 social events (Davis et al., 1941: Ch. 7).[14] Homans took these data, presented them in matrix form, and set out one of the first published statements of the method of 'matrix rearrangement' in social network analysis (see also Festinger, 1949). The Old City matrix shows 18 rows (women) and 14 columns (events), with a cross placed in a cell to represent the participation of a particular woman at a specific event. The raw matrix, argued Homans, was not necessarily arranged in any significant order: the columns, for example, were simply arranged in the date order of the events. For this reason, the crosses appear to be distributed at random across the matrix. A rearrangement of the rows and columns of the matrix, bringing together the events in which particular women predominate, would, he believed, uncover important structural features of the clique. He described his method as follows:

> we put in the center the columns representing events ... at which a large number of women were present, and we put toward the edges the columns representing the events ... at which only a few women were present. As far as the lines [rows] are concerned, we put together toward the top or bottom the lines representing those women that participated most often together in social events. A great deal of reshuffling may have to be done before any pattern appears. (Homans, 1951: 83)

Homans argued that this 'reshuffling' must go on until the distribution of the crosses in the cells shows a clear pattern, and he produced a rearranged matrix in which there were clear signs of a division into two 'cliques' among the women: there were two distinct clumps of crosses in the rearranged matrix. Homans's method is analogous to what has subsequently come to be called 'block modelling', but he made no use of any formal mathematical methods. In fact, his rearrangement seems to have been simply a trial-and-error process that continued until he was able to spot an apparently significant pattern.

Figure 2.6 shows a simplified version of the kind of reanalysis undertaken by Homans. The matrices show artificial data for the participation of eight people in eight events. In matrix (i), the crosses are scattered evenly across the whole matrix, but a rearrangement of the rows and columns into the order shown in matrix (ii) brings out a structural opposition between two distinct subgroups: Ann, Chris, Ed and Gill participate together in events 1, 3, 5 and 7, while Beth, Don, Flo and Hal participate jointly in events 2, 4, 6 and 8. There are two separate sets of people and two specific categories of events. It can be appreciated that rearrangement by trial-and-error would not be such an easy task, even for such a small matrix, when the data are not so tightly structured as in this artificial example. The real data on 18 women and 14 events would have taken a considerable amount of time to analyse. There is, furthermore, no certainty

**(i) Original matrix**

| | | Events | | | | | | | |
|---|---|---|---|---|---|---|---|---|---|
| | | 1 | 2 | 3 | 4 | 5 | 6 | 7 | 8 |
| People | Ann | X | | X | | X | | X | |
| | Beth | | X | | X | | X | | X |
| | Chris | X | | X | | X | | X | |
| | Don | | X | | X | | X | | X |
| | Ed | X | | X | | X | | X | |
| | Flo | | X | | X | | X | | X |
| | Gill | X | | X | | X | | X | |
| | Hal | | X | | X | | X | | X |

**(ii) Rearranged matrix**

| | | Events | | | | | | | |
|---|---|---|---|---|---|---|---|---|---|
| | | 1 | 3 | 5 | 7 | 2 | 4 | 6 | 8 |
| People | Ann | X | X | X | X | | | | |
| | Chris | X | X | X | X | | | | |
| | Ed | X | X | X | X | | | | |
| | Gill | X | X | X | X | | | | |
| | Beth | | | | | X | X | X | X |
| | Don | | | | | X | X | X | X |
| | Flo | | | | | X | X | X | X |
| | Hal | | | | | X | X | X | X |

**Figure 2.6**   Matrix rearrangement

that the final results produced by Homans would be the same as those produced by any other researcher, as there are no criteria by which a 'correct' result can be identified. It is for these reasons that later attempts at this kind of analysis have involved a search for programmable algorithms, so that computers can reliably undertake the task of rearrangement.

To illustrate his position further, Homans reanalysed the Hawthorne data on the bank wiring room. Using the sociograms constructed by the observers, he looked at the cliques that Roethlisberger and Dickson had identified (Homans, 1951: 66–70). Homans simply retained these original clique identifications and did not attempt a sociometric investigation of clique structure along the lines of his analysis of the Old City data. He did imply, however, albeit without any citation, that a matrix rearrangement method had been used by the original Hawthorne researchers (Homans, 1951: 84).[15]

The theoretical framework that Homans constructed to explain group behaviour was an elaboration of the model of the early small group researchers, in which the group is understood as a system within an environment. He divided the structure of any group into an 'internal system', which expresses the sentiments that arise through the interactions of its members, and an 'external system' through which group activities are related to the problem of environmental adaptation.[16] The environment itself consists of the physical, technical and social contexts of group behaviour. Homans's main concern was with the internal system, which he saw as a more scientific concept than that of the 'informal organisation' to which it referred. His interest, therefore, was in the scientific elaboration of the insights of research on informal organisation by translating these insights into propositions about the structure of internal systems.

To this end, he set up a number of hypotheses about the internal system, starting from the assumption that people who interact frequently with one another will tend to like one another and that, as the frequency of their interaction increases, so the degree of their liking for one another will also increase. If there are frequent interactions in the external system, because of such environmental constraints as the demands imposed by supervisors and managers, then the members of the workgroup will tend to develop sentiments of liking towards one another and will engage in further interactions unrelated to the needs of the external system. It is in this way, Homans argues, that the internal system gets elaborated into complex social configurations divisible into cliques.[17]

Despite the power of Homans's theoretical synthesis of sociometric and anthropological research, few major advances were directly inspired by his work. Homans himself became increasingly concerned to explore the explanation of social behaviour using behaviourist and rational choice models, and he came to be identified with the framework of 'exchange theory' (Homans, 1961). Robert Bales, a colleague of Homans, carried out some interesting small group research (Bales, 1950), but he did not use a sociometric approach in his work and he became increasingly linked with Parsonian structural functionalism (Parsons et al., 1953). The work of many who had contributed to the development of the idea of balance returned to exclusively psychological concerns, and the influential text of Festinger (1957) became an important charter statement in directing these researchers back into the social psychology of perception. The area of group dynamics all but stagnated, with most advances being in the purely mathematical problems of balance, cliques and clusters. While these mathematical explorations were to prove important and fertile sources for the advances later made by Harrison White, they had little impact on the shape of social research during the 1950s and 1960s.

# FORMAL MODELS OF COMMUNITY AND KINSHIP

It was in the work of a small group of active fieldworkers associated with the Department of Social Anthropology at Manchester University – most notably, John Barnes, Clyde Mitchell and Elizabeth Bott[18] – that the framework of social network analysis took a novel turn. The Manchester anthropologists were even more strongly influenced by Radcliffe-Brown than were their Harvard counterparts, and they sought to develop his ideas in a novel direction. Instead of emphasising integration and cohesion, they emphasised conflict and change. A central figure at Manchester was Max Gluckman, who combined an interest in complex African societies with a concern to develop a structural approach that recognised the important part played by conflict and power in both the mainte-nance and the transformation of social structures. For Gluckman, conflict and power were integral elements of any social structure, and his analyses stressed the ever-present activities of negotiation, bargaining, and coercion in the production of social integra-tion. Gluckman actively encouraged his colleagues and students who were undertaking investigations of small-scale interpersonal communities to pursue these themes.

The dominance during the 1950s of the Parsonian approach to sociology and of cultural approaches to anthropology was an important factor in directing the work of the Manchester school as a distinctly critical tradition. Where classical sociologists had emphasised that actions were to be understood in terms of their location in a struc-ture of social relations, Parsons held that actions must be explained as expressions of internalised value orientations. The work of the Manchester anthropologists, with its emphasis on seeing structures as networks of relations, combined formal techniques of network analysis with substantive sociological concepts. This proved an impres-sive and powerful mixture, which brought it close to the emerging framework of con-flict theory in sociology (see Rex, 1962), but their emphasis on interpersonal relations meant that it did not appear as a full-blown alternative to Parsonian theory. For this reason, social network analysis could not help but be seen as a specialised method of study rather than a critical alternative to conventional sociology.

The Manchester researchers, then, paid less attention to the formally institutional-ised norms and institutions of a society and rather more to the actual configurations of relations that arise from the exercise of conflict and power. The theoretical ideas inherited from the past, geared to the understanding of simple, kinship-based societies, were unable to handle these phenomena. It was in recognition of this inadequacy that they began to try to systematise such metaphorical notions as the 'web' and 'network' of social relations to which such writers as Radcliffe-Brown had pointed.

Initially, these researchers began to employ the idea of a social network simply in its metaphorical sense, but Barnes, in the early 1950s, took a lead in applying this idea in a more rigorous and analytical way. His approach had a considerable influence on the work of Bott, and the two began to explore more closely the work that had been undertaken in the sociometric tradition. Their various papers (Barnes, 1954; Bott, 1955, 1956) received a broad welcome among social anthropologists, the concept of the social network seeming to meet a need for appropriate concepts to use in under-standing complex societies. Siegfried Nadel espoused this approach in a set of lectures and an associated book (Nadel, 1957) that became a programmatic charter statement from a leading figure in the discipline. However, it was Clyde Mitchell who undertook the tasks outlined by Nadel and laid the basis for a systematic framework of social net-work analysis. Mitchell turned to the mathematics of graph theory that had emerged from the early sociometric concerns, and he reformulated these ideas as the basis of a distinctly sociological framework. Summarising the ideas that had begun to crystallise during the 1950s in his own work and that of his colleagues (Mitchell, 1969), he set out a body of sociological concepts that, he believed, could adequately grasp the structural properties of social organisation. Intriguingly, Mitchell's translation of graph theory and sociometry into a sociological framework led him to a concentration on exactly those features of informal and interpersonal organisation that had been highlighted by Mayo, Warner and Homans.

Barnes began his academic career at the Rhodes-Livingstone Institute in Central Africa, a major research centre for many of the Manchester anthropologists. After joining the Manchester Department in 1949, he decided to undertake some fieldwork in a fishing village in south-west Norway. Although it was a small village community, Bremnes was an isolated locale structured almost exclusively through the kinship relations of its members. It was an integral part of a complex and socially differentiated national society, but it had its own economic, political and other institutions, which were only imperfectly co-ordinated into an integrated system. Barnes was strongly drawn to the part played by kinship, friendship and neighbourliness in the production of commu-nity integration. These primordial relations were not directly tied to territorial locales or to formal economic and political structures. Instead, they formed a distinct and rela-tively integrated sphere of informal, interpersonal relations. Barnes claimed that 'the whole of social life' could be seen as 'a set of points some of which are joined by lines' to form a 'total network' of relations. The informal sphere of interpersonal relations was to be seen as one part, a 'partial network', of this total network (Barnes, 1954: 43).

Elizabeth Bott, a Canadian psychologist, had studied anthropology under Lloyd Warner at Chicago, and it may be assumed that, like Barnes, she had some familiar-ity with the Yankee City studies. She joined the Tavistock Institute in 1950 and soon began a fieldwork study of British families. Bott was principally concerned with their kinship relations, and employed the concept of a 'network' as an analytical device for investigating the varying forms taken by these kinship relations. This work was published in two influential articles and a book (Bott, 1955, 1956, 1957), and it was the basis of the PhD that Bott received from the London School of Economics in 1956. Although Elizabeth Bott is the daughter of the pioneering sociometrician Helen Bott, she feels that she developed her ideas independently.

The evolving theoretical framework of Bott's study was undoubtedly influenced by her colleagues at the Tavistock Institute, which had, in 1947, joined with the Research Center for Group Dynamics at Ann Arbor to publish the journal *Human Relations*. As a psychologist with an interest in psychotherapy, Bott was aware of the work that had been undertaken by Moreno. Indeed, both she and Barnes cited Moreno in their own papers. The more immediate influence on Bott's work, however, was Lewin's field theory, and even Barnes wrote of the existence of distinct 'fields' of activity in Bremnes society. *Human Relations* published articles by Lewin, Festinger, Newcomb, Cartwright and other American leaders of small group research, and it was there that both Bott and Barnes published their work on social networks.

Barnes had presented his initial ideas in seminars at Manchester and Oxford during 1953, and it was in 1954 that Bott learned of Barnes's work and adopted the term 'network' as the basis of her own theoretical interpretations. By the time that Barnes's article was published, he was working under Raymond Firth at the London School of Economics. Bott, already registered for her PhD, presented drafts of her own paper that year at both the LSE and at Manchester. These biographical details are not given for purely antiquarian reasons, nor are they given simply as illustrations of the importance of academic networks. My concern is to show how a small number of key individuals were responsible, in a very short space of time, for constructing the basis of a major theoretical innovation in British social anthropology. Once Barnes and Bott had made their breakthrough, the way was open for further developments that would consolidate their advances with further lessons from the American researchers.

A key voice in legitimating this direction of theoretical advance was Siegfried Nadel. An Austrian psychologist, influenced by Köhler and Lewin, Nadel had transferred to anthropological studies in the early 1930s, and in 1955 he presented a series of lectures on social structure at the LSE. Barnes and Bott had been important influences on the development of his work, and they were mentioned as both commentators and friends in the preface to the published version of these lectures (Nadel, 1957). Nadel's starting point was a definition of structure as the articulation or arrangement of elements to form a whole. By separating the forms of relations from their contents, he argued, the general features of structures can be described and can be investigated through using a comparative method. He advocated a mathematical approach for pursuing the aim of constructing formal models of social structure.

Social structure, according to Nadel, is 'an overall system, network or pattern' of relations (1957: 12), which the analyst abstracts from the concretely observable actions of individuals. By 'network' he meant 'the interlocking of relationships whereby the interactions implicit in one determine those occurring in others' (1957: 16). A particular claim made by Nadel was the idea that 'role' or position should be seen as the central concept in sociological theory. Social structures are structures of roles, and roles, together with their role sets, are defined through networks of interdependent activities. Nadel argued that algebraic and matrix methods should be applied to role analysis, but apart from one or two brief illustrations, he gave little indication of how this was to be done. His early death, in 1956, prevented him from contributing further to the advances that he had signposted.

Mitchell and others associated with Manchester and the Rhodes-Livingstone Institute attempted to systematise this view during the 1950s and 1960s. Indeed, Mitchell can be seen as the true inheritor of Nadel's aspirations. Mitchell's codification of social network analysis in 1969 generalised Barnes's conception of the sphere of interpersonal relations into that of the 'personal order'.[19] The personal order is the pattern of 'personal links individuals have with a set of people and the links these people have in turn among themselves' (Mitchell, 1969: 10). These patterns of interaction are, for Mitchell, the sphere of network analysis. Such interpersonal networks, he added, are built from two different ideal types of action that combine in varying ways to form concrete interaction networks. There is, first of all, 'communication', which involves the transfer of information between individuals, the establishment of social norms, and the creation of a degree of consensus. On the other hand, there is the 'instrumental' or purposive type of action, which involves the transfer of material goods and services between people (Mitchell, 1969: 36–9).[20] Any particular action will combine elements of both of these ideal types, and so particular social networks will embody, to varying degrees, both a flow of information and a transfer of resources and services.

Mitchell went on to conceptualise the 'total network' of a society as 'the general ever-ramifying, ever-reticulating set of linkages that stretches within and beyond the confines of any community or organisation' (Mitchell, 1969: 12). In actual research, he argues, it is always necessary to select particular aspects of the total network for attention, and these aspects he conceptualises as 'partial networks'. There are two bases on which such abstraction can proceed, though Mitchell concentrates his attention almost exclusively on one of these. First, there is abstraction that is anchored around a particular individual so as to generate 'ego-centred' networks of social relations of all kinds. Second, there is abstraction of the overall, 'global' features of networks in relation to a particular aspect of social activity: political ties, kinship obligations, friendship, or work relations, and so on. For Mitchell and for most of the Manchester researchers, it was individually anchored partial networks that were to be the focus of attention. In this kind of research, individuals are identified and their direct and indirect links to others are traced. Such research generates a collection of ego-centred networks, one for each of the individuals studied. A similar approach was taken in Bott's earlier investigation of the ego-centred networks of husbands and wives, where she measured the 'connectedness' of these networks and the degree of overlap between marital partners' networks.

Mitchell recognised the importance of the mode of abstraction that defines partial networks by the 'content' or meaning of the relations involved, but he saw this also as needing to be anchored around particular individuals. The 'partial networks' studied by sociologists and social anthropologists are always ego-centred networks focused on particular types of social relationship. Most such networks, Mitchell argues, are 'multi-stranded' or 'multiplex': they involve the combination of a number of meaningfully distinct relations. Thus, Barnes's original notion of the network, and that taken up by Bott, was a partial network in which kinship, friendship and neighbourliness are combined into a single, multi-stranded relationship that it is inappropriate to break down into its constituent elements.

Interpersonal networks, Mitchell claimed, can be analysed through a number of concepts that describe the quality of the relations involved. These are the 'reciprocity', the 'intensity' and the 'durability' of the relations (Mitchell, 1969: 24–9), concepts that echo Homans's distinctions between direction, frequency and intensity. Some, but not all, relationships involve a transaction or exchange, and so can be considered as 'directed' from one person to another. An important measure of such relations, therefore, is the degree to which the transaction or orientation is reciprocated. One person may, for example, choose another as a friend, but this choice may not be returned: the chooser may be ignored or spurned. Multi-stranded relationships can involve a complex balance of compensating relations, reciprocated and unreciprocated. Through these relations, financial aid, for example, might flow in one direction and political support in the other.[21] 'Durability' is a measure of how long-lasting are the underlying relations and obligations activated in particular transactions (Mitchell refers to Katz, 1966). Those that are constantly being activated in interaction are highly durable, while those that persist only for one or two activities are highly transient. While kinship obligations, for example, are very durable – they generally last for the whole of one's life – those that arise for a particularly limited purpose are more likely to be transient. 'Intensity' refers to the strength of the obligations involved in a relation. This reflects either the strength of the commitment to these obligations or the multiplexity of the relationship: multi-stranded relationships tend to be more intense because they are more diffuse in character.[22]

Mitchell added a further set of concepts to describe the texture of social networks, deriving these from a translation of graph theory into sociological language. 'Density', for example, he saw as the completeness of the network: the extent to which all possible relations are actually present. This is what Barnes and Bott had tried to describe with their notions of the 'mesh' and 'connectedness' of networks. 'Reachability' refers to how easy it is for all people to contact one another through a limited number of steps: how easy it is, for example, for gossip, ideas or resources to be diffused through the network. To these concepts, Barnes (1969) had added 'cliques' and 'clusters' as terms for identifying social groupings within networks, but these were not taken up in the empirical studies collected together by Mitchell (1969).

Institutionalised roles and positions are the framework within which interpersonal networks are constructed, but they exist only in and through the reproduction of interpersonal networks. But Mitchell and the Manchester tradition equivocated about whether the institutional structure of roles is itself a part of network analysis or is separate from it. While some of the Manchester school saw the institutional role structure as a network of relations that exists alongside the interpersonal network, Mitchell often distinguished networks of interpersonal relations from structures of institutional relations. Mitchell's discussion, therefore, tended towards a 'residual' definition of the social network: network analysis concerns only the interpersonal sphere that is left behind after formal economic, political and other roles are extracted (Whitten and Wolfe, 1973). To the extent that he saw social network analysis as a special method for the analysis of interpersonal relations, Mitchell departed from Nadel's aspiration for a general framework of structural sociology rooted in formal network analysis. This proved fateful for the development of social network analysis in Britain, which largely failed to attract adherents from outside the area of community studies.

## FORMAL METHODS TRIUMPHANT

The arguments of Mitchell, Barnes and Bott were extremely influential in Britain (see Frankenberg, 1966), but their very success meant that social network analysis came to be identified with the specific ideas of the Manchester anthropologists. That is to say, network analysis was seen to be concerned specifically with informal, interpersonal relations of a 'communal' type, and the method was seen as specifically concerned with the investigation of egocentric networks. As a result, the crucial breakthrough to the study of the global properties of social networks in all fields of social life was not made in Britain.

It was, in fact, at Harvard that this crucial breakthrough occurred. A decade after Homans's initial explorations, a trickle of papers began to appear from Harrison White and his associates. These pushed the analysis much further. Soon, the work of their students and colleagues produced a torrent of papers that firmly established social network analysis as a method of structural analysis.

The key elements in this breakthrough were two parallel mathematical innovations (see the discussion in Berkowitz, 1982). The first of these was the development of algebraic models of groups using set theory to model kinship and other relations in the spirit of Lévi-Strauss. This led to a reconsideration of the early work in graph theory and in other branches of mathematics and to the attempt to use algebraic methods to model the concept of 'role' in social structure (White, 1963; Boyd, 1969; Lorrain and White, 1971). White's continued explorations of 'block modelling' (see Chapter 8 below) can be seen as carrying forward the very emphasis on role structure to which Nadel had pointed. The second innovation was the development of multi-dimensional scaling, a technique for translating relationships into social 'distances' and for mapping them in a social space. Very much in the tradition of Lewin's work on field theory, these developments proved extremely powerful methods of analysis. (For early applications in sociology, see Laumann, 1966; Levine, 1972.)

The confluence of these two strands led to the important and influential work of the new Harvard group centred on White (see Mullins, 1973). White had moved to Harvard from Chicago, and his work retained important links with that of Davis and others, who had elaborated on the basic sociometric views through the 1960s. The Harvard group developed as mathematically oriented structural analysts, concerned with the modelling of social structures of all kinds. There was no single theoretical focus to their work, the unifying idea being simply that of using algebraic ideas to model deep and surface structure relations. It was network analysis as a method that united them. The public reception of Mark Granovetter's (1973) article on 'The strength of weak ties' popularised this viewpoint in American sociology and helped to stimulate many other studies. Although it was not a highly technical piece of mathematics – or, perhaps, because of this – Granovetter's work was of central importance as a charter statement for popularising and legitimating the position (see also Granovetter, 1982). Although many researchers continued to work in such areas as the analysis of community structure, others were interested in such phenomena as corporate interlocks and so helped to move network analysis away from its focus on purely interpersonal relations. In doing so, they stimulated numerous substantive applications of the techniques. Much of the effort of the Harvard group – no longer based solely at Harvard – was focused in the International Network for Social Network Analysis (INSNA), founded at Toronto, which acted as a focus for the development of social network analysis under the leadership of Wellman and Berkowitz, both former students of White.

## GETTING BY WITHOUT THE HELP OF YOUR FRIENDS

Two studies, by Granovetter and by Nancy Lee, became modern classics. They both grew out of the earliest discussions of the Harvard school, and while they were not explicitly algebraic in their approach, they became important exemplars for other researchers. This was not least because they offered both a substantive and analytical continuity with earlier sociometric work.

In *Getting a Job*, Granovetter (1974) started out from a critical consideration of attempts by labour economists to explain how people find work. In particular, he wanted to explore the ways in which people acquire information about job opportunities through the informal social contacts that they have. His interest was in the kinds of links involved in the transmission of information, whether these were 'strong' or 'weak', and how they were maintained over time. To this end, he selected a sample of male professional, technical, and managerial workers in a suburb of Boston, all of whom had changed their jobs during the previous five years. Granovetter found that informal, personal contacts were the primary channels through which individuals found out about job opportunities: 56 per cent of his respondents relied on this means, and this was particularly true for information about the higher-paying jobs. These results were not especially striking, being broadly in line with earlier research, and Granovetter set himself the task of identifying those who provided information and the circumstances under which they passed it on.

Granovetter showed that 'rational' choice was of little importance in deciding methods for acquiring job information. Individuals did not really compare the rewards and costs attached to different sources of information, and there was little active 'searching' for jobs. Instead, information was acquired accidentally, whenever contacts volunteered it. The most important people in providing information were work or work-related contacts. They were rarely family or friends, and they tended to be people who were in different occupations than the respondent. The probability that a person would make a job change was dependent on the proportion of work contacts who were in different occupations from him- or herself.

To explain these findings, Granovetter drew on an information diffusion model. Those people with job information were assumed to pass this on to a certain proportion of their immediate contacts, who passed it on, in turn, to a certain proportion of their contacts, and so on. Assuming that the information attenuates over time as it passes through subsequent links in the chain,[23] it is possible to track its passage through a social network and to discover the number of people who will acquire the information and their various locations in the network. The acquisition of information, therefore, depends upon, first, the motivation of those with information to pass it on, and second, the strategic location of a person's contacts in the overall flow of information (Granovetter, 1974: 52).

It was at this point in his argument that Granovetter introduced his now-famous argument on the strength of weak ties. The importance of strong ties is well understood. Those to whom a person is closest (family and close friends, workmates, etc.) have many overlapping contacts. They all tend to know and to interact with each other in numerous situations and so there is a tendency for them to possess the same knowledge about job opportunities. Information that reaches any one of them is more than likely to reach them all. Conversely, they are less likely to be the sources of new information from more distant parts of the network. The information received is likely to be 'stale' information, already received from someone else. It is through the relatively weak ties of less frequent contacts and of people in different work situations that new and different information is likely to become available. What this means is that 'acquaintances are more likely to pass job information than close friends' (Granovetter, 1974: 54). In almost all cases studied by Granovetter, information came directly from an employer or one of the employer's direct contacts: there was, typically, a maximum of one intermediary. Links through more than two intermediaries were very rare. It was the short, weak chains of connection that were of greatest significance in the receipt of useful job information.

A comparable, slightly earlier study was Lee's work in *The Search for an Abortionist* (1969). Lee wanted to discover how women acquired information about the opportunities for terminations in a situation where abortion is illegal. Doctors who undertake illegal terminations cannot advertise and must often operate from hotel rooms rather than from clinics. Those who seek an abortion must, therefore, try to obtain information from those of their friends and acquaintances who may have had some experience with abortion in the past, as these people are likely to have that information or to be able to put them in contact with others who can help.

To study this process, Lee contacted abortionists and women with recent experience of an abortion. In constructing her sample she was, interestingly, having to use information search techniques that were similar to those used by the women themselves. Like Granovetter, she used a mixture of interviews and questionnaires to gather her data. Having explored various aspects of their life and social background and their attitudes towards conception and abortion, Lee turned to an examination of their search for an abortionist. The search for an abortionist involved the making of informed guesses about who might be able to help, either by providing the name of an abortionist or mentioning a further contact that might help. Lee found that women approached an average of 5.8 people before successfully contacting an abortionist: the actual numbers of contacts ranged from 1 to 31. A number of the contacts, of course, were 'dead-ends', and the 'successful chains' varied in length from one to seven steps, the average length being 2.8. Over three-quarters of the successful chains involved two or fewer intermediaries (Lee, 1969: Ch. 5). Contacts tended not to be relatives or those in authority (employers, teachers, etc.), and the most important channels were female friends of the same age.

Both Granovetter and Lee explored network processes through the use of simple frequency tabulations, making only qualitative comments on the structure of the network relations that they discovered. Indeed, Lee argued that it is extremely difficult to trace the structure of overlapping personal networks in large-scale systems. These studies were, however, important as outgrowths of and contributions to the systematic and analytical development of social network analysis. Their studies showed the power of even the most basic of social network methods, and they suggested an immense power for the more rigorous techniques being developed by their Harvard colleagues.

# ENTRY OF THE SOCIAL PHYSICISTS

Sociologists have frequently borrowed concepts from physics to apply in their own studies in various specialist areas: ideas of attraction, energy, force and field, for example, all originated as borrowings from the work of physicists (Scott, 2011a). It is only recently, however, that physicists themselves have begun to undertake social network analysis. Barabási (2002), Buchanan (2002) and Watts (1999, 2003) have been the main proponents of this new social physics. Their work returns to the random graph models of Erdős and Rényi (1959), which they see as having demonstrated the existence of well-connected networks with quite distinctive properties that, they claim, have been overlooked by other researchers into the social world.

The key paper in establishing this work was by Watts and Strogatz (1998), who argued that real-world networks are not completely random but are clustered into well-connected zones. Barabási holds that sociologists had, until then, assumed that social structures comprised 'the random accumulation of social relationships' (2002: 62), and so the work of Watts and Strogatz had come as a complete surprise. Anyone who has read this far in my account of social network analysis will realise how far from the truth this is. Unaware of the prior work of sociologists and social anthropologists, the social physicists have claimed to have discovered the existence of order in social life and the mathematical principles that govern it. Behind the ignorance and the hype, however, there are some interesting discoveries that do, in fact, highlight some new directions in social network analysis.

Their key insight was into the significance of the 'small-world' properties of social networks. The research of Milgram (1967; Travers and Milgram, 1969) showed that randomly chosen individuals, even if geographically dispersed, are typically connected by social relations that pass through just five other individuals. This is the now-famous idea of 'six degrees of separation'. Thus, most people do live in a 'small world' of over-lapping acquaintances. In a small-world network the density of links is such that there are numerous 'shortcuts' from one individual to another.

It is in such small-world networks that the properties described by Granovetter are to be found. It is also in these kinds of networks that high levels of co-operation become possible. Watts's own crucial innovation was to turn this mathematical argument into an explanation of structural variations over time. That is, he constructed a model of network dynamics that provides a theory of change.

Networks develop, Watts argues, as a result of gradual, incremental changes that produce sudden, non-linear 'phase transitions' in network structure. Radical macro-level structural changes result from the unintentional accumulation of minor micro-level changes. The making and breaking of social relations by actors as they pragmatically adjust to their local social situations create the shortcuts that give a network its small-world properties. If their actions reduce the number of shortcuts below the level at which these properties emerge, then the efficiency of the network in the diffusion of information, for example, declines catastrophically. In a fragmented network it is more difficult for information or resources to flow, and so people are likely to become more dependent on their immediate local situation.

This argument allows us to see the significance of a network model developed from within sociology by Tom Snijders (2005; Snijders et al., 2010; see also Monge and Contractor, 2003). Using agent-based computational models, Snijders shows that agents tend to be 'myopic', following rules of action that make sense in their local situation but involve little or no awareness of the larger structures in which they are acting. This rule-following behaviour can be modelled – as Snijders has done in his SIENA program – and can show how and when radical macro-level changes in network structure will occur.

The long history of social network analysis has produced a powerful set of concepts and measures through which social networks of all kinds can be described and their changing structures explained. The most recent work has begun to provide ways of testing the strength of the effect that network structure can have on the actions of individuals. Social network analysis is a powerful method for exploring the relationship between structure and agency that has become so central to sociological analysis.

## FURTHER READING

Freeman, L.C. (2004) *The Development of Social Network Analysis: A Study in the Sociology of Science*. Vancouver: Empirical Press.

A comprehensive history of social network analysis and the key figures in its development.

# THREE

## Data Collection for Social Network Analysis

This chapter provides a discussion of:

- Types of data collection in social network analysis
- Data collection through surveys and interviews
- Data collection through observation
- Data collection from documents in libraries and archives
- Defining boundaries for social networks
- Issues in sampling social network data

Many of the general considerations that arise in handling relational data are not specific to this type of research. They are those that arise with all social science data: gaining access, designing questionnaires, drawing samples, dealing with non-response, storing data on computers, and so on. These issues are adequately covered in the many general and specialist texts on research methods, and it is not necessary to cover the same ground here. However, a number of specific problems do arise when research concerns relational data. As these problems are not, in general, covered in the existing texts on research methods, it is important to review them here before going on to consider the techniques of social network analysis themselves.

There are three ways of collecting data in social research: directly from the subjects of research through surveys and interviews (survey research); through our own observations of what people do and how they do it (observational research); and indirectly from written or electronic records of actions and events stored in libraries and archives (documentary research). All of these have their part to play in the collection of relational data for social network analysis.

Some of the earliest research was observational. Moreno observed schoolchildren in order to uncover patterns of observable play and friendship, though he supplemented this with some gentle questioning of children about their choices of friends and their feelings about them. The Hawthorn researchers also used evidence drawn from the observations made from the back of the bank wiring room while the subjects of their research went about their work tasks. Similarly, the important anthropological studies of community and kinship networks relied on the tried and tested ethnographic methods of participant observation.

Much of the research in the 1970s and later that was concerned with interlocking directorships and intercorporate relations drew its data from handbooks, yearbooks and directories that recorded information on company directors and corporate structures. It was generally assumed that such data would be more difficult to obtain from interviews, as corporate affairs would be regarded as confidential and not as matters to be shared with sociologists. Nevertheless, Pahl and Winkler (1974) carried out observational studies of directors to supplement – and throw into question – some of the findings of archival research.

Recent research has resurrected the use of survey and interview data, especially where the intention is to study informal, interpersonal relations. This approach had been used by Warner and his associates in the 1930s but it really became established in the important and ongoing studies initiated by Barry Wellman in the 1970s (Wellman, 1979). This provides a model for many, though the possibilities opened up by large-scale data sets collected by others and for other purposes raise distinct methodological issues.

## ASKING QUESTIONS

General issues of question and questionnaire design and the construction of interview schedules are common to all forms of social research and need not be pursued here.

Instead, I will look at the particular types and forms of question that can be designed in order to efficiently and accurately collect social network data. Questions can be asked in formal surveys or interviews, and many common issues apply.

When using a questionnaire or interview schedule the main choice is that between the use of a *roster* or list of people from which respondents may choose, or the use of free-response *nomination* (Marsden, 2011). When a roster is used the researcher must have identified the relevant members of the network before constructing and implementing the questionnaire or schedule. The respondent is typically asked a question of the form:

Which of the following people do you consider to be the most important in providing you with help and support in your everyday life?

or

Do you consider yourself to be a friend of any of the following people?

In each case the respondent is supplied with a list from which he or she can choose. The number of choices that can be made may be open or fixed, and the strength of the relationship may be recorded (for example, on a five-point scale from 'very weak' to 'very strong'). It will, of course, have been important to have provided sufficient information about what exactly is meant by 'help and support' or 'friend'. If this information is not supplied, each respondent will reply in terms of what she or he understands by the words, and the results from the survey may not be comparable from one individual to another.

The basic problem, as already noted, is that the roster must be full and complete. This may be possible for a relatively small group but in the case of larger networks it may be quite difficult and also very tedious for respondents to be presented with a very long list of names. With a long list of names, any attempt to measure the strength or frequency of relationship to any one individual is likely to make the task both tedious and unreliable.

For these reasons, many researchers have preferred an open nomination method in which respondents are free to name individuals of their own choice and the boundaries of the network are established from the responses made. Typically, questions take forms such as the following:

Please could you let us know the names of the people that you turn to most often when looking for help and support in everyday life?

or

Who would you regard as your four closest friends?

These questions illustrate a fundamental problem: do you limit the number of people who may be nominated as friends or helpers, or do you allow people to name as many or as few as they like? The answer is not straightforward. Analysis of the data is much easier – as will be seen later on – if the number of choices is the same for each respondent. On the other hand, people differ in the number of friends that they retain and so the naming of six close friends, for example, may require them to make a selection from a larger pool of friends or may be the upper limit of those they count as friends. There is a further problem of recall: respondents may forget to name certain people who are, nevertheless, important to them, and these data will be lost unless the researcher is able to probe with follow-up questions. The issue of recall is especially problematic when interviewees are being asked to remember contacts and connections from the distant past, for example, the early stages of their work careers.

It is rarely the case that one single question will be asked. The researcher's interest may be in more than one type of relationship or in the same relationship at various points in time. Where a roster question is repeated for a number of different relationships the same roster may be repeated in each question or the roster may be presented against a series of questions arranged in parallel. In either case, tedium may rapidly set in if the questions are at all complex. If the same relationship is being studied over time it may be necessary to identify a different roster for each time period if the composition of the group has changed over the period being studied. In these situations, free nomination questions may be preferred, but then the problem of recall becomes especially problematic.

Attempting to measure the frequency or intensity of a relationship is fraught with difficulties. Although 'frequency' may be specified by the researcher in conventional time periods – daily, once a week, once a month, and so on – frequency is likely to vary with distance. It may be physically impossible for a person to meet a friend living in another continent as often as he or she meets a friend in the same town, though the distant friend may be regarded as 'closer' or more intimate. The intensity of a relationship may be seen in terms of the degree of intensity, but if respondents are asked to assign an arbitrary number to this intimacy they may do so inconsistently. A close friend scored as '7' for one respondent may not be as intimate as that scored by another respondent at '5'. This may partly be avoided by using Likert scales with verbal descriptions of degrees of intimacy, but the meanings accorded to 'close' or 'intimate' may still vary significantly from one person to another.

## MAKING OBSERVATIONS

Ethnographic investigations using observational methods and conversational techniques of formal and informal interviewing are methods through which researchers can have far more control over the nature and form of the data collected.

Observation of social relations, whether as a participant observer or as a direct observer, avoids many of these problems, but it involves specific difficulties of its own.

In order to observe, a researcher must secure access to a group and its individual members. This may be easier for some kinds of groups than for others. Even when access is granted or behaviour takes place on public places, it may not be possible to observe everything relevant that occurs.

Where observations can be made, the researcher must have a device on which to record them. This might be a paper or electronic protocol on which a roster of members is listed who are checked off when a relationship is observed. In this type of research, the definition of a relationship is consistent across all of those observed because, of course, it is the definition adopted by the researcher rather than by the participants. This may not matter if the relationship is simple and straightforward, but it is more of a problem if the observer is attempting to assess the intensity of a relationship rather than just its frequency.

Observation does, however, allow a researcher to contextualise her or his relational data in ways that are not possible in survey research. By being party to open conversations and discussions, for example, the researcher obtains an understanding of the cultural meanings of relationships that are far more difficult to uncover in a questionnaire.

Observation is also a time-consuming way of collecting data as it is necessary for the observer to be present on numerous occasions and over long periods of time. In a survey or even an interview, each respondent takes a relatively short time to question and the various respondents can be scheduled flexibly to fit the needs of the researcher. Observational research must be more closely aligned to the needs and routines of those studied.

## USING DOCUMENTS

The use of written or electronic records has often appeared to be the most convenient way of obtaining some forms of relational data. While friendship choices are rarely written down, published, or stored in archives, economic and political information is frequently recorded in this way, as are some types of kinship information. Public records of birth, death, and marriage provide information on family relationships and on friends acting as witnesses or informants. Wills record information on family members given bequests and friends who are close enough to receive a bequest or act as an executor. Court cases record names of witnesses and those making depositions that may relate to inheritance relationships. One of the most common uses of documentary data is for purposes of corporate research. Names of directors and the company boards on which they sit, and lists of companies with the names of their directors, are recorded in annual handbooks, while companies and their shareholders are recorded in electronic form in public and private archives. Yearbooks for industries and sectors typically include full lists of members and their affiliations with constituent organisations and sections

(Scott, 1990, 2006). Biographical directories such as *Who's Who* list individuals with details on their careers and life histories, including organisational affiliations, kinship and residence. Newspapers and other media sources can often be used to collect relational data on individuals, though these are rarely in the pre-structured list format used by directories and yearbooks.

Collecting names from documents does not involve issues of question wording or respondent recall, but it must not be forgotten that these sources may themselves have been obtained through some form of questionnaire or official form and so may have some of the same underlying difficulties. Published sources are notoriously liable to errors and variations in transcription or recording: the Robert Brown identified in one source may or may not be the same person as the Bob Brown identified in another. As the data are generally compiled at various dates in the year there may have been changes during the course of the year: Bob Brown may have become Sir Robert Brown or even Lord Brown during the year. A researcher must, therefore, undertake a great deal of work to 'clean' the data and to ensure that all identities have been checked.

Much data in documentary form is now available electronically in computer databases. While the data may then be extracted more easily, the same questions of identity will arise. There are, however, a growing number of large databases that have been partially 'cleaned' and organised by commercial organisations that compile them for purposes other than academic research. We live in an age of 'big data' when information on shopping transactions, charitable donations, email traffic, Twitter feeds, and so on can be accessed and can yield relational data. Many readers may have used techniques readily available in Google, in IMDb, in the Web of Science, and in such social media as LinkedIn to generate social network models of professional linkages or scientific citations. Computer scientists have developed techniques of data mining that are specifically designed to generate social network information from big data sets.

## BOUNDARIES IN RELATIONAL DATA

Having clarified the ways in which relational data can be collected, it is possible to examine a number of important issues concerning the selection of relational data for analysis. The problem of sampling in social network analysis is apparent with friendship and acquaintance data. Estimates of the total number of acquaintances of an individual, in the contemporary United States, range from 3,500 to 5,000 (Pool, 1978; Freeman and Thompson, 1989). It is clearly impossible to ask a sample of people anything in detail about their acquaintances, and it is unlikely that the totality of their interactions could be observed. For these reasons, studies have typically focused on much smaller personal networks, making a selection on some defined basis. Even where large numbers of connections may be compiled from documentary sources, as may be the case with business information, decisions must be made on the size of the group that it is sociologically meaningful to study. The results must be interpreted in the light of all the familiar problems involved in collecting social science data through questionnaires and interviews.

These selection problems concern the boundedness of social relations and the possibility of drawing samples from relational data in order to make inferences about whole networks. Two broad approaches to identifying the boundaries of networks have been pursued. In the first an attempt is made to identify those boundaries that are perceived as real by the participants and so correspond to the actual boundaries of social groups and organisations. The alternative strategy involves the investigator using a formal criterion to identify the boundaries of a category that has some analytical significance but may not form a socially organised and recognised group (Laumann et al., 1989). Thus, the investigator must decide whether the study concerns a substantively real social group or a formal category or collection of units.

It has been common when studying small-scale social networks to try to identify all the members of a particular group and to trace their various connections with one another. In such small groups it seems relatively straightforward to aim to collect complete relational data on the whole group. There are, however, problems in clearly defining the relation that is to be reported. Social relations are social constructs, produced on the basis of participants' definitions of the situation. A relation of 'close friendship', as I have shown, may mean quite different things to different people, depending on their conceptions of what it means to be 'close'. The researcher who simply asks respondents to identify their 'close friends' cannot be sure that all respondents will have the same understanding of 'closeness'. Respondents with a restrictive definition of closeness will draw narrow boundaries around themselves, while those with a more inclusive conception of friendship will recognise more extensive boundaries. The very boundaries of the group of close friends, therefore, will vary from one person to another. Any boundaries identified by the researcher through an aggregation of these individual perceptions may be wholly artificial: they may be simple artefacts of question wording. If, on the other hand, the researcher explicitly defines 'close' – by, for example, frequency of interaction – he or she will be imposing a definition of closeness on the respondents, and the boundaries of friendship may again be artificial. Some researchers have taken advantage of this arbitrariness to explore subjective perceptions of friendship, asking people to map their various friends on a chart of concentric circles representing degrees of closeness around the focal individual – him- or herself (Spencer and Pahl, 2006).

This issue is important, as researchers may have inaccurate views about the boundaries of relational systems. It is often assumed that the social relations of individuals are confined to the particular group or locale under investigation. To the extent that connections outside this locale are ignored, the social network studied will be an imperfect representation of the full network. This is especially clear in the case of informal groups, such as street gangs, where the boundaries of the group are loosely drawn and where gang members' activities stretch well beyond its core membership

(Yablonsky, 1962). But the same is also true for more formal groups. Kerr and Fisher (1957), for example, discussed the 'plant sociology' that focuses attention on the physical boundaries of particular workshops and offices in isolation from the wider economy. Such investigations isolate their research locale from the larger regional, national and international systems in which they are embedded. Research that is confined to the local work situation may fail to identify those relations that extend beyond the plant.

In a similar vein, Stacey (1969) criticised locality studies for their assumption that bonds of 'communal' solidarity are confined within local social systems. She held that they must be seen as stretching out to entwine with the larger economic and political systems. Thus, a local study of the flow of money through a network ought not to limit its attention to that geographical locality. Many of the most important agencies involved in the circulation of money will lie outside the locality: there are federal government agencies, regional and national banks, multinational companies, and so on. If, as is likely, these are more important to the flow of money than are the local organisations and agencies, a locality-based research project faces the possibility of a totally inadequate view of the structure of the relevant network of transactions. This is particularly important at a time when electronic communication through email and the internet has created an extended cyberspace across which virtual relations can be established. The boundaries of such virtual communities are especially difficult to discern with any precision.

What these problems point to is the fact that the determination of network boundaries is not simply a matter of identifying the apparently natural or obvious boundaries of the situation under investigation. Although 'natural' boundaries may, indeed, exist, the determination of boundaries in a research project is the outcome of a theoretically informed decision about what is significant in the situation under investigation. A study of political relations, for example, might recognise that what counts as 'political', how this is to be distinguished from 'economic', 'religious' and other social relations, and the choice of boundaries for the relevant political unit, are all theoretically informed decisions. Researchers are involved in a process of conceptual elaboration and model building, not a simple process of collecting pre-formed data.

## POSITIONAL AND REPUTATIONAL APPROACHES

Assuming that relevant boundaries can be identified, the research may then define the target population for study. Two general approaches to this task have been identified: the 'positional' and the 'reputational' approaches.[1] In a positional approach, the researcher samples from among the occupants of particular formally defined positions or group memberships. First, the positions or groups that are of interest are identified, and then their occupants or members are sampled. Unless the population under investigation is very small, this is likely to require some kind of enumerated list that covers the whole of the target population. Examples of this kind of strategy would be samples drawn from a school class, a village, a workgroup, or from institutions such as a political elite or corporate directorate. A familiar problem with positional studies is that of determining which positions to include. Studies of elites, for example, have often been criticised for their identification of the top positions in institutional hierarchies, especially when the researcher offers no real justification for the cut-off threshold used to distinguish the 'top' from other positions in the institutional hierarchy. This problem is, of course, a reflection of the general boundary problem that has already been discussed, and it is important that researchers have theoretically and empirically justifiable reasons for the inclusion or exclusion of particular positions.

This may involve an assumption that there are 'natural' subgroups within the population. Research on business interlocks, for example, has often focused attention on the 'top 250' companies in an economy.[2] This research strategy involves assuming that the division between the 250th and the 251st companies forms a natural boundary between large-scale and medium-scale business. However, such boundaries can rarely be drawn with precision. There is a continuous gradation in size from large to small, and, while it may be possible to identify the points in the size distribution at which the gradient alters, it will not generally be possible to draw sharp boundaries. Indeed, most such research does not examine the overall size distribution for changes in gradient, but simply uses an arbitrary and a priori cut-off threshold: while some researchers investigate the top 250, others investigate the top 50, top 100, or top 500 slices of the distribution.[3]

In the positional approach the selection of cases for investigation may sometimes follow from an earlier decision about the selection of connections. A directorship, for example, can be regarded as a person's connection to a company, and a researcher may already have decided to limit attention to a particular group of companies. In such a situation, the selection of directors for study is determined by the selection criteria used for the companies.[4]

The reputational approach can be used where there are no relevant positions, where there is no comprehensive listing available, or where the knowledge of the agents themselves is crucial in determining the boundaries of the population. In the reputational approach, the researcher studies all or some of those named on a list of nominees produced by knowledgeable informants. Those included on the list are those who are reputed to be the members of the target population. The informants are asked to nominate, for example, 'powerful members of the community', 'people of high standing in business', and so on, depending on the purposes of the research. These nominations can then be combined into a target population. The choice of informants is obviously of crucial importance in the reputational approach. The researcher must have good reasons to believe that the informants will have a good knowledge of the target population and are able to report this accurately. Whether or not this is the case will often be known only when the research has been completed, and so there is an element of circularity in the strategy. For this reason, researchers should endeavour to come up with theoretical and empirical reasons for the choice of informant which are, as far as possible, independent of the particular social relations being investigated.

This will not always be possible, and one particular variant of this reputational strategy, using the so-called 'snowballing' technique, follows exactly the opposite procedure. In this approach, a small number of informants are studied and each is asked to nominate others for study. These nominees are, in turn, interviewed and asked for further nominations. As this procedure continues, the group of interviewees builds up like a snowball. Eventually, few new nominees are identified in each round of interviews. In the snowballing method, the social relation itself is used as a chain of connection for building the group. By its very nature, however, a snowball sample is likely to be organised around the connections of the particular individuals who formed its starting point. For this reason, the method of selection tends to determine many of the relational features of the resulting social network. This network is built from the relations of a group of connected agents and, as Laumann et al. (1989: 22) remark, 'it is scarcely informative to learn that a network constituted by a snowball sampling procedure is well-connected'.

A further strategy of selection, neither positional nor reputational, occurs when a researcher aims to select connections or affiliations directly. Such research might, for example, select the activities and events in which people are involved, independent of any positions or organisations that may have been used to identify the people themselves. In a study of New Haven, for example, Dahl (1961) used participation in the making of key decisions as the basis of selection. Involvement in decision-making, therefore, was seen as an action that allows people to be given a numerical value, measuring the importance of the decision, independently of whatever organisational positions they hold. Dahl held that this allowed him to assess the relative power of different categories of agents, instead of assuming that power was an automatic correlate of social position. A similar strategy was that of Davis et al. in *Deep South* (1941), where social events were studied, resulting in a matrix showing the participation of 18 women in 14 events. The problem in this kind of strategy, of course, is that of how to justify the choice of activity: have the most important events been chosen, and what is a 'key issue'? Selecting valid connections and affiliations, therefore, involves precisely the same problems as the direct selecting of cases. Activities and events can be chosen because they are regarded as objectively significant (a variant of the positional approach) or because knowledgeable informants believe them to be important (a variant of the reputational approach).

## DOES SAMPLING MAKE SENSE?

I have written, so far, mainly of the selection of whole populations through complete or quasi-enumeration. But it may often be necessary to use sample data, and these matters then become more complicated. Few sampling problems arise in small-group studies, where it is generally possible to undertake a complete enumeration of all group members and of their relations with one another. When research on large-scale social systems is being undertaken, however, a complete enumeration may not be a viable aim, and there will be particularly intractable sampling problems. The sheer scale of the resources needed will often preclude the complete enumeration of large populations, but, even if such research proves possible – for example, through a census of population – the scale of the resulting data set would make any analysis extremely difficult. Advances in computing have made such data sets containing attribute data relatively easy to handle for most statistical purposes. In the case of relational data, data sets may be a hundred times larger and require correspondingly more computer power. In the case of a fairly small village with a population of 5,000 people, there would be 25 million items of data, which is beyond the capacity of many computers. For a national population running into millions, the sheer quantity of data can hardly be imagined, and the computing power required to handle this will simply not be available to most social researchers.

It was, of course, similar problems that, in the pre-computer age, led to the development of sampling techniques that would allow, say, a sample of 1,000 to be used instead of a complete enumeration of a population of many thousands. The statistical theory of sampling sets out the conditions under which attribute data collected from a sample of cases can be generalised into estimates for larger populations. It might be assumed, therefore, that sampling from large populations would provide a similar workable solution for social network analysis. Figure 3.1 gives a schematic account of the ideal sampling process in social network analysis. A particular population of agents will be involved in a complex system of social relations of all types that make up the total network. Within this relational system, sociologists may identify such 'partial' networks as those comprising economic relations, political relations, religious relations, and so on. When a strategy of complete enumeration is followed, the researcher can attempt to ensure that full information is obtained on all the relevant relations, and so can construct adequate models of the partial networks.

The task of sampling would appear to be obvious and straightforward, involving nothing more than the general principles of sampling in survey research: a representative sample of cases is drawn from the population in question, their relations are investigated, and sample networks are constructed that will be homologous to the partial systems that occur in the population as a whole. But things are not, in fact, as simple as this. The general principles of sampling are based on the application of the theory of probability to large numbers of observations, and there are well-established mathematical rules for judging the reliability of sample data. There are no such rules for judging the quality of relational data derived from a sample, and there are good reasons for assuming that sampling may result in unreliable data. Although it is possible to draw a sample of 1,000 cases for analysis, there is no guarantee that the structure of this sample network will bear any relationship to the structure of the corresponding partial

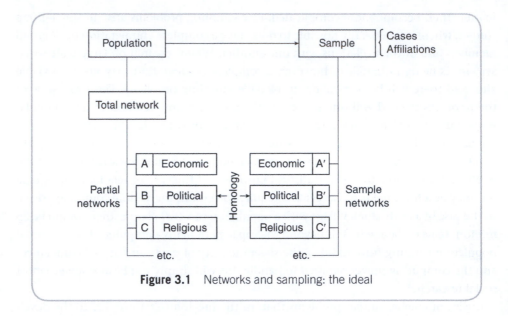

**Figure 3.1** Networks and sampling: the ideal

network. A representative sample of agents does not, in itself, give a useful sample of relations (Alba, 1982: 44).

It might seem, at first sight, that this is not a real problem. The overall distribution of relations among agents and their 'density' or 'connectedness',[5] for example, might seem an easy matter to estimate from sample data: the sample provides data on the network attributes of the individual cases, and these can be used to calculate overall network parameters. The density of the friendship ties in a country, for example, could be assessed by asking a random sample of people how many friends they have. If the sample is large enough, these estimates ought to be reliable. But it is almost impossible to go beyond such basic parameters to measure the more qualitative aspects of network structure.

The reasons for this relate to the sparsity of the relational data that can be obtained from a sample survey of agents. Even if there was a perfect response rate and all respondents answered all the questions in full, many of the contacts named by respondents will not themselves be members of the sample. This means that the number of relations among members of the sample will be a very small subset of all their relations, and there is no reason to believe that the relations identified among the agents in the sample would themselves be a random sample of all the relations of these same agents. With a very large population, such as that of a national study, it is very unlikely that any member of a random sample will have any kind of social relation with others in the same sample. The probability of a connection existing between two individuals drawn at random from a population of many millions is so low that the probability of drawing a sample containing significant numbers of mutually connected individuals is very considerably lower than the probability of winning a national lottery. It is, therefore, unlikely that a researcher could say anything at all about the relational structure of the national population with a random sample. Burt (1983a) has made a rough estimate that the amount of relational data lost through sampling is equal to 100 – k per cent, where k is the sample size as a percentage of the population. Thus, he argues that a 10 per cent sample involves the loss of 90 per cent of the relational data. Even a massive 50 per cent sample would involve the loss of half of the data. Such a loss of data makes the identification of most structural features virtually impossible in conventional sample research.

Sample data can also lead to difficulties in arriving at basic measures of the relational attributes of the particular individuals studied, especially if there is any amount of non-response in the survey. Imagine, for example, an attempt to estimate the sociometric popularity of agents in a network in which there is a very small number of very popular agents and a much larger number of less popular ones.[6] Because they exist in very small numbers, a sample is unlikely to include sufficient of the very popular agents to allow any generalisations to be made about the overall patterns of popularity in the network. This is akin to the problem of studying a small elite or dominant class through a national random sample survey. Unless the sample is very large indeed, they will not appear in adequate numbers, and a very large sample defeats much of the point of sampling. One way around this, of course, might be to use a stratified sample, in which popular agents have a higher probability of selection. The obvious difficulty with this, however, is that such a sampling strategy could be implemented only if the researcher already knew something about the distribution of popularity in the population.

There seem, at present, to be three different responses to these sampling problems. The first is to abandon any attempt to measure the global properties of social networks and to restrict attention to personal, individual-level networks. This research strategy involves looking at the unrestricted choices that people make, including those to others not included in the sample, and calculating the size and organisation of their particular groups of contacts. As no attempt is made to generalise about structure of the overall network, sampling poses few difficulties other than those that arise in any kind of social research. This is the strategy used in studies of friendship and community undertaken by Wellman (1979), Fischer (1982) and Willmott (1986, 1987).

The second response is to use a form of snowballing. Frank (1978a, 1979) argues that researchers should draw an initial sample of cases and then collect information on all the contacts of the sample members, regardless of whether these are members of the original sample. These contacts are added to the sample and their contacts are discovered in the same way. By extending this process through a number of stages, more and more of the indirect contacts of the members of the initial sample will be discovered. The researcher must decide how far to continue this snowballing. This will generally be to the point at which the number of additional members added to the sample drops substantially because names that have already been included are being mentioned for the second or third time. Frank has shown that such a snowballing method allows a reasonable estimate to be made of such things as the distribution of contacts and the numbers of dyads and triads. A snowball sample, of course, is not a random sample:

the structure that is discovered is, in fact, 'built in' to the snowball sampling method itself. But this is precisely what is necessary in order to avoid the sparsity of connections found in a random sample. The assumption of the snowball sampling method is that the connected segment of the network that forms the sample network is representative of all other segments of the network. The researcher, then, must have some knowledge about the population and their relations in order to make this assessment of representativeness. But snowballing does, at the very least, make it possible to try to estimate which features of the structure may be an artefact of the sampling method itself and so to control for these in the analysis.[7]

A third response to the sampling problem is that of Burt (1983a), who has suggested a way of moving on to some of the more qualitative features of social networks. In particular, Burt is concerned with the identification of 'positions' or structural locations, such as roles. If it is assumed that agents in a similar structural location in a network will have various social attributes in common, then it is possible to use survey data on the typical relations between agents with particular attributes as a way of estimating what structural locations might exist in the network. From each respondent it is necessary to obtain information about their social attributes and the attributes of those to whom they are connected (including people outside the sample). Agents can then be grouped into sets of agents with commonly occurring combinations of attributes, and these sets can be arranged into a sets-by-sets table that shows the frequency of relations between members of the various categories. It might be discovered, for example, that 70 per cent of white men have black male friends, while only 20 per cent of white women have black male friends. Such measures, argues Burt, provide estimates of the valued relations between social 'roles' that could be expected to occur if the researcher had undertaken a complete enumeration of all men and women in the population.

There are currently some glimmers of what can be achieved in the study of large-scale social systems using sampling methods. Though it might seem, at present, impossible to discover anything about such things as cliques and clusters from sample data, it is to be hoped that further advances in the techniques of network sampling will make this possible (Alba, 1982: 46; Frank, 1988, 2011).

---

## EXERCISE

Imagine that you are undertaking a study of power in the international economy.

- What published lists of companies are available for you to select companies for analysis? How would you decide how many companies to select, and would you select all those meeting a size criterion, or would you draw a sample? Can you apply the same selection criterion to all economic sectors (industrial, banking, insurance, etc.)?
- Are there organisations other than companies that should be included in your study? How would you select these for inclusion in your data set?

- Which positions within each company and organisation would be the appropriate level to take in order to identify the important or powerful individuals?
- What different issues would arise if you were to focus on participation in decision-making rather than following a positional approach?

Note: There are no right or wrong answers to these questions. You should explore the implications of the various choices made and try to compare your answers with those of a colleague. One such study is that of Stokman et al. (1985): what problems can you identify in their data selection procedures?

## FURTHER READING

There are no useful books on data collection, but you should consult the relevant chapters in any standard research methods text. A useful overview can be found at http://www.nsf.gov/pubs/2002/nsf02057/nsf02057_4.pdf

Frank, O. (2011) 'Survey Sampling in Networks', in J. Scott and P. Carrington (eds) *The Sage Handbook of Social Network Analysis*. London: Sage.

Rather technical, but written by the leading expert on issues of network sampling.

# FOUR

## Organising and Analysing
## Network Data

This chapter will explore:

- Ways of organising and storing network data
- Tables, matrices and sociograms
- Undirected, directed and valued data
- Computer programs for social network analysis

It is often quite straightforward to analyse very small data sets. Sociograms for four- or five-person groups, for example, can easily be constructed by hand and their properties can be visually inspected. However, this becomes much more difficult with larger networks. When dealing with data sets that have more than about ten cases and five relations, it is all but essential to use a computer. Computer processing saves a considerable amount of time: the data rearrangement undertaken by Homans in his investigation of the participation of 18 women in 14 social events, for example, can be undertaken on a computer in a few seconds at most. Use of a computer also allows analyses to be undertaken that are simply not possible by hand.

When relational data are properly prepared and stored, they can be managed and manipulated more efficiently. It is important, therefore, to consider how the logical structure of the data set can be translated into a computer file. The first step is often to sort names of individuals, organisations, or events in order to generate listings that can be analysed for their connections. Research on interlocking directorships, for example, involves generating a list of directors in the target companies, sorting this list into alphabetical order, and then identifying those names that appear two or more times. The most straightforward method for doing this is to use a word processor or spreadsheet program, as the names can be entered as text and then sorted and edited. These programs will allow data to be sorted into alphabetical or numerical order as an aid to its analysis and manipulation.[1] This is an essential first step whenever data are in a raw form that may require cleaning before use: it may be necessary to discover, for example, whether John Smith, J. Smith, and John H. Smith are the same person or, perhaps, two or three different people.

The most usual outcome of this kind of processing is a data set in a 'linked list' format. In a linked list, each line in the file shows a specific case followed by its affiliations or relations. It might show, for example, the name of a director followed by the names of all the companies of which he or she is a director (or it may show this in coded, label form). Specialist computer programs and general spreadsheets such as Excel, allow the use of linked lists and make it possible to store the labels and further data attributes (gender, age, income, etc.) for each case.

Even the simplest of spreadsheets can be used to store and to organise relational data, and they can be used to prepare these data in files readable by other specialist packages. The 'range' options can be used to specify particular parts of a table for copying to a new file. If, for example, a table of friendship relations among people is stored in a file, it is possible to select the male or the female data alone for separate analysis. A spreadsheet can also be used for basic network procedures. If the data have been converted from linked lists to tables in binary or valued form, a spreadsheet can be used to calculate basic statistical measures, such as row and column sums, frequency distributions, and correlations. Many of these measures can be converted into screen graphics and then printed out. Frequency distributions, for example, can be instantly plotted on a histogram or bar chart. While the major mathematical functions built into spreadsheets are the kind of financial and statistical procedures most appropriate for variable analysis, it is also possible to use matrix mathematics to calculate various structural properties of networks.[2] However, use of a spreadsheet beyond the most basic measures is probably best attempted only if other programs specifically designed for social network analysis are not available. The principal use of the spreadsheet should be to store the data and to carry out the straightforward data management functions of rearrangement and manipulation.[3]

The major software programs for social network analysis – discussed later in this chapter – store their data in simple table form as a linked list, and it is easy to transfer an appropriate file directly from a spreadsheet to these programs.[4] For most purposes, it is best to import data into one of the specialist packages as early as possible, reading it back into a spreadsheet only when attribute data have to be added and used in statistical analyses. In these circumstances, in fact, it may be preferable to export the data files to a specialist statistical package such as SPSS.

## MATRICES AND RELATIONAL DATA

The tables into which social research data can be entered are various kinds of 'data matrix' (Galtung, 1967). At its simplest, a data matrix appears as a pattern of rows and columns drawn on paper or displayed on a computer screen. Whatever the physical form that it takes, the logical structure of a data matrix is always that of a simple table. In research using attribute data, each case studied (for example, each respondent in a survey) is represented by a row in the matrix, and the columns refer to the variables that measure their attributes. This is a case-by-variable matrix, and Figure 4.1 shows a simple form of such a data matrix. This is the way in which data are organised for most standard statistical procedures.

The case-by-variable data matrix cannot be used for relational data. These data must, instead, be seen in terms of a case-by-affiliation matrix. The cases are the particular

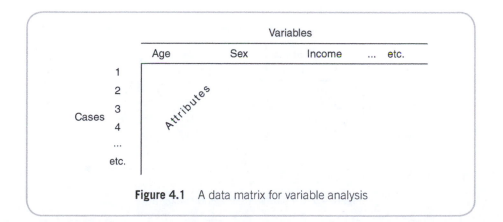

**Figure 4.1**   A data matrix for variable analysis

agents that form the units of analysis (for example, individuals or organisations), and the affiliations are the activities, organisations or events in which these agents are involved. The columns of the matrix, then, refer to the affiliations in terms of which the involvements, memberships or participations of the agents can be identified. The case-by-affiliation matrix is the logical form of what, in the previous section, was referred to as the linked list. From this case-by-affiliation matrix, information can be derived on the direct and indirect connections among the agents. In Figure 4.2, for example, a simple case-by-affiliation matrix is shown for the involvement of three people (labelled 1, 2 and 3) in three events (labelled A, B and C). Where a specific individual participates in a particular event, there is a '1' in the corresponding cell of the matrix; non-participation is shown by a '0' entry. It can be seen that all three people participate in event A, but none of them is involved in events B or C. Thus, the sociogram that can be drawn from this matrix shows a simple triad of mutual contacts among the individuals. The sociogram can be read as saying that each person meets the other two at a particular event.

It can be quite difficult to construct sociograms for even moderate-sized data sets. Lines will criss-cross one another at all sorts of angles to form a thicket of connections, and any visual appreciation of the structure is lost. Indeed, it may be quite impossible, using conventional manual methods of drawing, to construct a sociogram for a large network. For this reason, social network analysts have attempted to find alternative ways of recording the connections. Following the principle of the data matrix, the solution that has been most widely adopted has been to construct a case-by-case matrix in which each agent is listed twice: once in the rows and once in the columns. The presence or absence of connections between pairs of agents is represented by '1' or '0' entries in the appropriate cells of the matrix. This idea is not, perhaps, as immediately comprehensible as the sociogram, and so it is worthwhile spelling it out at greater length.

Figure 4.3 shows the general form of data matrices for social networks. The most general form for raw or coded data is what I have called the case-by-affiliation matrix, a linked list in which agents are shown in the rows and their affiliations in the columns.

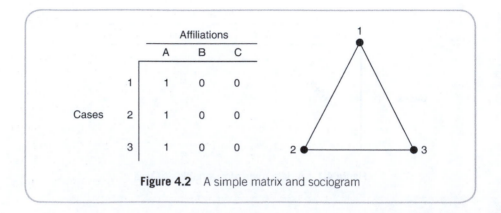

**Figure 4.2**   A simple matrix and sociogram

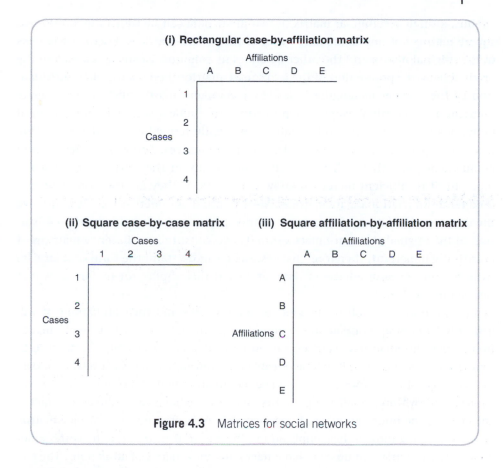

**Figure 4.3**   Matrices for social networks

Such a matrix is described as being 'two-mode' or 'rectangular', because the rows and columns refer to two different sets of data and so the number of rows and the number of columns are generally different.[5] From this basic rectangular data matrix can be derived two square, or 'one-mode', matrices. In the square case-by-case matrix both the rows and the columns represent the cases, and the individual cells show whether or not particular pairs of individuals are related through a common affiliation. This matrix, therefore, shows the actual relations or ties among the agents. It is exactly equivalent to the sociogram in the information that it contains. The second square matrix shows affiliations in both its rows and its columns, with the individual cells showing whether particular pairs of affiliations are linked through common agents. This matrix, the affiliation-by-affiliation matrix, is extremely important in network analysis and can often throw light on key aspects of the social structure that are not apparent from the case-by-case matrix. These one-mode matrices show the relations among the particular members of the network and much network data may be directly available in this form without having to be derived from a two-mode matrix. For example, friendship choices among the children in a particular secondary school class or kinship relations among those living in a particular village will take this form.

Thus, a single rectangular matrix of two-mode data can be transformed into two square matrices of one-mode data.[6] One of the square matrices describes the rows of the original matrix and the other describes its columns. Nothing is added to the original data, the production of the two square matrices being a simple transformation of the original rectangular one. The rectangular matrix and the two square matrices are equivalent ways of representing the same relational data. In social network analysis the rectangular matrix is generally termed an 'incidence' matrix, while the square matrices are termed 'adjacency' matrices. These terms derive from graph theory, and they will be explained more fully in the next chapter. For the moment, it is sufficient merely to know the names, as they are the most generally used terms for relational data matrices. Most techniques of network analysis involve the direct manipulation of adjacency matrices, and so also involve a prior conversion of the original incidence matrix into its two constituent adjacency matrices. It is critically important, therefore, that researchers understand the form of their data (whether incidence or adjacency data) and what this implies for the analyses that can be undertaken.

Where a researcher collects two-mode data on cases and their affiliations, it will generally be most appropriate to organise this information into an incidence matrix from which the adjacency matrices used in network analysis can later be derived. In some situations, however, it will be possible for a researcher to collect relational data in a direct case-by-case form. This would be the situation with, for example, friendship choices made within a small group. In this situation of what is called direct sociometric choice data, the information can be immediately organised in an adjacency matrix. Without entering into all the complications, there is, in this situation, no corresponding incidence matrix and no complementary adjacency matrix of affiliations. The reason for this, of course, is that all the agents have merely a single affiliation in common: the fact of having chosen one another as friends.[7]

For many social network purposes, the distinction between cases and affiliations may appear somewhat artificial. In a study of, say, the involvement of 18 women in 14 social events, it would seem only sensible to regard the women as the cases and the events as their affiliations. Indeed, this would be in line with the normal survey practice of treating the agents as the cases. But with such phenomena as overlapping group memberships, for example, the situation is far less clear-cut. This kind of research is interested in the extent to which a group of organisations overlap in their membership, and in how similar they are in their patterns of recruitment. Both the groups and their members are agents in the sociological sense, and so both have an equal right to be considered as the 'cases'. The members may be treated as the cases, in which case the organisations of which they are members will be treated as their affiliations; or the organisations may be treated as cases and the members that they share will be seen as their affiliations. The choice of which set of agents to treat as the cases for the purpose of network analysis will depend simply on which is seen as being the most significant in terms of the research design.

This decision will normally have been reflected in prior sampling decisions. If the organisations are assumed to be of the greatest importance, then a sample of organisations will be selected for study and the only people who will figure in the subsequent analysis will be those who happen to be members of these organisations. In such a research design, the organisations have a theoretical priority and it would seem sensible to treat the members as indicating affiliations between organisations. As far as the techniques of network analysis are concerned, however, it makes no difference which of the two are regarded as the cases. The same procedures may be applied whichever choice is made, and it is the task of the researcher to decide which of them may have a meaningful sociological interpretation.[8]

## MATRIX CONVENTIONS

The distinction between cases and affiliations, therefore, is generally to be regarded as a purely conventional feature of research designs for network analysis. Another aspect of this convention is to place the cases on the rows of the incidence matrix and the affiliations on its columns. This arrangement is based on the conventions employed in attribute analysis, where the cases are treated as rows and the variables are treated as columns.

Certain other conventions in the use of matrices must also be understood. These conventions can be recommended as the proper basis of best practice in network analysis, as they help to ensure maximum clarity in research discussions. Most readers will be familiar with the importance of various conventions in basic mathematics. It is conventional when drawing ordinary graphs of variables, for example, to use the vertical axis for the dependent variable and to label this as the $y$-axis. The horizontal axis is used for the independent variable and is labelled as the $x$-axis. This convention prevents any confusion about how the graph is to be read and it ensures that any statements made about the graph will be unambiguous. The conventions surrounding the relational data matrix have a similar purpose.

In the discussion of matrices, it is conventional to designate the number of rows in a matrix as $m$ and the number of columns as $n$. It is also customary to list the rows first when describing its size. The overall size of a matrix can, therefore, be summarised by referring to it as an $m \times n$ matrix. Incidence matrix (i) of Figure 4.3, for example, is a $4 \times 5$ matrix. It is also conventional to refer to the rows before the columns when describing the contents of any particular cell, and to use the letter $a$ to refer to the actual value contained in the cell. Thus, the value contained in the cell corresponding to the intersection of row 3 with column 2 would be designated as $a(3, 2)$. This can be generalised by using the convention of referring to the individual rows by $i$ and individual columns by $j$. Thus, the general form for the content of a cell is $a(i, j)$, where the researcher may then go on to specify the relevant values for $i$ and $j$. These conventions are summarised in Figure 4.4.

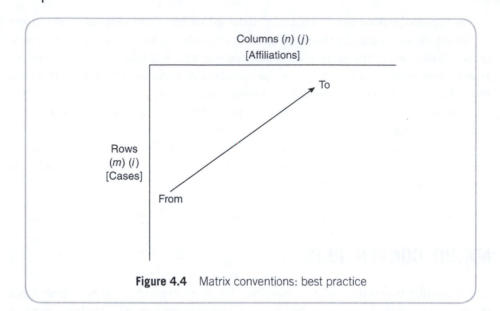

**Figure 4.4** Matrix conventions: best practice

# AN ANALYSIS OF DIRECTORSHIP DATA

The usefulness of the matrix approach to relational data can best be illustrated through a concrete example. Figure 4.5 contains some artificial data on interlocking directorships among companies. An interlocking directorship, or interlock, exists where a particular person sits as a director on the boards of two or more companies. His or her presence on the two boards establishes a relation between the companies. In many investigations of interlocking directorships, it is the companies that are of central interest. For this reason, they are generally treated as the cases and so are shown as the rows of incidence matrix (i) in Figure 4.5. The affiliations, shown in the columns of this matrix, are the directors that the companies have, or do not have, in common with one another. Each cell of the matrix contains a binary digit, '1' or '0', which indicates the presence or absence of each director on each company. Thus, company 1 has four directors (A, B, C and D), and director A sits on the board of company 2 as well as company 1. This means that there is an interlock between company 1 and company 2. The adjacency matrix – (ii) in Figure 4.5 – shows the interlocks that exist among all companies. In this matrix, each cell shows more than the mere presence or absence of an interlock, it shows the number of directors in common between a pair of companies. The cells contain actual values, rather than simply binary digits, because companies may have more than one director in common. Thus, company 1 and company 4 have just one director in common (director C), while companies 2 and 3 have two directors in common (directors B and C). This can be confirmed by examining the columns of the original incidence matrix, which show that director C sits on companies 1 and 4, and that directors B and C each sit on companies 2 and 3.

The simplest assumption to make about this adjacency matrix might be that the strength of a relation can be measured by the number of interlocks that it involves. The strongest relations, then, exist between companies 1 and 2 and between companies 1 and 3, each of these relations involving three directors. The weakest links would be those that involve just one director. The sociogram of companies indicates the structure of the matrix quite clearly, with the numbers attached to the lines indicating the

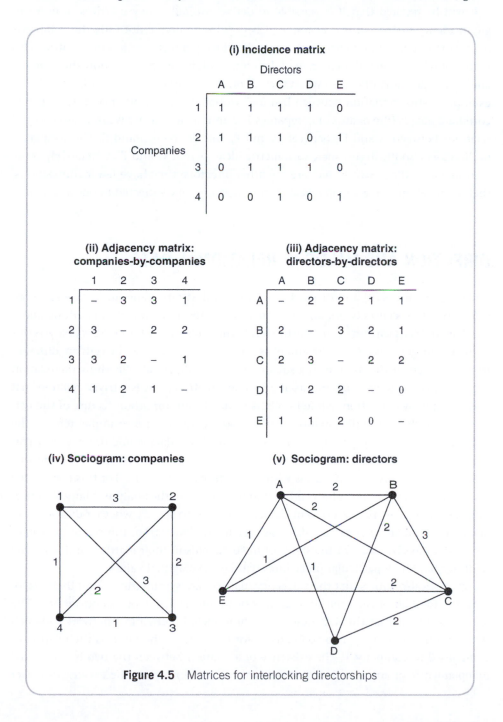

**Figure 4.5**  Matrices for interlocking directorships

strength or 'value' of the lines. This sociogram could equally well have been drawn in other ways: for example, with the thickness of the lines representing their value, or with the points connected by one, two, or three parallel lines. Each method would convey the same information about the structure of the matrix.

It will be recalled that it is possible to derive two adjacency matrices from a single incidence matrix. In this example, it is possible to derive not only the company-by-company adjacency matrix but also a director-by-director adjacency matrix. This matrix and its associated sociogram of directors – (iii) in Figure 4.5 – show the relations among the directors that exist when they sit on the same company board. There is, for example, a strong relation between B and C, who meet one another on three separate corporate boards (the boards of companies 1, 2 and 3), and rather weaker, single-board relations between A and D, between A and E, and between B and E. The sociogram of directors also illustrates such sociometric ideas as that D and E are relatively more 'peripheral' to the network than are the other directors: they have fewer connections, their connections are generally weaker, and they are not connected to one another.

## DIRECTION AND VALUE IN RELATIONAL DATA

Adjacency matrices (ii) and (iii) in Figure 4.5 also illustrate some further general considerations in social network analysis. First, it is important to note something about the diagonal cells running from the top left to the bottom right. In matrix analysis this particular diagonal is referred to simply as 'the diagonal', because the cells are different from all others in the matrix. In a square matrix the diagonal cells show the relation between any particular case and itself. In some situations this is a trivial relation that exists simply by definition, while in others it may be an important feature of the network. The cells on the diagonal of matrix (ii) of Figure 4.5, for example, refer to the relation of each company to itself. In this example, these data would not have any particular meaning. The fact that a company is connected to itself through all its directors is true but trivial, as our concern is with inter-company relations. For this reason, the diagonal cells contain no values and should be ignored in the analysis. Many technical procedures in network analysis require the researcher to specify whether diagonal values are to be included or excluded, if this is at all ambiguous. For this reason, researchers must always be aware of the status of the diagonals in their matrices and will need to understand how particular procedures handle the diagonal values.

Figure 4.5 also shows that the adjacency matrices are symmetric around their diagonals: the top half of each matrix is an identical, mirror image of its bottom half. The reason for this is that the data describe an 'undirected' network, a network in which the relation of company 1 to company 2, for example, is the same as the relation of company 2 to company 1. The existence of a relation between the two is considered independently of any question of whether the relation involves the exercise of power and influence in one direction but not in the other. For this reason, all the relational information in an adjacency matrix for an undirected network is contained in the bottom half of the matrix alone; the top half is, strictly speaking, redundant. Many analytical procedures in network analysis, therefore, require only the bottom half of the adjacency matrix and not the full matrix. For undirected networks, no information is lost in this method of analysis.

Undirected data are the simplest and easiest type of relational data to handle, and it is, perhaps, necessary to spend a little time in discussing some of the more complex types of data. One of the most important considerations in variable analysis is the level of measurement that is appropriate for a variable. This is the question of whether attribute data should be measured in nominal, ordinal, ratio, or interval terms. From this decision flow many other decisions about which particular analytical procedures can appropriately be used for the data. Similar measurement problems arise with relational data, according to whether the data are 'directed' and/or 'numbered'. Figure 4.6 uses these two dimensions to classify the four main levels of measurement in relational data.

The simplest type of relational data (type 1) is that which is both undirected and binary. This is the form taken by the data in the incidence matrix of Figure 4.5. The adjacency matrices in that figure contain relational data of type 2: the relations are undirected but valued.[9] I have already shown that the 'valued' data (type 2) in the adjacency matrices of Figure 4.5 are derived from the binary data of the original incidence matrix. Values typically indicate the strength of a relation rather than its mere presence. The signed data that were discussed in Chapter 2 in connection with theories of balance are relational data where a '+' or '−' is attached to each line. These relations can be regarded as intermediate between the binary and valued types. Such data show more than simply the presence or absence of a relation, as the presence is qualified by

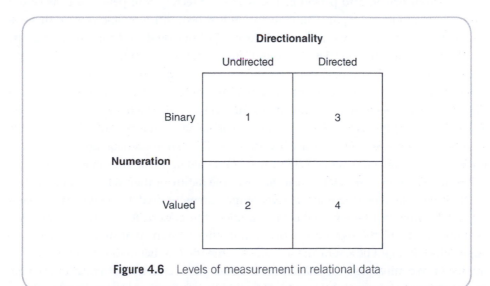

**Figure 4.6** Levels of measurement in relational data

the addition of a positive or negative sign; but the nature of the relation is indicated simply by the polarity and not by an actual value. It is, of course, possible to combine a sign with a value and to code relational data as varying from, say, –9 to +9. In such a procedure, the value could not represent simply the number of common affiliations between cases, as they cannot have a negative number of affiliations in common. The values must, therefore, be some other measure of the strength or closeness of the relation. Such a procedure would, of course, rest upon a sociological argument that produced solid theoretical or empirical reasons for treating the data in this way.

Valued data can always be converted into binary data, albeit with some loss of information, by using a cut-off value for 'slicing' or dichotomising the matrix. In a slicing procedure, the researcher chooses to consider only those relations with a value above a particular level as being significant. Values above this level are sliced off and used to construct a new matrix in which values at or below this level are replaced by '0' entries and values above it are replaced by '1' entries. This procedure of slicing the data matrix is a very important technique in network analysis, and will be discussed more fully in Chapter 6. Directed data can also take binary or valued forms, and similar slicing procedures can be applied to reduce valued and directed data (type 4) to binary and directed data (type 3). It is also possible to reduce directed data to undirected data, by the simple expedient of ignoring the direction. Thus, a researcher may decide that the important thing to consider is the mere presence or absence of a relation, and not its direction. In this case, then, it makes sense to ignore the directionality of the data. A further matrix convention may appropriately be mentioned at this point. In adjacency matrices that contain directed data, the usual convention is to present the direction of a relation as running 'from' a row element 'to' a column element. Thus, the entry in cell (3, 6) of a directed matrix would show the presence or strength of the relation directed from person 3 to person 6. The relation directed from person 6 to person 3 would be found in cell (6, 3). This convention is shown in Figure 4.4. It is for this reason that a directed matrix is asymmetric around its diagonal, and that, therefore, the whole matrix must be considered, and not simply its bottom half.

Complex types of relational data can always be reduced to simpler types and, in the last instance, any type of relational data may be treated as if it were undirected and binary (type 1). Techniques appropriate to this type of data, therefore, have the widest application of all the techniques of social network analysis. It is not, of course, possible to undertake the reverse operation, converting simple to complex data, unless additional information is available over and above that contained in the original data matrix.[10]

Researchers must always take great care over the nature of their relational data. They must, in particular, be sure that the level of measurement used is sociologically appropriate. The attempt to use valued data in studies of interlocks, for example, rests upon assumptions about the significance of multiple directorships that may or may not be appropriate. It might be assumed, for example, that the number of directors in common between two companies is an indicator of the strength or closeness of a relation. Having four directors in common, on this basis, would mean that two companies are 'closer' than those that have only two directors in common. But is this a valid sociological assumption? If it is not, the mathematical procedure should not be used. Mathematics itself cannot provide an answer for the researcher. The relevance of particular mathematical concepts and models is always a matter for the informed sociological judgement of the researcher. Even if it is decided that it is reasonable to use valued data, the researcher must be alive to other assumptions that might be contained in the mathematical procedures. Does a procedure, for example, treat the values as ordinal or as ratio variables? In the former case, a value of 4 would be regarded simply as being stronger than a value of 2; in the latter case the relationship would be regarded as being twice as strong. The choice of a level of measurement is, again, a sociological question and not a mathematical one.

# COMPUTER PROGRAMS FOR SOCIAL NETWORK ANALYSIS

There are now a variety of computer packages available for those who want to manipulate their matrices and calculate some social network measures. The most important programs, and the most easily available, are UCINET and Pajek, and I will be referring to the use of these programs at various points in the book.

UCINET was produced by a group of network analysts at the University of California, Irvine (UCI), and the current development team includes Stephen Borgatti, Martin Everett and Linton Freeman.[11] The program began as a set of modules written in BASIC, progressed to an integrated DOS program, and has been available as a Windows program for a number of years. It is a general purpose, easy to use program that operates through a hierarchical menu structure to reach particular options and commands. This is shown in this book in the form MENU1 > MENU2 > COMMAND so as to indicate the sequence of menu choices needed for any particular measure. The program covers all the basic graph-theoretical concepts, positional analysis, and multi-dimensional scaling. UCINET Version 6 data files are in matrix format and consist of simple alphanumeric files. The rows in a data file represent the rows in a basic network listing, but a header row contains details on the number of rows and columns and the labels that are used to identify them. The program contains in-built procedures for converting other data file formats. In addition to exporting in various formats, a number of conversion utilities are provided that allow UCINET to feed, almost seamlessly, into other social network analysis programs.

The easiest way to produce data files is by using the intuitive and built-in, spreadsheet-style, data entry system that is accessible from the DATA menu. This uses a linked list format that shows, for each unit (such as a person or an organisation), the code numbers of all the other units to which it is connected. As well as entering and editing data with the UCINET spreadsheet, it is possible to import (and export) data from Excel worksheets. The data file can be edited after the initial data entry, and various permutations and transformations can be performed on it so as to identify subsets for further analysis. For example, the rows and the columns can be permutated, sorted, or transposed, or the weightings of lines can be altered. This latter procedure is termed 'dichotomising' the matrix – accessed through the TRANSFORM menu – and makes it easy to prepare a series of data files for use in more complex analyses.

The principal social network analysis procedures are found under the NETWORK menu, where there are sub-menus for COHESION, CENTRALITY AND POWER, SUBGROUPS, ROLES & POSITIONS, and various more specialised procedures. COHESION gives access to basic calculations of distances and densities; CENTRALITY is the venue for all the various measures of closeness, betweenness and other measures of centrality and prominence. The SUBGROUPS menu gives access to a number of powerful techniques for the detection of cliques, while the REGION option detects the various zones and sectors within the network. Under ROLES & POSITIONS it is possible to run programs that analyse structural locations in a network. Finally, the TOOLS option is used to undertake multi-dimensional scaling, cluster analyses, factor analysis and correspondence analysis. All of these terms are explained in the course of this book. Display of network data can be handled through the separate NETDRAW program that is supplied with UCINET (but see below for an alternative).

The program called Pajek – the word is Slovenian for spider – was specifically devised to handle very large data sets, though it can also handle small ones. Produced by Vladimir Batagelj and Andrej Mrvar, it was released at the end of 1996 and has been periodically updated. Wooter de Nooy has taken the lead in producing a comprehensive manual for Pajek that includes numerous worked examples (de Nooy et al., 2005).[12]

The program displays its results and workings in a main window and various subsidiary windows. The options equivalent to DATA and TRANSFORM in UCINET are called FILES and NET in Pajek. The FILES menu has options to read, edit or sort data files – which are entered into data files as a list of points with their labels and a list of lines. These can be either the original matrices themselves or the results for partitioning or clustering the data. Using commands available from the NET menu, the networks can be transposed or reduced. This is also the place where the command to detect components can be found. A number of other menus allow a variety of partitioning and clustering options that are specifically designed to reduce the size of very large networks and make them more amenable to analysis. A large network can be analysed and partitioned, for example, and then the partitions can each be analysed separately and in greater detail.

Pajek concentrates on procedures that work efficiently on large data sets and does not contain the comprehensive array of network measures found in UCINET, but it does allow some powerful processing of large networks. For many users, however, the most interesting parts of the program will be the various options found under the DRAW menu. It is here that the user can gain access to procedures for the two-dimensional and three-dimensional drawing of network diagrams on screen, and the resulting diagrams can be coloured and labelled to bring out their central characteristics. Options are available to spin and rotate the diagrams for inspection from a variety of angles, and points can be moved easily by dragging them with the mouse. All aspects of these manipulations can be controlled in great detail. The diagrams created can be exported in a variety of graphical formats discussed later in this book. Pajek is also distributed along with UCINET, making it easy to move between one program and the other.

Numerous other programs exist and new programs are appearing all the time, often based around innovative – and sometimes unfamiliar – methods and measures.[13] Perhaps the most important of these is SIENA, which allows the analysis of network change over time. It is well worth checking these out, so long as you are clear about what they are trying to do. Most can be discovered from the INSNA home page by following through its connections, and many new programs are announced through the SOCNET information service.[14]

## EXERCISE

Download your preferred computer program and produce a data file for the data below. These data show the attendance of ten social workers at four national training sessions concerned with child welfare, professional ethics, record keeping and legal responsibilities. The attendance is as follows:

| | |
|---|---|
| Margery Allingham | Child welfare, Professional ethics, Record keeping, Legal responsibilities |
| Emily Bronte | Child welfare, Record keeping |
| Truman Capote | Professional ethics, Record keeping |
| Len Deighton | Child welfare |
| Mary Ann Evans | Legal responsibilities |
| Scott Fitzgerald | Professional ethics, Record keeping, Legal responsibilities |
| Elizabeth Gaskell | Professional ethics, Legal responsibilities |
| Geoffrey Household | Child welfare, Professional ethics |
| Hammond Innes | Child welfare, Legal responsibilities |
| Erica James | Child welfare, Record keeping |

Using the program, print the incidence matrix and then generate and print the adjacency matrix of social workers.

- Which social worker(s) attended the most courses?
- Which course was the most popular?
- Which social worker(s) met the most other social workers at courses?

*(Continued)*

*(Continued)*

- Which social worker(s) met the fewest other social workers at courses?
- Which social worker(s) met each other most frequently at the various courses?

You can probably, of course, discover many of these answers directly from the above list, but the point of the exercise is to familiarise yourself with using the program so that you can use it on larger and more complex data sets.

If you feel brave, see if you can use the drawing facilities of the program to produce a sociogram.

## FURTHER READING

Crossley, N., Bellotti, E., Edwards, G., Everett, M., Koskinen, J., and Tranmer, M. (2015) *Social Network Analysis for Ego-Nets*. London: Sage.

Concerned with personal networks (which I introduce in Chapter 5), but also introduces the use of UCINET.

De Nooy, W., Mrvar, A., and Batagelj, V. (2005) *Exploratory Social Network Analysis with Pajek*. New York: Cambridge University Press.

A good manual for using Pajek, which also covers many key issues in social network analysis.

# FIVE

## Terminology for Network Analysis

This chapter provides:

- An overview of the basic concepts required to describe the structure of social networks
- A review of concepts of points, lines, neighbourhood, distance and density
- Consideration of ego-focused networks and whole networks
- An extensive discussion of network density
- A study of face-to-face and online communities

Social network analysis involves the description of the structural features of the social relations of individuals and groups. These structural properties figure as the concepts in social theories that aim to explain patterns of action and processes of change. Those interested in social network analysis have devised a set of concepts that can be expressed in a formal language – that of mathematics – and so can give a precise summary of the structural features of particular systems of social relations. In this chapter I will outline a set of basic concepts that will allow a researcher to make the most general description of a social network and that are the building blocks of the more complex concepts introduced in later chapters. First, however, it is necessary to look at the types of social networks and the ways in which they are built.

Social networks are of two broad kinds, depending on whether the focus is on the agent (individual or collective) or on the whole structure of social relations connecting different individuals. A network based on a particular individual is called an egocentric network or 'egonet'. An egonet comprises all the relations that a focal agent has with others. Collecting information on friendship choice among a sample of individuals, for example, will yield a large collection of egonets, one for each person in the sample. It is possible to analyse the types of people with whom a person is friendly and the variation in the numbers of friends that each person has. A number of other measures, which will be discussed later, can also be made on these egonets.

Egonets are not, however, completely separate from each other. A person's friends each have their own friendship networks and so the relations of friendship will extend through long chains: I am a friend of Harry, who is a friend of Deborah, who is a friend of Jim, who is a friend of Jean, who is completely unknown to me. In a sample survey this may not be apparent, as it is unlikely that the friends of the respondent will also have been selected as respondents in the same survey. However, if data have been collected for a whole population, such as a school class or a set of companies, it is possible to connect the various egonets together as the building blocks of a larger structure that may connect all members of the population together. This larger structure is called the 'whole network'.

Social network analysis can be used to study networks of both types, though the concepts used will sometimes have a slightly different meaning or method of calculation according to whether the research is concerned with egonets or whole networks. In this chapter I will highlight these variations wherever they are relevant.

## THE LANGUAGE OF NETWORK ANALYSIS

Many of the fundamental features of social networks can be analysed through the direct manipulation of matrices – transposing, adding and multiplying matrices will all produce information on their structure. Matrix algebra, however, is rather complex for most researchers (but see the simple introduction in Meek and Bradley, 1986). Although matrices are useful for the organisation and storage of relational data, specialist computer programs allow an easier and more direct approach to network analysis. This has typically been achieved through a mathematical language that directly operationalises the idea of the sociograms. This is the approach called 'graph theory', which provides a formal language for describing networks and their features. Graph theory translates matrix data into formal concepts and theorems that can be directly related to the substantive features of social networks. If the sociogram is one way of representing relational matrix data, the language of graph theory is a more general way of doing this. While it is not the only mathematical theory that has been used for modelling social networks, it is the starting point for many of the most fundamental ideas in social network analysis.

The concepts of graph theory are the basis of the principal procedures provided in the UCINET program, though it keeps as much of the mathematics as possible hidden from the user. Data in matrix form can be read by the programs, and suitable graph-theoretical concepts can be explored without the researcher needing to know anything at all about the mechanics of the theory or of matrix algebra. Nevertheless, an understanding of graph theory will significantly help to improve the sophistication of a researcher's analyses, helping to ensure that he or she chooses procedures that are appropriate for the particular questions being investigated.

Graph theory concerns sets of elements and the relations among these, the elements being termed 'points' and the relations 'lines'.[1] A matrix describing the relations among a group of people can be converted into a graph of points connected by lines, and therefore a sociogram is a 'graph'. It is important to be clear about the difference between this idea of a 'graph' and the graphs of variables used in statistics and other branches of quantitative mathematics. These more familiar graphs are graphs of variables that plot, for example, frequency data on axes that represent the variables. The graphs of graph theory are graphs of relations that express the qualitative patterns of connection among points. Indeed, graph diagrams themselves are of secondary importance in graph theory. As has already been suggested, it is often very difficult to draw a clear and comprehensible diagram for large sets of points with complex patterns of connection. By expressing the properties of the graph in a more abstract mathematical form, it is possible to dispense with the need to draw a sociogram and so ease the task of understanding very large graphs.

Nevertheless, the drawing of graph diagrams has always been of great illustrative importance in graph theory, and many will be used in this book. Because of the visual simplicity of small sociograms, I will begin with an introduction to the principles involved in drawing graph diagrams.

A graph diagram[2] aims to represent each row or column in an incidence matrix – each of the cases or affiliations under investigation – by a point on paper or on a computer screen. Once the appropriate adjacency matrix has been derived, the '1' and '0' entries in the cells of the matrix, representing the presence or absence of a relation, can be indicated by the presence or absence of lines between the points. In Figure 4.5, for example, the symmetric 4 × 4 adjacency matrix of companies can be drawn as a four-point graph containing six lines, which correspond to the non-zero entries in the matrix.

In a graph, it is the pattern of connections that is important, and not the actual positioning of the points on the page or screen. The graph theorist has no interest in the relative position of two points, the lengths of the lines that are drawn between them, or the size of the character used to indicate the points. While graph theory does use concepts of length and location, these do not correspond directly to the ideas of physical length and location with which we are most familiar. It is usual in a graph diagram to draw all the lines with the same physical length, wherever this is possible, but this is a purely aesthetic convention and a matter of practical convenience. Indeed, it is not always possible to maintain this convention if the graph is to be drawn with any clarity. For this reason, there is no one correct way to draw a graph. The graph diagrams in Figure 5.1, for example, are equally valid ways of drawing the same graph – all convey exactly the same graph-theoretical information.

## MORE THAN JOINING UP THE LINES

The concepts of graph theory, then, are used to describe the patterns of connections among points. At its simplest, the social researcher represents each case by a dot on the page and proceeds to join up the dots to produce a pictorial representation of the network. The simplest of graph-theoretical concepts refer to the properties of the individual points and lines from which such a graph is constructed. However, lines are not simply lines; they differ in important ways that allow us to disclose the salient features of a social network.

Lines can correspond to any of the types of relational data distinguished in Figure 4.6: undirected, directed, valued, or both directed and valued. The graphs in Figure 5.1 consist of undirected lines. These graphs derive from a symmetric data matrix where it is simply the presence or absence of a relation that is of importance. If, however, the relations are directed from one agent to another, then they can be represented in a directed graph, sometimes termed a 'digraph'. A directed graph is represented in drawn form by attaching an arrow head to each line, the direction of the arrow indicating the direction of the relation. A directed line is sometimes referred to as an 'arc'. Figure 5.2 shows a simple directed graph.

If, on the other hand, the intensity of the relation is an important consideration and can be represented by a numerical value, the researcher can construct a valued graph in which numerical values are attached to each of the lines. I have already shown that a matrix for a directed graph may not be symmetric, as relations may not be reciprocated. Similarly, a matrix for a valued graph may or may not be symmetric, but it will contain values instead of simple binary entries.[3] An example of a valued graph is that shown in Figure 4.5. One of the simplest and most widely used measures of intensity is the 'multiplicity' of a line. This is simply the number of separate contacts that make

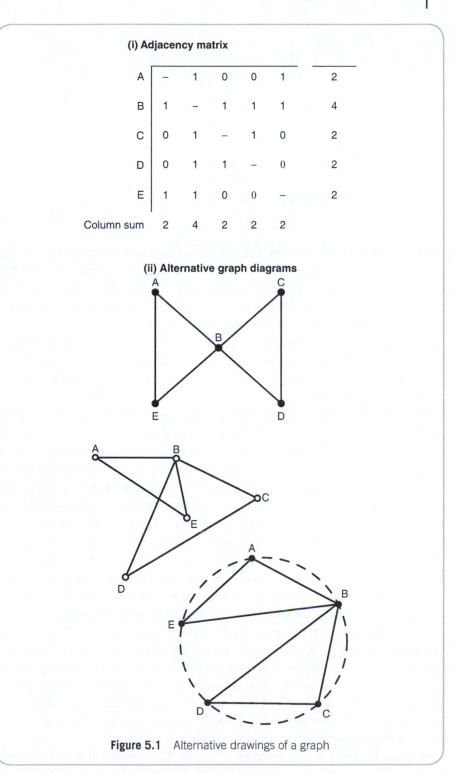

**(i) Adjacency matrix**

| | A | B | C | D | E | |
|---|---|---|---|---|---|---|
| A | – | 1 | 0 | 0 | 1 | 2 |
| B | 1 | – | 1 | 1 | 1 | 4 |
| C | 0 | 1 | – | 1 | 0 | 2 |
| D | 0 | 1 | 1 | – | 0 | 2 |
| E | 1 | 1 | 0 | 0 | – | 2 |
| Column sum | 2 | 4 | 2 | 2 | 2 | |

**(ii) Alternative graph diagrams**

**Figure 5.1** Alternative drawings of a graph

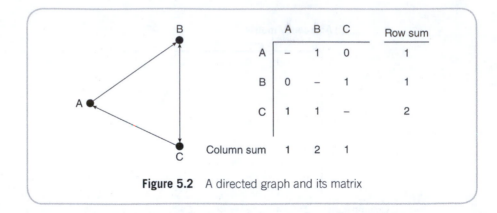

**Figure 5.2**  A directed graph and its matrix

up the relationship. If, for example, two companies have two directors in common, the relation between the companies can be represented by a line of multiplicity 2. If they have three directors in common, the interlocking directorship can be seen as a line with multiplicity 3. The values in a graph can, of course, relate to any other suitable measure of intensity, such as the frequency of a relationship.

The fundamental ideas of graph theory can most easily be understood in relation to simple undirected and unvalued graphs. A number of apparently straightforward words are used to refer to graph-theoretical terms, and it may appear pedantic to define these at great length. However, these definitional matters are important, as the apparently simple words are generally used in highly specific and technical ways. It is essential that their meanings are clarified if the power of graph theory is to be understood.

Two points connected by a line are said to be adjacent to one another. 'Adjacency' is the graph-theoretical expression of the fact that two agents represented by points are directly related or connected with one another. Those points to which a particular point is adjacent are termed its 'neighbourhood', and the total number of other points in its neighbourhood is termed its 'degree' (strictly, its 'degree of connection'). Thus, the degree of a point is a numerical measure of the size of its neighbourhood – how many others it is adjacent to. The degree of a point is shown by the number of non-zero entries in the corresponding row or column entry in the adjacency matrix. Where the data are binary, as in Figure 5.1, the degree is simply the row or column sum for that point.[4] Because each line in a graph connects two points – it is 'incident' to two points – the total sum of the degrees of all the points in a graph must equal twice the total number of lines in the graph. The reason for this is that when calculating the degrees of the various points each line is counted twice, once each for the points at its two ends. This can be confirmed by examining Figure 5.1. In this graph, point B has degree 4 and all the other points have degree 2. Thus, the sum of the degrees is 12, which is equal to twice the number of lines (6). Degree measures can be computed in Pajek using the NET > PARTITIONS > DEGREE menu option.

Points may be directly connected by a line, or they may be indirectly connected through a sequence of lines. A sequence of lines in a graph is called a 'walk', and a

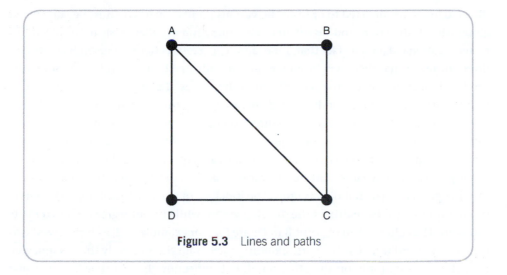

**Figure 5.3**  Lines and paths

walk in which each point and each line are distinct, when there is no returning or repetition, is called a path. The concept of the path is, after those of the point and the line, one of the most basic of all graph-theoretical concepts and is the basis of concepts of 'length' and 'distance'. The length of a path is measured by the number of lines that make it up; the number of 'steps' necessary to get from one point to another. In Figure 5.1, for example, points A and D are not directly connected by a line but they are connected through the path ABD, which has a length of 2. A particularly important concept in graph theory is that of the distance between two points. This is the length of the shortest path (sometimes called the 'geodesic') that connects them.

These concepts are illustrated in the simple graph in Figure 5.3. In this graph, AD is a path of length 1 (it is a line), while ABCD is a path of length 3. The walk ABCAD is not a path, as it passes twice through point A. It can be seen that points A and D are connected by three distinct paths: AD at length 1, ACD at length 2, and ABCD at length 3.[5] The distance between A and D, however, is the length of the shortest path between them, which, in this case, is 1. The distance between points B and D, on the other hand, is 2. Many of the more complex graph-theoretical measures take account only of geodesics – shortest paths – while others consider all the paths in a graph.

## THE FLOW OF INFORMATION AND RESOURCES

A directed line is particularly useful for representing the flow of information or resources from one agent to another and so a directed graph allows us to chart the diffusion of information and resources through a network. The same concepts discussed above can be used with directed graphs, though some modifications must be made. The lines in a directed graph are directed to or from the various points. Each line must be considered along with its direction, and there will not be the symmetry that exists in simple, undirected relational data. The fact that, for example, person A chooses person B as a friend does not mean that there will be a matching friendship choice from B to A. Similarly, the fact that company C invests £500,000 in the shares of company D does not mean that there will be a corresponding investment – or any investment – from D to C. For this reason, the 'degree' of a point in a directed graph comprises two distinct elements, called the 'indegree' and the 'outdegree'. These are defined by the direction of the lines that represent the social relations. The indegree of a point is the total number of other points that have lines directed towards it; and its outdegree is the total number of other points to which it directs lines. The indegree of a point, therefore, is shown by its column sum in the matrix of the directed graph, while its outdegree is shown by its row sum. The column sum of point B in Figure 5.2, for example, is 2, as it 'receives' two lines (from A and from C). The corresponding sociogram shows clearly that its indegree is 2. The row sum for B, on the other hand, is 1, reflecting the fact that it directs just one line, to point C.

A path in a directed graph is a sequence of lines in which all the arrows point in the same direction. The sequence CAB in Figure 5.2, for example, is a path, but CBA is not: the changing direction of the arrows means that it is not possible to 'reach' A from C by passing through B.[6] It can be seen that the criteria for connection are much stricter in a directed graph, as the researcher must take account of the direction of the lines rather than simply their presence or absence. The distance between two points in a directed graph, for example, must be measured only along the paths that can be identified when account is taken of direction. When agents are regarded as either 'sources' or 'sinks' for the flow of resources or information through a network, for example, it is sensible to take serious account of this directionality in analysing the graph of the network.

The flow of information through directed networks has been central to studies of diffusion. This was explored in topological terms by Tarde (1890), but it was not until the work of Rogers (1962) and Coleman et al. (1966) that it was investigated in true network terms. These studies showed the crucial effects of network structures in shaping the flow and speed of diffusion and the effects of distance on the attenuation of information.

Sometimes, however, the direction of the lines can legitimately be ignored. If it is the mere presence or absence of a line that is important, its direction being a relatively unimportant factor, it is possible to relax the usual strict criteria of connection and to regard any two points as connected if there is a sequence of lines between them, regardless of the directions of the arrows. In such an analysis it is usual to speak of the presence of a 'semi-path' rather than a path. CBA in Figure 5.2 is a semi-path. Treating directed data as if they were undirected, therefore, means that all the usual measures for undirected data may then be used.

# DENSITY OF CONNECTIONS

One of the most widely used concepts in graph theory is that of 'density'. This describes the general level of linkage among the points in a graph. Uses of density in social network analysis can best be illustrated by considering unvalued and symmetrical data, though the issues about value and symmetry discussed in the previous section must still be borne in mind.

Density is the overall level of connectedness in a network. Its measurement depends upon two other parameters of network structure: the inclusiveness of the graph and the sum of the degrees of its points. Inclusiveness refers to the number of points included within the various connected parts of the graph. Put in another way, the inclusiveness of a graph is the total number of points minus the number of isolated points. The most useful measure of inclusiveness for comparing various graphs is the number of connected points expressed as a proportion of the total number of points. Thus, a 20-point graph with five isolated points would have an inclusiveness of 0.75. An isolated point has no connections and so can contribute nothing to the density of the graph. Thus, the more inclusive the graph, the denser it will be. Those points that are connected to one another, however, will vary in their degree of connection. Some points will be connected to many other points, while others will be less well connected. The higher the degrees of the points in a graph, the denser it will be. In order to measure density, then, it is necessary to use a formula that incorporates these two parameters. This involves comparing the actual number of lines present in a graph with the total number of lines that would be present if the graph were complete. A 'complete' graph is one in which all the points are adjacent to one another: each point is connected directly to every other point. Such completion is very rare, even in very small networks, and the concept of density is an attempt to summarise the overall distribution of lines in order to measure how far the graph is from this state of completion. A complete graph has a density of 100 per cent, conventionally expressed as 1.0. A graph in which half of all possible connections are present has a density of 50 per cent or 0.5, so density varies on a scale of 0 to 1.0.

The actual number of lines in a graph is a direct reflection of its inclusiveness and the degrees of its points. This may be calculated directly in small graphs, but in larger graphs it must be calculated from the adjacency matrix. The number of lines in any graph is equal to half the sum of the degrees. In Figure 5.1, as I have already shown, half the sum of the row or column totals is 6. The maximum number of lines that could be present in this graph can be easily calculated from the number of points that it contains. Each point may be connected to all except one other point (itself), and so an undirected graph with $n$ points can contain a maximum of $n(n - 1)/2$ distinct lines. Calculating $n(n - 1)$ would give the total number of pairs of points in the graph, but the number of lines that could connect these points is half this total, as the line connecting the pair A and B is the same as that connecting the pair B and A. Thus, a graph with three points can have a maximum of 3 lines connecting its points; one with four points can have a maximum of 6 lines; one with five points can have a maximum of 10 lines; and so on. It can be seen that the number of lines increases at a much faster rate than the number of points. Indeed, this is one of the biggest obstacles to computing measures for large networks. A graph with 250 points, for example, can contain up to 31,125 lines.

The density of a graph is formally defined as the number of lines in a graph, expressed as a proportion of the maximum possible number of lines. The formula for the density is

$$\frac{l}{n(n-1)/2}$$

where $l$ is the number of lines present.[7] As already indicated, this measure can vary from 0 to 1.0, the density of a complete graph being 1.0. The densities of various graphs can be seen in Figure 5.4: each graph contains four points and so could contain a maximum of 6 lines. It can be seen how the density varies with the inclusiveness and the sum of the degrees.[8] In Pajek, density measures are computed from the INFO > NETWORKS > GENERAL menu choice and in UCINET these are calculated using NETWORK > COHESION > DENSITY.

In directed graphs the calculation of the density must be slightly different. The matrix for directed data is asymmetric, as a directed line from A to B will not necessarily involve a reciprocated line directed from B to A. For this reason, the maximum number of lines that could be present in a directed graph is equal to the total number of pairs that it contains. This is simply calculated as $n(n-1)$. The density formula for a directed graph, therefore, is $l/n(n-1)$.

It is also possible to use the density measure with valued graphs, though there is very little agreement about how this should be done. The simplest solution, of course, is

| | | | | | | |
|---|---|---|---|---|---|---|
| No. of connected points | 4 | 4 | 4 | 3 | 2 | 0 |
| Inclusiveness | 1.0 | 1.0 | 1.0 | 0.7 | 0.5 | 0 |
| Sum of degrees | 12 | 8 | 6 | 4 | 2 | 0 |
| No. of lines | 6 | 4 | 3 | 2 | 1 | 0 |
| Density | 1.0 | 0.7 | 0.5 | 0.3 | 0.1 | 0 |

**Figure 5.4** Density comparisons

to disregard the values of the lines and to treat the graph as a simple directed or undirected graph. This involves a considerable loss of information. It might be reasonable, for example, to see lines with high multiplicity as contributing more to the density of the graph than lines with low multiplicity. This would suggest that the number of lines in a valued graph might be weighted by their multiplicities: a line with multiplicity 3 might be counted as being the equivalent of three lines. Simple multiplication, then, would give a weighted total for the actual number of lines in a graph. But the denominator of the density formula is not so easy to calculate for valued graphs. The denominator, it will be recalled, is the maximum possible number of lines that a graph can contain. This figure must be based on assumptions about the maximum possible value that could be taken by the multiplicity in the network in question. If the maximum multiplicity is assumed to be 4, then the weighted maximum number of lines would be equal to four times the figure that would apply for a similar unvalued graph. However, it is not at all obvious how a researcher might decide on an estimate of what the maximum multiplicity for a particular relation would be. One solution is to take the highest multiplicity actually found in the network and to use this as the weighting (Barnes, 1969). There is, however, no particular reason why the highest multiplicity actually found should correspond to the theoretically possible maximum. In fact, a maximum value for the multiplicity can be estimated only when the researcher has some independent information about the nature of the relationships under investigation. In the case of company interlocks, for example, average board size and the number of directorships might be taken as weightings. If the mean board size is 5, for example, and no person can hold more than two directorships, then the mean multiplicity would be 5 in a complete and fully connected graph.

In the case of the company sociogram in Figure 4.5, for example, the weighted total of lines measured on this basis would be 5 times 6, or 30. The actual total of weighted lines in the same sociogram, produced by adding the values of all the lines, is 12, and so the multiplicity-based density would be 12/30, or 0.4. This compares with a density of 1.0 which would be calculated if the data were treated as if they were unvalued. It must be remembered, however, that the multiplicity-based calculation is based on an argument about the maximum number of directorships that a person can hold. If it were possible for a person to hold a maximum of three directorships, for example, then the density of the company sociogram would fall from 0.4 to 0.2. Typically, of course, there is no fixed limit to the number of directorships that a person can hold, and so such calculations are impossible to make unless an arbitrary limit is chosen by the researcher. The problem in handling valued data may be even more complex if the values do not refer to multiplicities. For other measures of intensity, there is no obvious way of weighting lines.

The density measure for valued graphs, therefore, is highly sensitive to assumptions that a researcher makes about the data. A measure of density calculated in this way, however, is totally incommensurable with a measure of density for unvalued data. For this reason, it is important that a researcher does not use a measure simply because it is available in a standard program. A researcher must always be perfectly clear about the assumptions involved in any particular procedure, and must report these along with the density measures calculated.

## DENSITY IN EGONETS

The discussion so far has assumed that we are dealing with whole networks. Barnes (1974) and Mitchell (1969) have discussed the application of density measures to egonets such as 'personal networks' (Crossley et al., 2015). In such an analysis a measure of density would be concerned with the density of the links surrounding particular agents. From this socio-centric standpoint, the density is that of the overall network, and not simply of the 'personal networks' of focal agents.

In an egonet constructed from sample data the network will typically include the agent ('ego') and his, her or its direct connections to others. In such a case, the egonet is necessarily complete and so its density will always be 1.0, which is not very informative. The density of an egonet, therefore, is more usually calculated for egonets that have been derived from a whole network, as the data include the contacts among the others involved in the egonet. Density then becomes a measure of the connections among ego's contacts. In the case of friendship, for example, it measures whether they are strongly mutually connected – everyone knowing everyone else – or whether the various friends are segregated from each other and are connected only through ego. An important qualification is often made to the way in which density is measured in an egonet. It is common to disregard the focal agent and his or her direct contacts, concentrating only on the links that exist among these contacts. Figure 5.5 shows the consequences of this. Sociogram (i) shows a network of five individuals anchored around ego. The sociogram shows ego's direct contacts and the relations that exist among these contacts. There is a total of 6 lines, and the density of the sociogram is 0.60. But the density is at this relatively high level principally because of the four lines that connect ego to B, C and D. These relations will exist almost by definition. If these data had, for example, been obtained through a questionnaire that asked respondents to name their four best friends, the high density would be an artefact of the question wording. The relations to the four nominated contacts of each respondent will swamp any information about the relations among those who are named by each respondent and for this reason should usually be ignored in calculations of density. The significant fact about sociogram (i) is that there are relatively few connections among ego's own contacts. In sociogram (ii), where ego's direct contacts are shown as dotted lines, there are two relations among A, C and D (shown as solid lines), and the four-person network has a density of 0.33. It is for this reason that many analysts regard this as a more useful measure of the density of the egonet.[9] It can be argued, however, that both measures are useful and that they highlight different features of the networks.

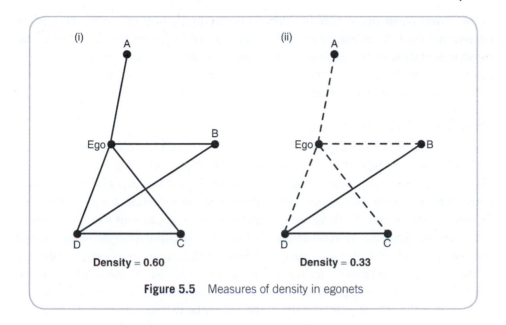

**Figure 5.5**  Measures of density in egonets

# PROBLEMS IN DENSITY MEASURES

A far more fundamental problem that affects all measures of density must now be considered. This is the fact that the density depends on the size of a graph. This prevents density measures being compared across networks of different sizes (see Niemeijer, 1973; Friedkin, 1981; Snijders, 1981). Density, it will be recalled, varies with the number of lines present in a graph, this being compared with the number of lines that would be present in a complete graph. There are very good reasons to believe that the maximum number of lines achievable in any real graph may be well below the theoretically possible maximum. If there is an upper limit to the number of relations that each agent can sustain, the total number of lines in the graph will be limited by the number of agents. This limit on the total number of lines means that larger graphs will, other things being equal, have lower densities than small graphs. This is linked, in particular, to the time constraints under which agents operate. Mayhew and Levinger (1976) argue that there are limits on the amount of time people can invest in making and maintaining relations. The time that can be allocated to any particular relation, they argue, is limited, and it will decline as the number of contacts increases. Agents will, therefore, decide to stop making new relations – new investments of time – when the rewards decline and it becomes too costly. The number of contacts they can sustain, therefore, declines as the size of the network increases. Time constraints, therefore, produce a limit to the number of contacts and, therefore, the density of the network. Mayhew and Levinger have used models of random choice to suggest that the maximum value for density that is likely to be found in actual graphs is 0.5.[10]

The ability of agents to sustain relations is also limited by the particular kind of relation involved. A 'loving' relation, for example, generally involves more emotional commitment than an 'awareness' relation, and it is likely that people can be aware of many more people than they could love. This means that a network of loving relations, other things being equal, is likely to have a lower density than any network of awareness relations.

I suggested in Chapter 3 that density was one of the whole-network measures that might reasonably be estimated from sample data. Now that the measurement of density has been more fully discussed, it is possible to look at this suggestion in greater detail. The simplest and most straightforward way to measure the density of a large network from sample data would be to estimate it from the mean degree of the cases included in the sample. With a representative sample of a sufficient size, a measure of the mean degree would be as reliable as any measure of population attributes derived from sample data, though I have suggested some of the reasons why sample data may fail to reflect the full range of relations. If the estimate is, indeed, felt to be reliable, it can be used to calculate the number of lines in the network. The degree sum – the sum of the degrees of all the points in the graph – is equal to the estimated mean degree multiplied by the total number of cases in the population. Once this sum is calculated, the number of lines is easily calculated as half this figure. As the maximum possible number of lines can always be calculated directly from the total number of points (it is always equal to $n(n - 1)/2$ in an undirected graph), the density of the graph can be estimated by calculating

$$\frac{(n \times \text{mean degree}) / 2}{n(n-1) / 2}$$

which reduces to $(n \times \text{mean degree})/n(n-1)$.

Granovetter (1976) has gone further than this and attempted to provide a method of density estimation that can be used when the researcher is uncertain about the reliability of the initial estimate of the mean degree. In some situations there may be a highly reliable estimate. With company interlock data, for example, the available directories of company information allow researchers to obtain complete information on the connections of sample companies to all companies in the population, within the limits of accuracy achieved by the directories. In such circumstances, an estimate of mean degree will be reliable. In studies of acquaintance, on the other hand, such reliability is not normally the case, especially when the population is very large. Granovetter's solution is to reject a single large sample in favour of a number of smaller samples. The graphs of acquaintance in each of the subsamples (the 'random subgraphs') can be examined for their densities, and Granovetter shows that an average of the random subgraph densities results in a reliable estimate of the population network density. Using standard statistical theory, Granovetter has shown that, for a population of 100,000, samples of between 100 and 200 cases will allow reliable estimates to be made. With a sample size of 100, five such samples would be needed; with a sample size of 200, only two samples would be needed.[11] These points have been further explored in field research, which has confirmed the general strategy (Erickson et al., 1981; Erickson and Nosanchuck, 1983).

It is hardly surprising that density has become one of the commonest measures in social network analysis. It is an easily calculated measure for both undirected and directed graphs, it can be used for both egonets and whole-network studies, and it can be reliably estimated from sample data. I hope that I have suggested, however, some of the limits on its usefulness. It is a problematic measure to use with valued data, it varies with the type of relation and with the size of the graph, and, for this reason, it cannot be used for comparisons across networks that vary significantly in size. Despite these limitations, the measurement of density will, rightly, retain its importance in social network analysis. If it is reported along with such other measures as the inclusiveness and the network size, it can continue to play a powerful role in the comparative study of social networks.

# A DIGRESSION ON ABSOLUTE DENSITY

The crucial problem with the existing measures of density is that density is relative to size, which makes it difficult to use the measure in comparisons of radically different sized graphs. This raises the question of whether it might not be possible to devise a measure of absolute density that would be of more use in comparative studies. This is not an essential element in my discussion, however, and it may be ignored by those readers who wish to proceed directly to the illustration of the uses of graph theory in social research in the following section. Some readers may prefer to skip-read this section and return to it after completing Chapter 6.

A concept of density modelled on that used in physics for the study of solid bodies would require measures of 'radius', 'diameter' and 'circumference'. The radius of a circular or spherical object is the distance from its centre to its circumference, on which are found its most distant reachable points. This idea of the absolute centre is discussed in the following chapter but can be taken in its common-sense meaning for now: the absolute centre is simply the point that lies 'in the middle' of a graph. Translating this into graph-theoretical terms, the eccentricity of the absolute centre of a graph can be regarded as the 'radius' of the graph. This can be illustrated by referring to some of the features of Figure 5.6, the details of which will be examined more formally in Chapter 6. The 'diameter' of a graph is defined as the greatest distance between any pair of its points. In sociogram (iv) of Figure 5.6, for example, the radius is 1.5 and the diameter is 3. In this case, then, the diameter is equal to twice the radius, as would be the case in the conventional geometry of a circle or a sphere. This will not, however, be true for all graphs.

In geometry there is a definite relationship between the area and the volume of a body, these relationships being generalisable to objects located in more than three dimensions. The area of a circle is $\pi r^2$ and the volume of a sphere is $4\pi r^3/3$, where $\pi$ is the ratio of the circumference of a circle to its diameter. The general formula for the area of a circle, therefore, is $cr^2/d$, and that for the volume of a sphere is $4cr^3/3d$, where $c$ is the circumference, $r$ is the radius and $d$ is the diameter. Applying this to sociogram

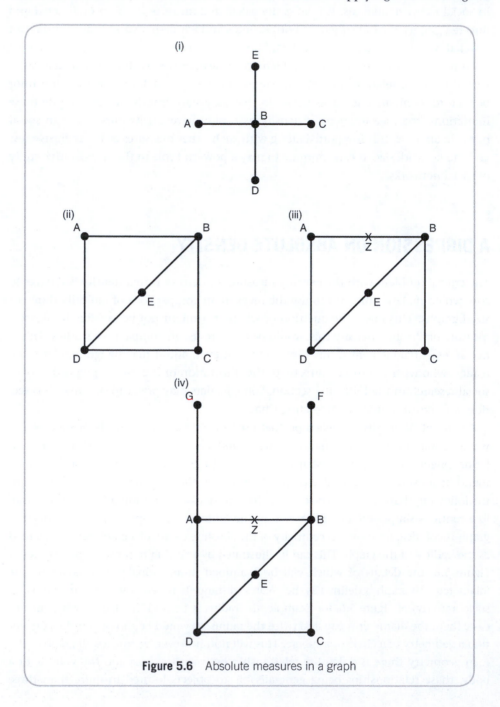

**Figure 5.6**   Absolute measures in a graph

(iv) of Figure 5.6 would show that it has a volume of $4c(1.5)^3/9$, or $1.5c$.[12] But what value is to be given to $c$ in this formula? If the diameter of a graph is taken to be the length of the geodesic between its most distant points (the longest geodesic), the circumference might most naturally be seen as the longest possible path in the graph. In sociogram (iv), this is the path of length 5 that connects point G to point F. Thus, the 'volume' of the example sociogram is 7.5.

Relatively simple geometry has, therefore, enabled us to move a part of the way towards a measure applicable to the absolute density of a graph in three dimensions. Density in physics is defined as mass divided by volume, and so to complete the calculation a measure of the 'mass' of a graph is required. Mass in physics is simply the amount of matter that a body contains, and the most straightforward graph-theoretical concept of mass is simply the number of lines that a graph contains. In sociogram (iv) of Figure 5.6 there are eight lines, and so its absolute density would be 8/7.5, or 1.07.

Generalising from this case, it can be suggested that the absolute density of a graph is given by the formula $l/(4cr^3/3d)$, where $l$ is the number of lines. Unlike the relative density measure discussed earlier in this chapter, this formula gives an absolute value that can be compared for any and all graphs, regardless of their size. But one important reservation must be entered: the value of the absolute density measure is dependent on the number of dimensions in which it is measured. The absolute density measure given here has been calculated for graphs in three dimensions. The concept could be generalised to higher dimensions, by using established formulae for 'hyper-volumes', but such an approach would require some agreement about how to determine the dimensionality of a graph. This issue will be approached again in Chapter 9, drawing on the arguments of Freeman (1983).[13] Unfortunately, no available software makes the calculation of absolute density a real possibility for social network analysts.


## COMMUNITY STRUCTURE AND DENSITY

The power and utility of density analysis can be illustrated through some concrete studies of community relations. Barry Wellman (1979, 1982), a member of Harrison White's original cohort of network analysts at Harvard, has undertaken a number of studies of community structure, in which the measurement of density has played a key role. He took as his starting point the long-standing tradition of community studies, in which writers on 'community' had generally been concerned to investigate whether the communal solidarities associated with small-scale, rural villages had been able to withstand the modernising forces of industrialisation and urbanisation. Wellman wanted to use social network analysis to see whether the development of modern societies had resulted in the disappearance of community and the emergence of urban anomie. It had been pointed out by some critics of community studies that social relations of all kinds had become detached from specific localities, with relations having an increasingly national or international scope (see the discussion in Bulmer, 1985). Wellman's early research aimed to investigate this issue for a particular urban area in Toronto – East York – and, like Fischer (1977, 1982), he focused on the question of whether 'personal communities', investigated as egonets, had stretched beyond the bounds of the local neighbourhood itself.

East York is an inner-city suburb of private houses and apartment blocks and was, at the time of the research in 1968, occupied mainly by skilled manual workers and routine white-collar workers. Wellman's fieldwork involved interviews with a random sample of 845 adults, and a key question in the interviews involved asking people to name their six closest associates. They were then asked to say whether those named were themselves close to one another (see also McCallister and Fischer, 1978). This was an attempt to go beyond direct connections by asking people about their knowledge of the relations among their friends. This is an ingenious way of going beyond the limits of sample survey data but is limited by the accuracy and completeness of the knowledge that a person has about his or her friends' friendship choices. The responses to these questions were then used to construct egonets of intimate association for each respondent, at least as these were perceived by the respondent. By asking about the connections among the persons who were named by each respondent, Wellman was able to measure the density of each personal network. This calculation of density followed the procedure outlined earlier, and ignored the direct links between respondents and their intimates. That is, data were collected on ego and his or her six intimate associates, but the densities of the egonets were calculated for the links among the six associates only.

Wellman discovered that many of the intimate associates (about a half) were relatives of the respondents, but kin and non-kin associates were all to be found across a wide geographical area. The majority of all links were with people who lived in the city itself, though very few of these links were based in the immediate locality of East York. A quarter of all the intimate associates named by respondents lived outside the city, some living overseas. Having summarised the broad shape of people's personal networks, Wellman turned to a comparison of their densities. The mean density of these egonets was 0.33,[14] only one-fifth of networks having a density greater than 0.50 (Wellman, 1979: 1215). A density of 0.33 meant that five out of the 15 possible links among intimate associates were actually present.[15] Wellman discovered that the densest networks tended to be those that were composed mainly of kin, owing to the fact that it was more likely that the kin of the respondents would maintain mutual contacts. Where kinship obligations were absent, such contacts were less likely to be maintained.

Wellman's principal findings on personal networks are summarised in Figure 5.7. He interprets these data as indicating that people were involved in networks that were 'sparsely knit'. That is, the networks were of low density. 'Communal' links were neither solidaristic nor localised. People did have particular others to rely on, but the low density of their personal networks, their lack of mutual cross-linkages, meant that such help

| Density | % of networks | % of network members who are kin |
|---|---|---|
| 0–0.25 | 47.1 | 36.4 |
| 0.26–0.50 | 31.7 | 56.9 |
| 0.51–0.75 | 7.9 | 56.9 |
| 0.76–1.00 | 13.3 | 73.7 |
| | 100.0 (n = 824) | |

**Figure 5.7**  Density of personal networks

was likely to be limited. These personal networks were, nevertheless, important sources of help and support, on both an everyday basis and in emergencies: 'East Yorkers can almost always count on help from at least one of their intimates, but they cannot count on such help from most of them' (Wellman, 1979: 1217). Those intimate associates who were less likely to give help and support were more likely to be significant for sociability. Helpers were more likely to be kin, while those who were most important for sociability were more likely to be co-residents or co-workers.

To pursue some further issues, a follow-up study was undertaken in which in-depth interviews were carried out, during 1977–78, with 34 of the original respondents. The aim was to get more 'qualitative' contextual data for the structural data of the earlier study. Although the detailed results of this stage of the inquiry go beyond the immediate concerns of this chapter, some of the directions pursued can usefully be outlined. Wellman discovered that the interpersonal networks of households were differentiated by gender divisions and by the involvement of household members in paid work. He found, for example, a number of differences between households where women were involved in paid employment and those where they were involved only in domestic work. He discovered that the social relations of a household and their access to interpersonal support from kin, friends, neighbours and co-workers were most likely to be maintained by women rather than by men. This was especially true of households where women were engaged solely in domestic work. Households where women were involved in both domestic work and in paid employment had far less dense networks of relations and were, therefore, able to obtain less support and fewer services from their contacts (Wellman, 1985).[16]

Wellman's studies relied on survey methods to generate the relational data used, but similar methods and measures can be used on other forms of relational data. Smith (1979), for example, used historical data derived from documentary sources to investigate communal patterns in an English village in the thirteenth century. Smith's data came from the records of the manor court of Redgrave in Suffolk, these records showing such things as patterns of landholding, property transactions, and financial disputes among the villagers. In total, he considered 13,592 relations among 575 individuals over the period 1259–93. Initially, he analysed the different types of relations and their frequency, which showed that about two-thirds of the relations were 'pledging' relations. These were relations in which one person gave a specific legal commitment in support of another person in relation to debt repayments and other financial arrangements.

Smith's concern was with the role of kinship and other local ties in organising these relations and in structuring communal relations.[17] Homans (1941) had previously undertaken a similar historical study of communal solidarity, but had not applied any social network concepts in his study. By contrast, Smith used the idea of the egonet as his principal orientating concept. The 425 Redgrave landholders of the year 1289 were divided into four categories according to the size of their landholdings, and equal-sized random samples were drawn from each category. This gave 112 individuals for analysis, and their documented relations with all other people over the ten-year period from 1283 to 1292 were extracted from the database. The personal egonets of the 112 people, taking account of the distance 1 relations, were then analysed in terms of their social bases and geographical spread. The distribution of the densities of the personal networks showed a curvilinear relation to landholding. Thus, density increased steadily with size of landholding among those with four acres of land or less, and it decreased steadily with the size of holding for those with more than four acres. Those with three or four acres, therefore, had the densest personal networks, median density among these households being between 0.2 and 0.4. They were also the most involved in multiplex relations. It was, therefore, the middling landholders who were best integrated into their village community. In the light of the earlier discussion of the relation between network size and density, it is interesting to note that Smith discovered a correlation of just 0.012 between the two measures. He concluded, therefore, that the observed variations in network density were not a mere artefact of network size, but reflected real variations in the quality of interpersonal relations.

Taking account of all his network data, Smith rejected the idea that Redgrave was a tightly knit organic community organised around kin and neighbours. The network structure of the medieval village, at least as far as Redgrave was concerned, was much looser than this image. Neither were distant kin an especially important source of social support:

> those individuals who interacted most frequently with near neighbours also interacted most frequently with kin, although probably on most occasions residing apart from them. These kin, however, tended to be close: siblings, uncles, nephews, nieces, fathers and mothers, sons and daughters. (Smith, 1979: 244)

Wellman recognised that the egonets that he studied in East York were linked into chains of connection through overlapping associations: there was, he held, a 'concatenation of networks' with personal networks being 'strands in the larger metropolitan web' (Wellman, 1979: 1227). However, he did not directly investigate these overall features of the whole network of East York. Some pointers to the shape that this 'concatenation' might take are provided in Grieco's (1987) extension of the work of White (1970) and Granovetter (1974). Grieco's research concerned the giving and receiving of information about job opportunities, and she showed that the flow of help from particular individuals to their network contacts produces an alteration in the global structure of the network. Where information is received indirectly, from contacts at a distance of 2 or more, there is a tendency for a new direct link, albeit a weak one, to be established between the originator of the information and those who received it (Grieco, 1987: 108ff.). The overall density of the network, therefore, increases, and some of these links may be solidified and strengthened through feelings of solidarity and obligation. Thus, some of the initial increase in density will persist. When others in the network acquire the ability to reciprocate for the help that they have received they will, in turn, tend to create new direct links and a further alteration in the density of the network. In this way, changes at the individual level of egonets result in a continual transformation of the density and the other features of the whole network.

Recent work by Wellman and others has investigated changes in network relations consequent upon advances in communications technology. Personal community links have gradually been extended in geographical scope and ease of communication by use of the car, aeroplane and telephone, but electronic computer communication through the internet and mobile phone has, perhaps, had the most extensive consequences. Cheap or no-cost communication by email, Skype and messaging services allows communication to be stretched in both time and space, enabling people to stay in touch over extended distances. Contrary to some public commentary, computer use has not led to autistic, withdrawn and isolated individuals, but to individuals integrated into online communities that are more or less connected to localised geographical communities. Indeed, growth in the number of friends has been found to be directly related to the amount of internet activity: people make *more* friends through the internet (Wellman et al., 2006; Wang and Wellman, 2010).

Websites such as Facebook and Twitter have become central nodes in an extensive network of interpersonal communication that has been described as a cyberspace. People can communicate and participate in large and extensive groups that can simulate face-to-face interaction but introduce a variety of subtle and complex alterations to communication. Individuals may use aliases and build misleading identities that, because of the absence of immediate face-to-face cues, may make for a stronger element of fictional self-presentation than in other forms of interaction. These new communities may, however, be easy for sociologists to study as electronic communication leaves digital traces that can be accurately and unobtrusively tracked and mapped using data mining techniques (Gruzd and Haythornthwaite, 2011). Sociologists are only just beginning to model these cybercommunities and to chart the patterns of solidarity and cohesion that they make possible.

------------------------------ EXERCISE ------------------------------

Using the data set that you created in Chapter 4, carry out the tasks below. If you have not created that data set, choose one of the example data sets provided with your preferred computer program. (You should try to use a small data set.)

Disregard the values attached to the lines, and through visual inspection of the matrix or sociogram try to identify the following:

- The point with the highest degree
- The longest path in the network

Load the data set into your program and make the same calculations to check your results.

Compute the density of the network and consider whether your calculation suggests a high or low level of connection for the data that you are using.

------------------------------ FURTHER READING ------------------------------

Crossley, N., Bellotti, E., Edwards, G., Everett, M., Koskinen, J., and Tranmer, M. (2015) *Social Network Analysis for Ego-Nets*. London: Sage.

An excellent introduction and comprehensive coverage of egonets.

Gruzd. A. and Haythornthwaite, C. (2011) 'Networking Online: Cybercommunities', in J. Scott and P. Carrington (eds) *The Sage Handbook of Social Network Analysis*. London: Sage.

Explores particular issues in the investigation of online networks.

# SIX

## Popularity, Mediation and Exclusion

This chapter explores:

- The concept of centrality, distinguishing between local and overall centrality
- Intermediaries in networks
- The relationship of central agents to peripheral agents
- Studies of bank centrality in corporate networks

One of the earliest concepts to be utilised in social network analysis was the idea of the sociometric concept of the 'star': that person who is the most 'popular' in his or her group or who stands at the centre of attention. Moreno (1934) reported the popularity of particular pupils within their school class by examining the friendship choices that were made. A popular individual is a centre of attention and appears in a sociogram at the centre of a radiating set of directed lines. This idea of the sociometric star has been formalised by Bavelas (1950) as the concept of 'centrality'. Since this pioneering work, a number of competing concepts of centrality have been proposed. What unites the majority of the approaches to centrality is a concern for the relative centrality of the various points in the graph. This is the question of so-called 'point centrality'. But from this common concern they diverge sharply. Some of the concepts have been especially formulated as ways of understanding how some central individuals or organisations may be able to act as intermediaries, mediating the demands and influence of the other members of their network. This highlights the fact that there are a number of different ways in which an agent can be 'central' to their network. Alongside the idea of popularity is that of unpopularity and of exclusion from participation with those who are the centre of attention. Low measures of centrality can therefore be taken as measures of various forms of exclusion or peripherality.

In this chapter I will review the various approaches to centrality and I will discuss whether these measures also provide a way of identifying a subset within the network of especially prominent agents who may be regarded as collectively holding a central position within their network.

## LOCAL AND OVERALL CENTRALITY

The concept of point centrality, I have argued, originated in the sociometric concept of the 'star'. A central point is one that is literally at the centre of a number of connections. It is a point with a great many direct contacts with other points. The simplest and most straightforward way to measure point centrality, therefore, is by the degrees of the various points in the graph. The degree, it will be recalled, is simply the number of other points to which a point is adjacent. A point is central, then, if it has a high degree: the corresponding agent is central in the sense of being 'well connected' or 'in the thick of things'. A degree-based measure of point centrality, therefore, corresponds to the intuitive notion of how well connected a point is within its local environment – whether, for example, it has a large number of direct contacts. Because this is calculated simply in terms of the number of points to which a particular point is adjacent, ignoring any indirect connections it may have, the degree can be regarded as a measure of 'local centrality'. The most systematic elaboration of this concept is to be found in Nieminen (1974). Degree-based measures of local centrality can also be computed for points in directed graphs, though in these situations each point will have two measures of its local centrality, one corresponding to its indegree and the other to its outdegree. In directed graphs, then, it makes sense to distinguish between the 'in-centrality' and the 'out-centrality' of the various points (Knoke and Burt, 1983).

A degree-based measure of point centrality can be extended beyond direct connections to those at various path distances. In this case, the relevant neighbourhood is widened to include the more distant connections of the points. A point may, then, be assessed for its local centrality in terms of both direct (distance 1) connections and distance 2 connections: or, indeed, whatever cut-off path distance is chosen. The principal problem with extending this measure of point centrality beyond distance 2 connections is that in graphs with even a very modest density the majority of the points tend to be linked through indirect connections at relatively short path distances. Thus, comparisons of local centrality scores at distance 4, for example, are unlikely to be informative if most of the points are connected to most other points at this distance. Clearly, the cut-off threshold which is to be used is a matter for the informed judgement of the researcher who is undertaking the investigation, but distance 1 and distance 2 connections are likely to be the most informative in the majority of studies.

It is important to recognise that the measurement of local centrality does not involve the idea that there will be any unique 'central' point in the network. In Figure 6.1, for example, points A, B and C can each be seen as local centres: they each have degree 5, compared with degrees 1 or 2 for all other points. Even if point A had many more direct connections than points B and C it would not lie at 'the' centre of the network: it lies physically towards one 'side' of the chain of points, and its centrality is a purely 'local' phenomenon. The degree, therefore, is a measure of local centrality, and a comparison of the degrees of the various points in a graph can show how well connected the points are with their local environments.

This measure of local centrality has one major limitation. This is that comparisons of centrality scores can only meaningfully be made among the members of the same graph or between graphs that are the same size. The degree of a point depends on, among other things, the size of the graph, and so measures of local centrality cannot be compared when graphs differ significantly in size. The use of the raw degree score may, therefore, be misleading. A central point with a degree of 25 in a graph of 100 points, for example, is not as central as one with a degree of 25 in a graph of 30 points, and neither can be easily compared to a central point with a degree of 6 in a graph of 10 points. In an attempt to overcome this problem, Freeman (1979) proposed a *relative* measure of local centrality in which the actual number of connections is related to the maximum number that it could sustain. Thus, a degree of 25 in a graph of 100 points can be translated into a relative local centrality of 0.25. A degree of 25 in a graph of 30 points equates to a relative centrality of 0.86, and a degree of 6 in a graph of 10 points equates to a relative centrality of 0.67.[1] Figure 6.1 shows that relative centrality also allows a comparison to be made between points within the same network. This idea can be extended to directed graphs. A relative measure, therefore, gives a far more standardised approach to the measurement of local centrality.

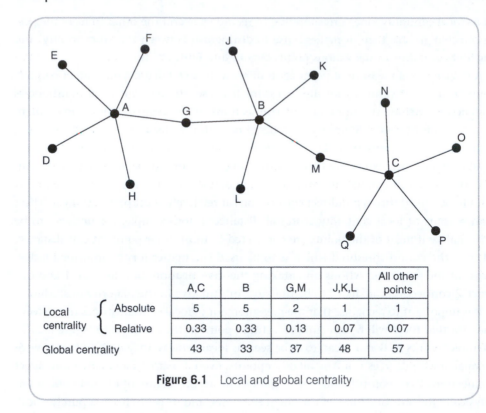

| | A,C | B | G,M | J,K,L | All other points |
|---|---|---|---|---|---|
| Local centrality { Absolute | 5 | 5 | 2 | 1 | 1 |
| Relative | 0.33 | 0.33 | 0.13 | 0.07 | 0.07 |
| Global centrality | 43 | 33 | 37 | 48 | 57 |

**Figure 6.1**  Local and global centrality

The problem of comparing raw degree measures of centrality is closely related to the problem discussed in the previous chapter of comparing densities between different graphs. Both measures are related to the size of the graph. It will be recalled, however, that the density level also depends on the type of relation that is being analysed. The density of an 'awareness' network, I suggested, will tend to be higher than that of a 'loving' network. Because both density and point centrality are computed from degree measures, exactly the same consideration applies to measures of point centrality. Centrality measured in a loving network, for example, is likely to be lower, other things being equal, than centrality in an awareness network. Relative measures of point centrality do little to help with this problem. Even if local centrality scores are calculated in relative terms, they should be compared only for networks that involve similar types of relations.

Local centrality is, however, only one way of measuring point centrality. Freeman (1979, 1980) proposed a measure of overall centrality, often called 'global centrality', based around what he terms the 'closeness' of the points. Local centrality measures, whatever path distance is used, are expressed in terms of the number or proportion of *points* to which a focal point is connected. Freeman's measure of global centrality is expressed in terms of the *distances* among the various points. It will be recalled that two points are connected by a path if there is a sequence of distinct lines connecting them, and the length of a path is measured by the number of lines of which it is composed. In graph theory, the length of the shortest path between two points is a measure of the distance between them. The shortest distance between two points on the surface of the earth lies along the geodesic that connects them, and, by analogy, the shortest path between any chosen pair of points in a graph is termed a geodesic. A point is globally central if it lies at short distances from many other points. Such a point is 'close' to many of the other points in the graph. It has a position of strategic significance in the overall structure of the network.

The simplest notion of closeness is, perhaps, that calculated from the 'sum distance', the sum of the geodesic distances to all other points in the graph (Sabidussi, 1966). If the matrix of distances between points in an undirected graph is calculated, the sum distance of a point is its column or row sum in this matrix (the two values are the same). A point with a low sum distance is 'close' to a large number of other points, and so closeness can be seen as the reciprocal of the sum distance. In a directed graph, of course, paths must be measured through lines that run in the same direction, and, for this reason, calculations based on row and column sums will differ. Global centrality in a directed graph, then, can be seen in terms of what might be termed 'in-closeness' and 'out-closeness'.

The table in Figure 6.1 compares a sum distance measure of global centrality with degree-based measures of absolute and relative local centrality. It can be seen that A, B and C are equally central in local terms, but that B is more globally central than either A or C. In global terms, G and M are less central than B, but more central than the locally central points A and C. These distinctions, made on the basis of the sum distances measure, therefore, confirm the impression gained from a visual inspection of the graph. This is also apparent in the measures for the less central points. All the remaining points have a degree of 1, indicating low local centrality, yet the sum distance measure clearly brings out the fact that J, K and L are more central in global terms than are the other points with degree 1.

## MEDIATION AND BETWEENNESS

Freeman (1979) adds yet a further concept of point centrality, which he terms the 'betweenness'. This measures the extent to which a particular point lies 'between' the various other points in the graph: a point of relatively low degree may play an important 'intermediary' role and so be very central to the network. Points G and M in Figure 6.1, for example, lie between a great many pairs of points. The betweenness of a point measures the extent to which an agent can play the part of 'broker' or 'gate-keeper', with a potential for control over others.[2] G could, therefore, be interpreted as an intermediary between the set of agents centred around B and that centred around A, while M might play the same role for the sets associated with B and C.

Freeman's approach to betweenness is built around the concept of 'local dependency'. A point is dependent on another if the paths that connect it to others pass through this point. Burt (1992) has described this in terms of 'structural holes'. A structural hole exists where two points are connected at distance 2, but are otherwise separated by a long path. The third point can act as a broker or intermediary that bridges the structural hole. In Figure 6.1, for example, point E is dependent on point A for access to all other parts of the graph, and it is also dependent, though to a lesser extent, on points G, B, M and C.

Betweenness is, perhaps, the most complex of the measures of point centrality to calculate. The 'betweenness proportion' of a point Y for a particular pair of points X and Z is defined as the proportion of geodesics connecting that pair that passes through Y: it measures the extent to which Y is 'between' X and Z.[3] The 'pair dependency' of point X on point Y is then defined as the sum of the betweenness proportions of Y for all pairs that involve X. The 'local dependency matrix' contains these pair dependency scores, the entries in the matrix showing the dependence of each row element on each column element. The overall 'betweenness' of a point is calculated as half the sum of the values in the columns of this matrix, that is, half the sum of all pair dependency scores for the points represented by the columns. Despite this rather complex calculation, the measure is intuitively meaningful, and it is easily computed with the UCINET program, and in Pajek with the NET > VECTOR > CENTRALITY menu option.

In Freeman's work, then, can be found the basis for a whole family of point centrality measures: local centrality (degree), betweenness, and global centrality (closeness). I have shown how comparability between different social networks can be furthered by calculating local centrality in relative rather than absolute terms, and Freeman made similar proposals for his other measures of centrality. He produced his own relative measure of betweenness, and used the formula of Beauchamp (1965) for a relative closeness measure. In UCINET these measures are calculated using the NETWORK > CENTRALITY > DEGREE, NETWORK > CENTRALITY > CLOSENESS and NETWORK > CENTRALITY > BETWEENNESS menu options. All these measures, however, are based on raw scores of degree and distance, and it is necessary to turn to Bonacich (1972, 1987) for an alternative approach that uses weighted scores.

# CENTRALITY BOOSTS CENTRALITY

Bonacich holds that the centrality of a particular point cannot be assessed in isolation from the centrality of all the other points to which it is connected. A point that is connected to central points has its own centrality boosted, and this, in turn, boosts the centrality of the other points to which it is connected (Bonacich, 1972). There is, therefore, an inherent circularity involved in the calculation of centrality. According to Bonacich, the local centrality of point $i$ in a graph, $c_i$, is calculated by the formula $\sum_j r_{ij} c_j$, where $r_{ij}$ is the value of the line connecting point $i$ and point $j$ and $c_j$ is the centrality of point $j$. That is to say, the centrality of $i$ equals the sum of its connections to other points, weighted by the centrality of each of these other points.[4]

Bonacich (1987) has subsequently generalised his initial approach, as did Freeman, to a whole family of local and global measures. The most general formula for centrality, he argued, is $c_i = \sum_j r_{ij}(\alpha + \beta c_j)$. In this formula, the centrality weighting is itself modified by the two parameters $\alpha$ and $\beta$. The parameter $\alpha$ is introduced simply as an arbitrary standardising constant which ensures that the final centrality measures will vary around a mean value of 1. The parameter $\beta$, on the other hand, is of more substantive significance. It is a positive or negative value that allows the researcher to set the path distances that are to be used in the calculation of centrality.[5] When $\beta$ is set as equal to zero, no indirect links are taken into account, and the measure of centrality is a simple degree-based measure of local centrality. Higher levels of $\beta$ increase the path length, so allowing the calculation to take account of progressively more distant connections. Bonacich claims that measures based on positive values of $\beta$ correlate highly with Freeman's measure of closeness.

A major difficulty with Bonacich's argument, however, is that the values given to $\beta$ are arbitrary choices made by researchers. It is difficult to know what theoretical reasons there might be for using one $\beta$ level rather than another. While the original Bonacich measure may be intuitively comprehensible, the generalised model is more difficult to interpret for values of $\beta$ that are greater than zero. On the other hand, the suggestion that the value of $\beta$ can be either positive or negative does provide a way forward for the analysis of signed graphs. Bonacich himself suggests that negative values correspond to 'zero-sum' relations, such as those involved in the holding of money and other financial resources. Positive values, on the other hand, correspond to 'non-zero-sum' relations, such as those involving access to information.

I have discussed centrality principally in terms of the most central points in a graph, but it should be clear that centrality scores also allow the least central points to be identified. Those points with the lowest centrality, however this is measured, can be regarded as the peripheral points of the graph. This is true, for example, for all the points in Figure 6.1 that have degree 1. They are locally peripheral in so far as they are loosely connected into the network. The global centrality scores in Figure 6.1, however, show that points J, K and L are not as globally peripheral as the other points with degree 1. The extreme of peripherality occurs with the isolated point, the point that has no connections with any other point in the network.

## CENTRALISATION AND GRAPH CENTRES

I have concentrated, so far, on the centrality of particular points. But it is also possible to examine the extent to which a whole graph has a centralised structure. Centrality and 'centralisation' of a graph have sometimes been confused by the use of the same term to describe them both. Freeman's important and influential (1979) study, for example, refers to both 'point centrality' and 'graph centrality'. Confusion is most likely to be avoided if the term 'centrality' is restricted to the idea of point central-ity, and the term 'centralisation' is used to refer to particular properties of the graph structure as a whole. Centralisation, therefore, refers not to the relative prominence of points, but to the overall cohesion or integration of the graph around a particular set of points. Graphs may, for example, be more or less centralised around particular points or sets of points. A number of different procedures have been suggested for the measurement of centralisation, contributing further to the confusion that besets this area. The concepts of density and centralisation refer to differing aspects of the overall 'compactness' of a graph. Density describes the general level of cohesion in a graph; centralisation describes the extent to which this cohesion is organised around particu-lar focal points. Centralisation and density, therefore, are important complementary measures.

Figure 6.2 shows a simplified model of a highly centralised graph: the whole graph is organised, in important respects, around point A as its focal point. How is this level of centralisation to be measured? Freeman (1979) has shown that measures of point centrality can be converted into measures of the overall level of centralisation found in different graphs. A graph centralisation measure is an expression of how tightly the graph is organised around its most central point. Freeman's measures of centralisation are attempts to isolate the various aspects of the simplified notion of centralisation. On this basis, he identified three types of graph centralisation, rooted in the varying conceptions of point centrality already defined.

The general procedure involved in any measure of graph centralisation involves look-ing at the differences between the centrality scores of the most central point and those of all other points. Centralisation, then, is the ratio of the actual sum of differences to the maximum possible sum of differences. The three different ways of operationalising this general measure that Freeman discusses follow from the use of one or other of the three concepts of point centrality. Freeman (1979) shows that all three measures vary from 0 to 1 and that a value of 1 is achieved on all three measures for graphs structured in the form of a 'star' or 'wheel'. He further shows that a value of 0 is obtained on all three measures for a 'complete' graph. Between these two extremes lie the majority of graphs for real social networks, and it is in these cases that the choice of one or other of the measures will be important in illuminating specific structural features of the graphs. A degree-based measure of graph centralisation, for example, seems to be particularly sensitive to the local dominance of points, while a betweenness-based measure is rather more sensitive to the 'chaining' of points.

More usefully, Everett and Borgatti (1999, 2005) have shown how Freeman's meas-ures of point centrality can be extended to an analysis of the centrality of sets of points. Whether defined by a particular attribute (gender, age, ethnicity, etc.) or by the sociometric criteria discussed in the following chapters, the centrality of a category or

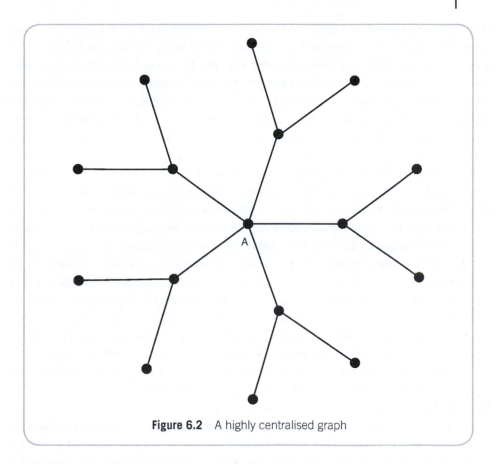

**Figure 6.2**  A highly centralised graph

group cannot be calculated simply by adding or averaging individual scores because of the need to take account of group size. The way that this must be achieved varies from measure to measure. Everett and Borgatti argue that a degree-based measure of centrality comprises the number of points outside the group that are connected to its members, normalised by the total number of points outside the group. This measure allows centrality to be compared across networks of varying sizes. A more complex measure of group centrality is that based on closeness, which it will be recalled is a measure in which low numbers indicate high levels of closeness. Everett and Borgatti argue that in this case, normalised group closeness is the total number of network members outside the group divided by the summed closeness for group members. Finally, a betweeness-based measure of group centrality takes the summed between-ness and divides by half the maximum possible number of connections. The authors of these measures conclude that they provide useful assessments of the social capital of a group, as opposed to the social capital of its individual members.

Assessing the centralisation of a graph around a particular focal point or a defined set of points is the starting point for a broader understanding of centralisation. The measures of centralisation discussed can tell us whether a graph is organised around its most central points or a defined set of points, but they do not tell us whether these central points comprise a distinct set of points that themselves cluster together in a particular part of the graph. The points in the graph that are individually most central, for example, may be spread widely through the graph, and in such cases a measure of centralisation might not be especially informative. It is necessary, therefore, to investigate whether there is an identifiable 'structural centre' to a graph. The structural centre of a graph is a single point or a cluster of points that, like the centre of a circle or a sphere, is the pivot of its organisation.

An approach to this issue has been outlined by Stokman and Snijders.[6] Their approach is to define the set of points with the highest point centrality scores as the 'centre' of the graph. Having identified this set, researchers can then examine the structure of the relations between this set of points and all other points in the graph. A schematic outline of the Stokman and Snijders approach is shown in Figure 6.3.

If all the points in a graph are listed in order of their point centrality – Stokman and Snijders use local centrality – then the set of points with the highest centrality scores are the centre. The boundary between the centre and the rest of the graph is drawn wherever there appears to be a 'natural break' in the distribution of centrality scores. The decrease in the centrality score of each successive point may, for example, show a sharp jump at a particular point in the distribution, and this is regarded as the boundary between the centre and its 'margin'. The margin is the set of points that clusters close to the centre and that is, in turn, divided from the 'peripheral' points by a further break in the distribution of centrality scores.

The Stokman and Snijders concept applies only to highly centralised graphs. In a graph such as that in Figure 6.2, which is centralised around a particular set of central points, as measured by one of Freeman's indicators, it may be very informative to try to identify the sets defined by Stokman and Snijders. There will, however, be an inevitable arbitrariness in identifying the boundaries between centre, margin and periphery. The location of the boundaries cannot be determined with any precision, as it depends on the identification by the analyst of 'breaks' in the distribution of scores. Indeed, the number of boundaries identifiable is a matter of researcher judgement. The attempt to identify central and peripheral sets of points in a network is, however, an important analytical device in describing network structure. A solution to these problems, though not one pursued by Stokman and Snijders, is to use a clique or cluster analysis to identify the boundaries of the structural centre: if the most central points, for example, constitute a clearly defined and well-bounded 'clique', as discussed in Chapter 7, then it may make sense to regard them as forming the structural centre of the graph.[7] But not all graphs will have such a hierarchical structure of concentric sets. Where the central points do not cluster together as the nucleus of a centralised graph, the Stokman and Snijders 'centre' will constitute simply a set of locally central, though dispersed, points. In such circumstances, it is not very helpful to use the term 'centre'.

An alternative approach to centralisation is that of Borgatti and Everett (1999; Everett and Borgatti, 2005), who have derived ways of identifying a centre and a periphery in

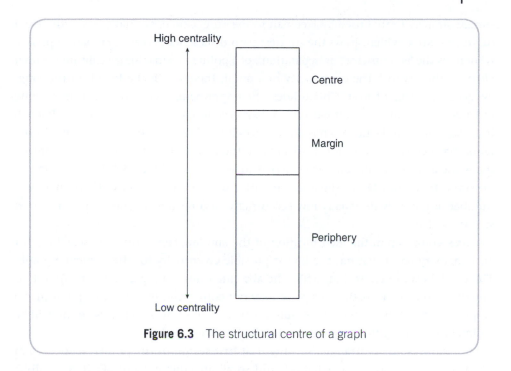

**Figure 6.3** The structural centre of a graph

any network.[8] Their method, implemented in UCINET, computes the 'concentration' of each point in relation to maximum centrality and progressively increases the size of the centre until the maximum possible concentration score is reached. This procedure dichotomises the network into a connected centre and a surrounding periphery of points that are less well connected to the central points.

## THE ABSOLUTE CENTRE OF A GRAPH

It is possible to extend the analysis of centralisation a little further by considering the possibility that there might be an 'absolute centre' to a graph. The idea of an absolute centre is based on the idea of the centre of a circle or a sphere: it is the focal point around which the graph is structured. The structural centre, as a set of points, does not meet this criterion. The absolute centre must be a single point. The centre of a circle, for example, is that unique place that is equidistant from all points on its circumference. By strict analogy, the absolute centre of a graph ought to be equidistant from all points in the graph. This idea is difficult to operationalise for a graph, and a more sensible idea would be to relax the criterion of equidistance and to use, instead, the idea of minimum distance. That is to say, the absolute centre is the point that is 'closest' to all the other points in terms of path distance.

Christofides (1975: Ch. 5) has suggested using the distance matrix to conceptualise and compute the absolute centre of a graph. The first step in his argument follows a similar strategy to that used by Freeman to measure 'closeness'. Having constructed a distance matrix, which shows the shortest path distances between each pair of points, he defines the 'eccentricity', or 'separation', of a point as its maximum column (or row) entry in the matrix.[9] The eccentricity of a point, therefore, is the length of the longest geodesic incident to it. Christofides's first approximation to the idea of absolute centrality is to call the point with the lowest eccentricity the absolute centre. Point B in sociogram (i) of Figure 5.6 has an eccentricity of 1, and all the other points in the graph have eccentricity 2. In this sociogram, then, point B, with the lowest eccentricity, is the absolute centre and was referred to as such in Chapter 5.[10] In other graphs, however, there may be no single point with minimum eccentricity. There may be a number of points with equally low eccentricity, and in these circumstances a second step is needed.

This second step in the identification of the absolute centre involves searching for an imaginary point that has the lowest possible eccentricity for the particular graph. The crucial claim here is that, while the absolute centre of a graph will be found on one of its constituent paths, this place may not correspond to any *actual* point in the graph. Any graph will have an absolute centre, but in some graphs this centre will be an imaginary rather than an actual point. It is a virtual centre.

This claim is not as strange as it might at first seem. All the points in sociogram (ii) in Figure 5.6 have eccentricity 2, and so all are equally 'central'. It is possible, however, to conceive of an imaginary point, Z, mid-way between points A and B, as in sociogram (iii). 'Point' Z is distance 0.5 from both A and B, and it is distance 1.5 from points C, D and E. The artificial point Z is more central than any of the actual points, as its eccentricity is 1.5. But it is still not possible to find a single absolute centre for this sociogram. The imaginary point Z could, in fact, have been placed at the mid-point of any of the lines in the sociogram with the same results, and there is no other location for the imaginary point that would not increase its minimum eccentricity. The best that can be said for this graph, therefore, is that there are six possible locations for the absolute centre, none of which corresponds to an actual point. Moving to the second step of searching for an imaginary point as the absolute centre, then, will reduce the number of graphs for which there is no unique absolute centre, but it does not ensure that a single absolute centre can be identified for all graphs.[11]

Thus, some graphs will have a unique absolute centre, while others will have a number of absolute centres. Christofides provides an algorithm that would identify, through iteration, whether a graph contains a mid-point or actual point that is its unique absolute centre.[12] In sociogram (iv) of Figure 5.6, for example, there is a unique absolute centre. Its 'point' Z has an eccentricity of 1.5, compared with eccentricity scores of 2.5 for any other imaginary mid-point, 2 for points A and B, and 3 for points C, D, E, F and G. Alternative approaches to identifying the absolute centre of a graph depend upon the spatial models of network structure discussed in Chapter 10.

# BANK CENTRALITY IN CORPORATE NETWORKS

Studies of interlocking directorships among corporate enterprises are far from new, but most of the studies carried out prior to the 1970s made little use of the formal techniques of social network analysis. Despite some limited use of density measures and cluster analysis, most of these studies took a strictly quantitative approach, simply counting the numbers of directorships and interlocks among the companies. Levine's influential (1972) paper marked a shift in the direction of this research while, at about the same time, Mokken and his associates in the Netherlands began a pioneering study in the systematic use of graph theory to explore corporate interlocks (Helmers et al., 1975). The major turning point, however, occurred in 1975, when Michael Schwartz and his students presented a major conference paper that applied the concept of centrality to corporate networks (Bearden et al., 1975). This long paper was circulated widely in cyclostyled form and, despite the fact that it was unpublished until 2002, it has been enormously influential. The work of Schwartz's group, and that which it has stimulated, provides a compelling illustration of the conceptual power of the idea of point centrality.

Michael Schwartz and Peter Mariolis had begun to build a database of top American companies during the early 1970s, and their efforts provided a pool of data for many subsequent studies (see, for example, Mariolis, 1975; Sonquist and Koenig, 1975). They gradually extended the database to include the top 500 industrial and the top 250 commercial and financial companies operating in the United States in 1962, together with all new entrants to this 'top 750' for each successive year from 1963 to 1973. The final database included the names of all the directors of the 1,131 largest American companies in business during the period 1962–73: a total of 13,574 directors. This database is, by any standard, for a large social network. As such, it lends itself to the selection of substantial subsets of data for particular years. One such subset is the group of the 797 top enterprises of 1969 studied by Mariolis (1975).

The path-breaking paper of Schwartz and his colleagues (Bearden et al., 1975) drew on the Schwartz–Mariolis database and analysed the data using Granovetter's (1973) conceptual distinction between strong and weak ties. The basis of their argument was that those interlocks that involved the full-time executive officers of the enterprises could be regarded as the 'strong' ties in the corporate network, while those that involved only the part-time non-executive directors were its 'weak' ties. The basis of this theoretical claim was that the interlocks carried by full-time executive officers were the most likely board-level links to have a strategic salience for the enterprises concerned. For this reason, they tended to be associated with intercorporate shareholdings and trading relations between the companies.[13] Interlocks created by non-executive directors, on the other hand, involved less of a time commitment and so had less strategic significance for the enterprises concerned.

The top enterprises were examined for their centrality, using Bonacich's (1972) measure. This, it will be recalled, is a measure in which the centrality of a particular point could be measured by a combination of its degree, the value of each line incident to it, and the centrality of the other points to which it is connected. This is a 'recursive', circular measure that, therefore, requires a considerable amount of computation. A network containing 750 enterprises, for example, will require the solution of 750 simultaneous equations. The first step in Bearden et al.'s analysis was to decide on an appropriate measure for the value of the lines that connected the enterprises. For the weak, undirected lines, they hold that the value of each should be simply the number of separate interlocks, weighted by the sizes of the two boards. This weighting rested on the supposition that having a large number of interlocks was less significant for those enterprises with large boards than it was for those with small boards. The formula used in the calculation was $b_{ij}/\sqrt{d_i d_j}$ , where $b_{ij}$ is the number of interlocks between the two companies $i$ and $j$, and $d_i$ and $d_j$ are the sizes of their respective boards. This formula allows Bonacich's centrality measure to be calculated on the basis of all the 'weak ties' in the graph.

A more complex formula was required to measure centrality in terms of the strong ties. In this case, the measure of the value of each line needed to take some account of the direction attached to the lines in the graph. For those companies that were the 'senders' of lines, the value of the lines was calculated by the number of directors 'sent', weighted by the board size of the 'receiving' company. The attempt in this procedure was to weight the line by the salience of the interlock for the receiving board. Conversely, for those companies that were the 'receivers' of interlocks, the number of directors received was weighted by the sender's board size.[14] For the final calculation of centrality scores, Bearden et al. introduced a further weighting. Instead of taking the raw weighted scores, they took 90 per cent of the score for the senders and 10 per cent of the score for the recipients. The reasoning behind this weighting of the scores was the theoretical judgement that, in the world of corporate interlocking, it is 'more important to give than to receive': the sending of a director was more likely to be a sign of corporate power than was the receiving of a directorship. Thus, the arbitrary adjustment to the centrality scores was introduced as a way of embodying this judgement in the final results. It should be noted, however, that centrality will not always be a sign of power. In some situations, the prominent and most visible actors may be among the weakest (Mizruchi, 1994: 331–2).

The Bonacich measure of centrality that was calculated for the companies in the study correlated very highly, at 0.91, with the degrees of the companies. Bearden et al. hold, however, that the more complex Bonacich measure was preferable because it had the potential to highlight enterprises with a low degree but that were, nevertheless, connected to highly central companies. Such a position, they argued, may be of great importance in determining the structural significance of the companies in the economy.

Schwartz and his colleagues also used a further approach to centrality, which they termed 'peak analysis'. This was later elaborated by Mizruchi (1982) as the basis for an interpretation of the development of the American corporate network during the twentieth century. A point is regarded as a 'peak' if it is more central than any other

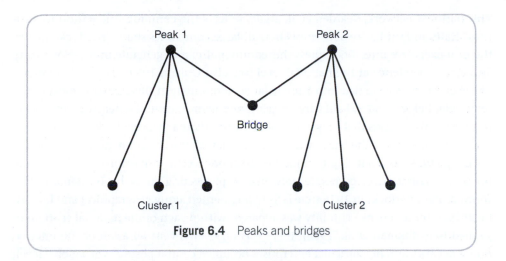

**Figure 6.4** Peaks and bridges

point to which it is connected. Mintz and Schwartz (1985) extend this idea by defin-ing a 'bridge' as a central point that connects two or more peaks (see Figure 6.4). They further see a 'cluster' as comprising all the direct contacts of a peak, except for those that have a similar distance 1 connection to another peak. Thus, peaks lie at the hearts of their clusters.[15]

The results arrived at through the use of these techniques for the measurement of point centrality have become widely accepted as indicating some of the most funda-mental features of intercorporate networks. In summary, Bearden et al. argue that the American intercorporate network shows an overall pattern of 'bank centrality': banks are the most central enterprises in the network, whether measured by the strong or the weak ties. Bank centrality is manifest in the co-existence of an extensive national interlock network (structured predominantly by weak ties) and intensive regional groupings (structured by the strong ties). Strong ties had a definite regional base to them. The intensive regional clusters were created by the strong ties of both the finan-cial and the non-financial enterprises, but the strong ties of the banks were the focal centres of the network of strong ties. The intercorporate network of 1962, for exam-ple, consisted of one very large connected component,[16] two small groupings each of four or five enterprises, and a large number of pairs and isolated enterprises. Within the large connected component, there were five peaks and their associated clusters. The dominant element in the network of strong ties was a regional cluster around the Continental Illinois peak, which, with two other Chicago banks, was connected with a group of 11 Midwestern enterprises with extensive connections to a larger grouping of 132 enterprises. The remaining four peaks in the network of strong ties were Mellon National Bank, J.P. Morgan, Bankers Trust and United California Bank, their clusters varying in size from four to ten enterprises.

Overlying this highly clustered network of strong, regional ties was an extensive national network created by the weak ties that linked the separate clusters together.

This national network, Bearden et al. argue, reflects the common orientation to business affairs and similarity of interests that all large companies share. Interlocks among the non-executive directors express this commonality and generate integration, unity and interdependence at the national level (see also Useem, 1984). The great majority of the enterprises were tied into a single large component in this network, most of the remainder being isolates. Banks are, once more, the most central enterprises, especially those New York banks that play a 'national' rather than a 'regional' role. It is the non-executive directors of the banks who cement together the overall national network.[17]

This picture has been slightly modified in more recent discussions of the transnational centralisation of corporate networks. A pioneering study by Fennema (1982) showed that interlocks in 1976 were largely fragmented along geographical and linguistic lines. Although bank centrality was apparent within each of the national economies studied (see Stokman et al., 1985), there was no overall centralisation of the international network and no particular enterprises occupied central positions at a global level. The development of a more extensive and intensive globalisation of economic relations since the time of that study has increased the number of transnational links and transformed the position of banks in the transnational network. National economies became more fragmented and those banks that had transnational operations tended to increase their centrality within their national economies (Carroll, 2002, 2004). Sklair (2001) has suggested that a transnational capitalist class has developed, while Bauman (1998) has suggested the emergence of global financial decision-makers detached from national commitments. It appears, however, that the extent of transnational integration at board level has been considerably exaggerated (Carroll and Fennema, 2002).

--- EXERCISE ---

Regarding the intercorporate network for 1962 discussed above, consider the following questions:

- Is it correct to see interlocks as power relations? Why is this?
- Do the network data provide any evidence to support the claim that bank centrality is an indicator of bank power?
- What additional evidence might be needed to strengthen this claim?

Imagine a network of friendship choices with a similar pattern of centrality.

- Can the friendship relations be seen as indicators of popularity?
- How would you interpret the social significance of the most central individuals?
- How would your interpretation vary with the use of different measures of centrality?
- If a structural centre could be identified in the friendship network, how would you interpret its reality as a social group?

## FURTHER READING

Freeman, L.C. (1979) 'Centrality in Social Networks: I. Conceptual Clarification', *Social Networks*, 1: 215–39.

The classic foundational statement of centrality concepts.

Everett, M.G. and Borgatti, S. (2005) 'Extending Centrality', in P.J. Carrington, J. Scott and S. Wasserman (eds) *Models and Methods in Social Network Analysis*. Cambridge: Cambridge University Press.

Proposes an innovative advance in centrality analysis using two-mode data.

Bearden, J., Atwood, W., Freitag, P., Hendricks, C., Mintz, B. and Schwartz, M. (1975) 'The Nature and Extent of Bank Centrality in Corporate Networks'. Paper presented to the American Sociological Association. Reprinted in J. Scott (ed.) *Social Networks: Critical Concepts in Sociology*, Volume 3. London: Routledge.

The classic study of bank centrality from the pioneer researchers in this area.

## FURTHER READING

# SEVEN

## Groups, Factions and Social Divisions

This chapter examines:

- Graphs and subgraphs
- The component structure of networks
- Cycles and circuits in networks
- Cliques and other subgroups
- Ways of examining the overall group structure of a network and the shape of its social structure
- Studies of citations in scientific publications and their implications for professional and disciplinary organisation

A key issue in the study of social relations is the question of the extent to which the members of a network are formed into more or less cohesive social groups: friendship groups, families, work groups, political parties, churches, sectarian organisations, and so on. Some aspects of this question were touched on in the previous chapter, where I discussed the ways in which a central core of network members can be identified. However, sets of central agents may be divided into competing factions or into 'insider' and 'outsider' groups, and group formation is just as important among intermediate and peripheral agents.

The early researchers who undertook the Hawthorne and Yankee City studies took up the idea of the 'clique' as a way of identifying the cohesive subgroups into which a network can be divided. They held that people's informal and reciprocal social relations tied them into cohesive subgroupings with their own norms, values, orientations and subcultural outlook, which may run counter to the 'official' or formal social structure of the larger organisation. These cliques were, they held, among the most important sources of a person's identity and sense of belonging, and their existence was widely recognised in the everyday terms – such as 'our set' and 'the group in the back' – that people used to describe their social world.

Once analysts began to formalise the idea of the clique and to devise mathematical measures of the number and cohesion of cliques in a network, it was discovered that the idea was not limited to informal relations. There were also similarly structured political cliques and factions, economic cliques and interest groups, and so on. It was also recognised that there were a number of different ways of operationalising the apparently simple idea of the 'clique': cliques could, for example, be seen as groups of mutually connected individuals or as pockets of high density. A number of different theoretical models of subgroups were developed from the original idea of the 'clique'. These models – 'clusters', 'components', 'cores' and 'circles' – have very little in common with one another, apart from beginning with the letter 'c'. In this chapter I shall discuss their varying theoretical bases, though I will leave the issue of 'cluster analysis' until the next chapter.

# IDENTIFYING SUBGRAPHS

The starting point for all of these measures of group structure is the idea of a 'subgraph'. A subgraph is any collection of points selected from the whole graph of a network, together with the lines connecting those points. Any aspect of the graph can be chosen for identifying its subgraphs, though not all of these criteria will be substantively useful in research. A random sample of points, for example, could be treated as a subgraph and its structural properties could be examined. But a random subgraph is not, in general, likely to correspond to a meaningful social group. A more useful approach to the identification of subgraphs might be to divide the members of a network by, say, gender and to investigate the separate subgraphs of men and women. Any such choice will depend on the theoretical and empirical concerns of the researcher. The general aim would simply be to define a meaningful category of agents and to explore their distinct patterns of network formation. From this point of view, therefore, the identification of subgraphs is no different from the initial identification of the graphs themselves. All the considerations of boundaries and sampling that have been considered in earlier chapters will be equally relevant here and no new issues are involved (see, for example, Frank, 1978b).

The analysis of cliques and similar group concepts normally involves a different approach to the study of subgraphs. Here the aim has been to investigate the structural properties of a whole graph itself in order to discover the 'naturally existing' subgraphs into which it can be divided. From this point of view, a subgraph must have some defining characteristic drawn from the mathematical principles of graph theory: the connectedness of its points, the intensity of their connection, and so on. It must be *maximal* in relation to a particular defining structural characteristic. A maximal subgraph is the largest subgraph that can be formed without this defining quality disappearing. The choice of a particular characteristic depends on the researcher's judgement that a particular mathematical criterion can be given a meaningful and useful sociological interpretation. Unfortunately, this is rarely made explicit, and far too many researchers assume that whatever mathematical procedures are available in social network analysis programs *must*, almost by definition, be useful sociological measures. My aim in this chapter is to uncover the mathematical assumptions of the various available procedures so that researchers can make an informed decision about those that might be relevant to their particular investigations.

# THE COMPONENTS OF A NETWORK

The simplest of the various subgraph concepts is that of the 'component', which is formally defined as a maximal connected subgraph. A subgraph is 'connected' when all of its points are linked to one another through paths: all points in a connected subgraph can 'reach' one another through one or more paths, but they have no connections outside the subgraph. Within a component, all points are connected through paths, but no paths run to points outside the component. A connected subgraph is maximal when it is impossible to add any new members without destroying the quality of connectedness. Isolated points, for example, cannot be added to an existing component, as they have no connections to any of its members. The boundary of a component, therefore, is identified by tracing through the paths from its potential members to test for their connectedness.

A computer algorithm for identifying components might start from a randomly chosen point and trace all the other points to which it is directly connected. This same procedure can then be repeated for each of these points in turn, and so the component gradually increases in size through a 'snowballing' method. When no further points can be added to the component, its full membership has been identified. If any points remain outside the component, the same procedure can be repeated for them, so as to see what other components can be identified in the graph.

Components, then, are sets of points that are linked to one another through continuous chains of connection. The paths connecting points are traced through until the boundaries of the component are discovered. A 'connected graph', of course, simply comprises a single component. Other graphs typically consist of one or more separate components, together with a number of isolated points (see Figure 7.1). This idea is readily interpretable in sociological terms. The members of a component can, in principle, communicate or exchange with one another, either directly or through chains of intermediaries. Isolates, on the other hand, have no such opportunities. The pattern of components found in a graph – their number and size – can, therefore, be taken as an indication of the opportunities and obstacles to communication or the transfer of resources in the associated network. To this extent, then, the identification of components embodies the ideas behind the 'topological regions' of the early field theorists. A basic step in the structural description of a network, therefore, is to identify the number and size of its components.

The simplest of algorithms to detect components in a graph would search all possible paths in order to discover the geodesics between points. The lengths of these geodesics will vary from a minimum of 1 (direct connection) to a maximum of $n - 1$. In a graph of size 100, for example, the maximum possible path length would be 99.

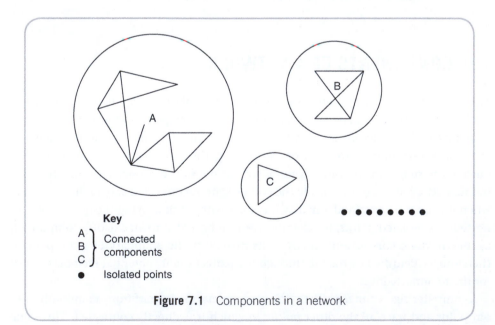

**Key**

A ⎫
B ⎬ Connected components
C ⎭

● Isolated points

**Figure 7.1**   Components in a network

In large graphs, however, the longest geodesic in a component – its 'diameter' – is generally much shorter than this.[1] However, the diameter of a component will not generally be known before the boundaries of the component have been identified, and so such an algorithm must search all paths up to the maximum level of $n - 1$ in its search for components.

Because such a procedure is very time-consuming and inefficient, social network programs generally use an alternative procedure in which components are discovered by building up 'spanning trees' by using a back-tracking method from chosen points. The algorithm looks for any point that is connected to its random starting point, and then looks for any point that is connected to this additional point. This is repeated until no further connections can be found. The algorithm then back-tracks along the chain that it has discovered until it is able to make a connection to a new point. It continues in the same way until it again comes to a halt. By repeated back-tracking of this kind, the boundaries of a component are discovered very efficiently and the procedure can search the remaining points for other components. In UCINET components are investigated through the NETWORK > REGIONS > COMPONENTS menu option, and in Pajek through the NET > COMPONENTS menu option.

# THE STRENGTH AND STABILITY OF COMPONENTS

Components can be identified in both undirected and directed graphs, but there are important differences between the two situations. In the case of directed graphs, two distinct types of component can be identified: 'strong components' and 'weak components'. A strong component is one in which the lines that make up the paths are aligned in a continuous chain without any change of direction. Any paths that do not meet this criterion are disregarded. The justification for this restriction is that the direction of a line is assumed to indicate the possible flow of some resource or facility, such as money, power, or information. It is only when the lines in a path run in a constant direction that this flow can continue without interruption. A strong component, then, represents a set of agents among whom such resources can easily and freely flow.

An alternative, weaker interpretation can also be placed on directed lines. It can be assumed that the mere presence of a relationship, regardless of its direction, allows some possibility for communication. From this point of view, components can be identified from the semi-paths in the graph. Components in a directed graph that are identified in this way, disregarding the direction of the lines that make up the paths and taking account simply of the presence or absence of a connection, are termed weak components.

The distinction between strong and weak components does not, of course, exist in undirected graphs. In these situations the researcher is dealing with what might be called 'simple components': as no directions are attached to the lines, all paths are acceptable connections. Computer algorithms for identifying simple components in an undirected graph are, in principle, identical to those for identifying weak components in a directed graph. It is only when the question of direction has to be explicitly dealt with that the algorithms differ.

Component analysis is able to decompose any graph into one or more components (simple, weak or strong components) and a number of isolated points. Graphs of relatively dense social networks have been found to show – typically – the dominance of a single large component, especially where the analysis focuses on simple or weak components. Indeed, this is probably one of the mathematical features of the 'small-world' networks (Watts, 1999) that I discuss in Chapter 9. In order to achieve a finer-grained analysis of network structure, it is generally necessary to attempt to probe the internal structure of components.

A useful way of probing the internal structure of components is to see whether there are particular points with a pivotal significance in holding components together. Hage and Harary (1983) approached this through a concept they designated as a 'block', which refers to those subgraphs within simple components (or within the weak components of a directed graph) that have no 'cut-point'.[2] A cut-point is a point whose removal would increase the number of components by dividing the subgraph into two or more separate subsets between which there are no connections. In the graph component (i) shown in Figure 7.2, for example, point B is a cut-point, as its removal would create the two disconnected components shown in sociogram (ii). None of the other points is a cut-point. Thus, cut-points are pivotal points of articulation between the elements that make up a component. These elements, together with their cut-points, are what Hage and Harary described as the 'blocks'. In order to avoid the conceptual confusion which results from the varying usages that have been given to the word 'block', I use the more descriptive term 'knot'. The component in Figure 7.2, then, comprises the two knots {A, B, C} and {B, D, E, F}. The various cut-points in a graph, therefore, will be members of a number of knots, with the cut-points being the points of overlap between the knots.[3]

It is relatively easy to give a substantive sociological interpretation to the idea of a cut-point. It can, for example, be seen as indicating some kind of local centrality for the corresponding agent. Hage and Harary (1983) have argued that knots ('blocks' in their terminology) can be seen as being, for example, the most effective systems of communication or exchange in a network (see also Hage and Harary, 1991, 1998, for applications of this view). Because they contain no cut-points, acts of communication and exchange among the members of a knot are not dependent upon any one member. There are always alternative paths of communication between all the points in a knot, and so the network that it forms is both flexible and unstratified.

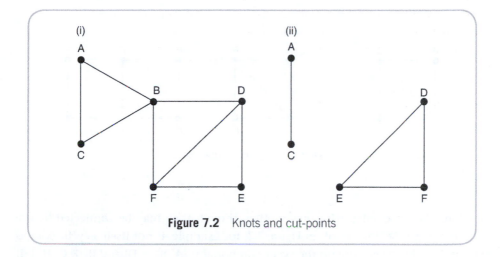

**Figure 7.2** Knots and cut-points

# CYCLES AND CIRCUITS

Everett has proposed an extension to the idea of the component that aims to achieve a fine-grained view of the texture of dense networks. His approach (1982, 1983a, 1983b, 1984) is based on a graph-theoretical concept that he terms the 'block'. As already indicated, there is a great deal of confusion over the word 'block', as it has been used in a number of radically different ways in social network analysis. To try to avoid some of this confusion, I propose some terminological innovations. For reasons that will soon become apparent, I shall refer to Everett's concept not as the 'block', but as the 'cyclic component'.[4]

The concept of the cyclic component follows from that of the cycle. A cycle is a path that returns to its own starting point, and, like a path, a cycle can be of any length. The cycles in a graph can be described by their length as 3-cycles, 4-cycles, and so on. Putting this in its most general form, graph theorists can identify what Everett terms $k$-cycles, where $k$ is any specified cycle length. A useful first step in the analysis of cycles is to decide on a maximum cycle length for consideration and to ignore any cycle of greater length than this. If a maximum cycle length of 4 is chosen, for example, sociogram (i) in Figure 7.3 contains four cycles of length 4 (ABCDA, BCDAB, CDABC and DABCD) and six cycles of length 3 (ABDA, BDAB, DABD, BCDB, CDBC and DBCD).[5] At a maximum cycle length of 3, only the shorter cycles remain and points A and C are not connected by any cycle. Everett goes on to define a bridge as a line that does not itself lie on a cycle but that may connect two or more cycles.[6] Sociogram (ii) in Figure 7.3, for example, contains, at maximum cycle length 4, the bridge BE.

A cyclic component can be defined as a set of intersecting cycles connected by those lines or points they have in common. The separate cyclic components of a graph,

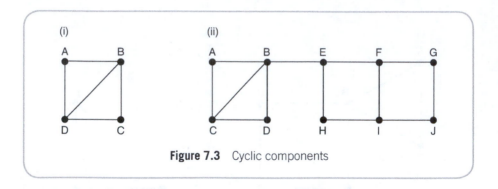

**Figure 7.3**  Cyclic components

therefore, do not overlap with one another, though they may be connected by one or more bridges. Sociogram (ii) in Figure 7.3, for example, is not itself a cyclic component; it does, however, contain the cyclic components {A, B, C, D} and {E, F, G, H, I, J}. The latter set of points contains the line FI, which is common to the cycles EFIHE and FGJIF. It can be seen, therefore, that a cyclic component consists of a chain of intersecting cycles, where the intersections are lines or points common to the overlapping cycles.[7] The cyclic components of a graph are identified by removing from a graph all those lines that are bridges at the specified cycle length (termed the 'k-bridges'). The sets of points that remain are the cyclic components.

Where an analysis of simple, weak, or strong components results merely in the identification of components and isolates, an analysis of cyclic components generally produces more complex results. This is because the cyclic components will be connected to various points that are not themselves members of cyclic components. Everett (1982) has shown that there are five types of network element:

- *Cyclic components.*
- *Hangers.* These are points that are connected to a member of a cyclic component, but do not themselves lie on a cycle. Hangers simply 'hang' on to a cyclic component.
- *Bridgers.* These are points that are 'intermediaries' or 'waverers' between two or more cyclic components, but are not members of any of them. A bridger, then, 'hangs' on to two or more cyclic components.
- *Isolated trees.* These are chains of points (including dyads) that are not connected to any cyclic component. The members of these 'trees' are linked to one another in a non-cyclic way.[8]
- *Isolates.* Those points that have no connections at all, that is, those which have degree 0.

It can sometimes be difficult to give a substantive sociological interpretation to long paths of connection. This is a particular problem where long cycles tie large numbers of points together. There is, as noted, a tendency for connected graphs to comprise a single, large cyclic component. Everett holds that, for most purposes, it is realistic to limit an analysis to relatively short cycles of length 3 or 4. At cycle length 3, for example, an analysis would be concerned simply with cyclic components built

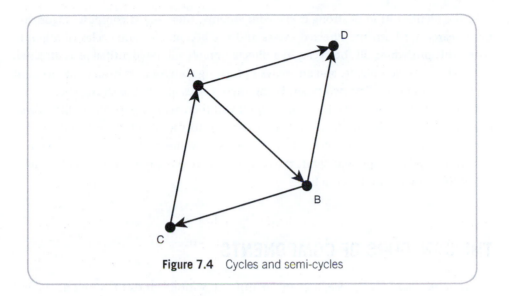

**Figure 7.4**  Cycles and semi-cycles

out of triads, to which a number of substantive interpretations can be given. At cycle length 4, an analysis would be concerned with those cyclic components that are built from either triads or 'rectangles'. If a researcher intends to use cycle lengths much greater than 4, where distances between points may increase substantially, it is particularly important that a clear and meaningful sociological interpretation can be given to the mathematical structures found.

An analysis of cyclic components can also be undertaken for directed graphs. The simplest way of doing this would be to disregard the directions attached to the lines. Such an analysis, based on the semi-paths in the graph, would identify 'semi-cycles'. These are cycles in which no account is taken of the direction of the lines. This does, of course, involve some loss of information, but the procedure allows the identification of what can be termed weak cyclic components. In order to analyse strong cyclic components, the information on directionality must be retained. Everett recommended that this kind of analysis should, in fact, also include some of the semi-cycles. In a directed cycle the direction runs consistently through all the constituent lines. In Figure 7.4, for example, the path ABCA is a directed cycle. The path ABDA, on the other hand, involves a reversal of direction between A and D, and so is merely a semi-cycle. Everett defines a semi-cycle as being an 'acceptable semi-cycle' if points that do not lie on a directed cycle are, nevertheless, connected by two or more distinct directed paths. Thus, points A and D are not connected through a directed cycle, but they are connected through the directed paths ABD and AD. For this reason, ABDA is an acceptable semi-cycle. The reasoning behind this is that the various members of the semi-cycle are connected through intersecting directed paths and so have a relatively 'strong' connection to each other.

In the identification of strong cyclic components, therefore, a computer algorithm must search for both the directed cycles and the acceptable semi-cycles of a graph. Using this procedure, all the cycles in a directed graph will be identifiable as directed, acceptable or unacceptable, and an analysis of strong components would take account only of cycles of the first two types. Using these cycles alone, the strong cyclic components of the graph can be identified, and it will then also be possible to distinguish between 'hangers-on' and 'hangers-off', according to the direction of the lines that connect them. The hangers-on are those hangers that direct a line towards a member of a strong cyclic component, while the hangers-off are those hangers to which a member of the component directs a line.[9]

## THE CONTOURS OF COMPONENTS

I have looked so far at procedures for identifying various kinds of components and sub-components, and I have reviewed some proposals for analysing the elements that make up these components (the knots and cut-points) and those which lie outside the components (the hangers, bridgers, trees and isolates). In this section I will pursue the question of the internal structure of components by exploring how the 'contours' of components can be charted by identifying their 'cores'.

I showed in Chapter 2 that the work of the Yankee City researchers involved an attempt to identify the core and peripheral members of what they called 'cliques'. This procedure can more usefully be applied to the internal structure of components. The contours of components can be disclosed by a procedure that is usually termed the 'nesting' of components.[10] The nesting of successive analyses of components involves using progressively stronger cut-off criteria for drawing the boundaries of components at each step of the analysis. When combined into a single model, the result of such a procedure is a series of concentric sets of points. The basic image in a nested analysis is that of a contour map or a set of Russian babushka dolls, each component being 'nested' within a larger component. A component can be understood as having a core of especially cohesive or intensely connected points, with the boundaries of the core being gradually extended to include more and more points as the cut-off level of cohesion or intensity is weakened. At the weakest level of connection, all connected points are included in a single component.

Figure 7.5 illustrates a simple case of nesting. The points in set A are the most tightly connected, and they comprise the core of their component. The boundary of set B is drawn with a weaker criterion of connection and so includes all the points of set A together with the additional points that are connected at this weaker level. Finally, set C has its boundary determined by the very weakest criterion of connectedness and so includes all connected points. Sets D, E and F in the second component can be interpreted in the same way. Thus, each of the components in a graph can be decomposed into its core elements and a contour diagram of the graph can be drawn.

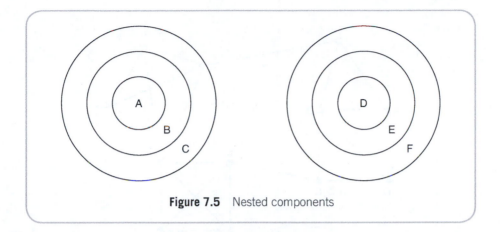

**Figure 7.5** Nested components

Basic component detection algorithms treat all connections as binary data, as indicating simply the presence or absence of a relation. A valued graph, therefore, must be analysed by converting its actual values into binary values of 1 or 0. This is done by comparing entries in the matrix for the valued graph with a 'slicing' or 'dichotomising' threshold.[11] Entries above or below the specified threshold are dichotomised into binary values: those above it are given the value 1 and those below it are given the value 0. These binary values can then be used in the search for components. A valued adjacency matrix might, for example, contain entries that show the multiplicities of the lines, and this matrix could be 'sliced' by choosing progressively stronger levels of intensity. By studying the components identified at each threshold level, the researcher can construct a contour diagram of nested components such as that shown in Figure 7.5. The boundaries of the components are drawn as concentric loops, and the diagram shows the 'peaks' of high intensity that comprise its core and the 'plains' of low intensity.

This method can be extended to the analysis of nesting in relation to cyclic components. Cyclic components can, of course, be identified in valued graphs by using an appropriate 'slicing' value. By varying the slicing criterion it is possible to arrive at an analysis of nested components: in this case, of nested cyclic components.[12]

Two alternative methods of nesting have been proposed: one based on the use of the degrees of the points as a measure of cohesion, and the other based on the use of the multiplicities of the lines as a measure of intensity. The degree-based measure results in the identification of 'k-cores', while the multiplicity-based measure results in the identification of 'm-cores'.[13]

Seidman (1983) proposed that the structure of components can be studied by using a criterion of minimum degree to identify areas of high and low cohesion. An analysis of the resulting k-core structure of a graph, he argued, is an essential complement to the measurement of density, which I have shown fails to grasp many of the global features of graph structure. A k-core is a maximal subgraph in which each point is adjacent to at least k other points: all the points within the k-core have degree greater than or

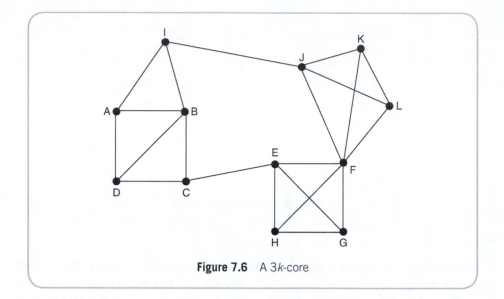

**Figure 7.6** A 3*k*-core

equal to *k*.[14] Thus, a simple component is a '1*k*-core'. All its points are connected to one another and so have a degree of at least 1. To identify a 2*k*-core, all points with degree 1 are ignored and the structure of connections among the remaining points is examined. The 2*k*-core consists of those remaining connected points that have degree 2. A 3*k*-core is identified by deleting all points with a degree of 2 or less, and so on. Figure 7.6 illustrates a 3*k*-core. In this subgraph, all points have degree at least 3. Although there are two points with degree 4 (points B and J) and one point with degree 6 (point F), there are no 4*k*- or 6*k*-cores in this graph, as a *k*-core must have at least *k* + 1 members each with degree *k*.

A *k*-core, then, is an area of relatively high cohesion within the whole graph. But it is not necessarily a maximally cohesive subgraph: there may be areas of very high cohesion that are connected to one another rather loosely. In Figure 7.6, for example, the cohesive areas {E, F, G, H, J, K, L} and {A, B, C, D, E, I} are connected through the weaker links CE and IJ. The *k*-cores, then, constitute areas of the component within which cohesive subgroups, if they exist, will be found.[15]

Seidman also shows how the overall fragmentation of a network can be assessed by looking at what he calls the core collapse sequence. The points in a *k*-core can be divided into two sets: those that are in a *k* + 1 core and those that are not. Seidman terms the latter group the '*k*-remainder'. The remainder in any core comprises those points that 'disappear' from the analysis when *k* is increased by 1. It is the disappearance of these less well-connected points that causes the core to 'collapse' as *k* is increased. Seidman proposed that the proportion of points that disappear from a core at each increase in *k* can be arranged in a vector (a simple row of figures) that describes the structure of local density within the component.[16]

This can be illustrated through the sociogram in Figure 7.7. All six points are connected, and so the increase in *k* from 0 to 1 involves no loss of points. At *k* = 1 all points are contained in a core, but there is a remainder of 2 (points A and F) that will disappear when $k$ is increased to 2. At $k = 2$, points B, C, D and E remain, each with degree greater than or equal to 2. As these points are, in fact, mutually connected at degree 3, there is no remainder at $k = 2$. When $k$ is increased to 3, however, the remainder is 4, as all points will disappear when $k$ is increased to 4. Arranging the sequence of remainders from $k = 0$ in a vector gives the core collapse sequence (0, 0.33, 0, 0.67).

The core collapse sequence gives a summary of the 'clumpiness' of the component. A slow and gradual collapse in the core, argues Seidman, indicates an overall uniformity in the texture of the network. An irregular sequence of values, as shown in Figure 7.7, shows that there are relatively dense areas surrounded by more peripheral points. The persistence of zero values in the vector up to high levels of $k$ indicates a uniformity of structure within the component; the appearance and persistence of zero values after low levels of $k$ indicates the existence of clumps of high density. The $k$-cores of a network are computed in Pajek through the NET > PARTITIONS > CORE menu choice and in UCINET through the NETWORK > SUBGROUPS > K-CORE menu choice.

By contrast with $k$-cores, which are based around the degrees of the points, '$m$-cores' are based around the multiplicities of the lines.[17] An $m$-core can be defined as a maximal subgraph in which each line has a multiplicity greater than or equal to $m$. An $m$-core is a chain of points connected by lines of the specified multiplicity. As in the case of a $k$-core, a simple component is a $1m$-core, as all of its points are connected with a multiplicity of at least 1. In a $2m$-core, lines of multiplicity 1 are ignored, and components are identified on the remaining lines. In a $3m$-core, lines of multiplicity 1 and 2 are ignored, and so on. Figure 7.8 shows a simple $3m$-core. All the points are connected through paths of multiplicity greater than or equal to 3, the weaker connections of the

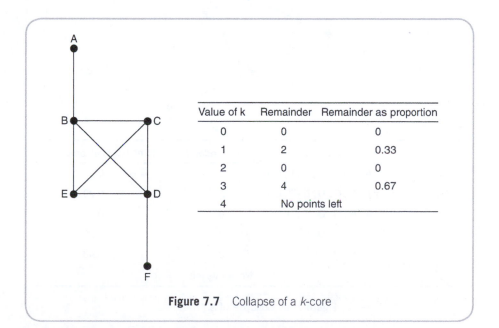

| Value of k | Remainder | Remainder as proportion |
|---|---|---|
| 0 | 0 | 0 |
| 1 | 2 | 0.33 |
| 2 | 0 | 0 |
| 3 | 4 | 0.67 |
| 4 | No points left | |

**Figure 7.7** Collapse of a $k$-core

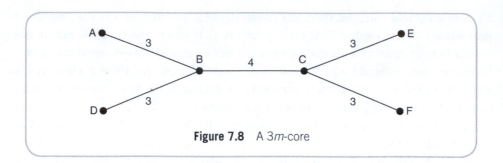

**Figure 7.8** A 3*m*-core

points to those outside the core being disregarded. As points B and C are connected by a line of multiplicity 4, they form a two-member 4*m*-core. It is the nesting of cores within each other that discloses the overall shape of the network.[18]

Seidman's idea of the core collapse sequence can be extended to *m*-cores: indeed, the idea is far simpler to apply to them. This can be illustrated with the sociogram in Figure 7.9. Lines are progressively removed as the value of *m* is increased, and the remainder at each level of *m* is the number of points that will disappear when *m* is increased to *m* + 1. Two points disappear when *m* is increased from 1 to 2, but no further points disappear until *m* reaches 4. If *m* is increased to 5, all points will disappear, as the highest multiplicity in the graph is 4. Thus, the *m*-core collapse sequence for this component is: (0, 0.29, 0, 0.29, 0.43). De Nooy et al. (2005: 111–13) refer to the *m*-core as an *m*-slice and discuss its measurement in Pajek.

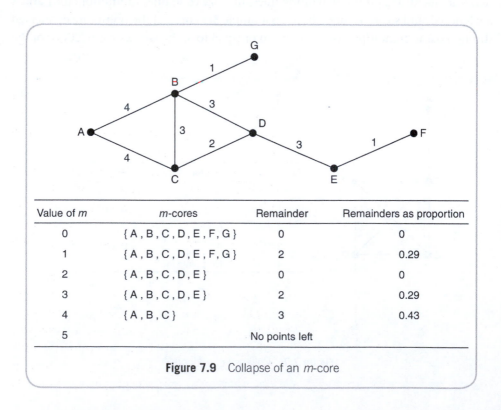

| Value of *m* | *m*-cores | Remainder | Remainders as proportion |
|---|---|---|---|
| 0 | { A , B , C , D , E , F , G } | 0 | 0 |
| 1 | { A , B , C , D , E , F , G } | 2 | 0.29 |
| 2 | { A , B , C , D , E } | 0 | 0 |
| 3 | { A , B , C , D , E } | 2 | 0.29 |
| 4 | { A , B , C } | 3 | 0.43 |
| 5 | | No points left | |

**Figure 7.9** Collapse of an *m*-core

Taken together, the various extensions of the basic idea of the simple component provide a powerful set of concepts for analysing the level of fragmentation in a network. They supplement the measurement of density and help to overcome many of its limitations by highlighting the overall shape of the network. A full outline comparison of the global structures of networks of comparable size would involve measures of the overall density of the networks and their inclusiveness, the number and sizes of their components and their densities, and the nested structures of the components and their core collapse sequences.

# CLIQUES WITHIN COMPONENTS

The concepts discussed so far in this chapter have gone some way towards formalising the ideas of those early writers on social networks who talked about the 'cliques' discovered in the Hawthorne works and in Yankee City. However, the idea of the clique implies something more than simply connectedness. It implies that there is a certain closeness and mutuality among those who can be regarded as a clique. A number of competing meanings have been given to the sociometric concept of the clique. The most widely held view is that its essential meaning is that of the maximal complete subgraph (Luce and Perry, 1949; Harary, 1969). That is to say, a clique is a subset of points in which every possible pair of points is directly connected by a line and the clique is not contained in any other clique.[19] As Figure 7.10 shows, a three-member clique contains 3 lines, a four-member clique contains 6 lines, a five-member clique contains 10 lines, and so on.[20] While a 'component' is maximal and connected (all points are connected to one another through paths), a 'clique' is maximal and complete (all points are adjacent to one another).

Doreian (1979: 51–2) has spelled out some of the formal properties of cliques. The basic consideration is that all cliques are maximal subsets of points in which each point is in a direct and reciprocal relation with all others. In an undirected graph all lines are, by definition, reciprocal relations, and so a clique detection procedure will consider all the lines in the graph. In a directed graph, however, this is not the case: its matrix is asymmetric, and only the reciprocated lines should be considered. In directed graphs, therefore, network analysis identifies what might be called strong cliques. On the other hand, if the direction of the lines is disregarded and simply the presence or absence of a relation is considered, the analysis treats all lines as if they were reciprocated and results in the identification of weak cliques.[21]

This concept of the maximal complete subgraph is rather restrictive for real social networks, as such tightly knit groups are very uncommon. For this reason, a number of extensions to the basic idea have been proposed.[22] The earliest of these extensions was the concept of the n-clique, which, it was claimed, is much closer to people's everyday understanding of the word 'clique'. In this concept, n is the maximum path length at which members of the clique will be regarded as connected. Thus, a 1-clique is the maximal complete subgraph itself, the set in which all pairs of points are directly

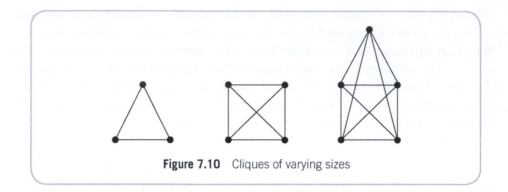

**Figure 7.10** Cliques of varying sizes

connected at distance 1. Such a clique is, necessarily, both a 1$k$-core and a 1$m$-core, but not all such cores will be cliques. A 2-clique, on the other hand, is one in which the members are connected either directly (at distance 1) or indirectly through a common neighbour (distance 2).

The value of $n$ that is used in an analysis is chosen by the researcher, and a progressive increase in the value of $n$ results in a gradual relaxation of the criterion for clique membership (see Figure 7.11). A 3-clique, for example, is a looser grouping than a 2-clique. The maximum value that can be given to $n$ is one less than the total number of points in the graph. In practice, however, most large connected graphs are joined into a single $n$-clique at much shorter path lengths than this.

An $n$-clique can be identified through the relatively simple matrix multiplication methods available in many spreadsheet programs. Multiplying the adjacency matrix by itself, for example, produces a matrix of path distances. The square of the matrix shows all distance 2 connections, the cube of the matrix shows distance 3 connections, and so on. Matrix multiplication is, however, a rather inefficient method of clique detection, and specialist network analysis programs such as UCINET and Pajek use a variant of the back-tracking procedure used for component detection. It is possible to analyse $n$-cliques in a valued graph by applying a slicing criterion, and such an analysis generates a set of nested cliques for each level of $n$: nested 2-cliques, nested 3-cliques, and so on. Cliques can be computed easily in UCINET, through the NETWORK > SUBGROUPS > CLIQUE menu, and with rather more difficulty in Pajek (see de Nooy et al., 2005: 74–7).

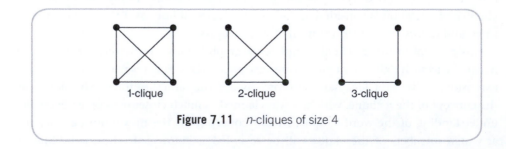

| 1-clique | 2-clique | 3-clique |

**Figure 7.11** $n$-cliques of size 4

There are two important limitations on the use of the *n*-clique idea. The first and most important is that values of *n* greater than 2 can be difficult to interpret socio-logically. Distance 2 relations can be straightforwardly interpreted as those involving a common neighbour who, for example, may act as an intermediary or a broker to cover a structural hole. Path lengths greater than 2, however, involve rather more distant and weak links. While long, weak chains of connection may be very important for the overall structure of the network, as Granovetter and the 'small-world' analysts have argued, it is not at all clear that they are appropriate for the definition of cliques. The very idea of a clique seems to demand relatively close linkages. It is, therefore, difficult to justify the identification of *n*-cliques with values of *n* greater than 2.

The second limitation on the use of the *n*-clique concept is the fact that intermedi-ary points on the paths of the *n*-clique may not themselves be members of the clique. For example, points A, B, C, D and E in graph (i) of Figure 7.12 form a 2-clique, but the distance 2 path that connects D and E runs through the non-member F. The 'diam-eter' of the clique – the path distance between its most distant members – may, then, be greater than the value of *n* used to define the clique. Thus, the set {A, B, C, D, E} comprises a 2-clique, but it has a diameter of 3. Both Alba (1973, 1982) and Mokken (1974) have taken up this problem and proposed some further extensions to the idea of the *n*-clique. Mokken proposed that a more useful concept is one that would limit the diameter of the clique to *n*. That is to say, the researcher accepts, for example, distance 2 paths for the identification of clique members, but also requires that the diameter of the clique be no greater than 2. This concept he terms the '*n*-clan'. Graphs (ii) and (iii) in Figure 7.12 are, unlike graph (i), 2-clans.[23]

A different extension of the basic clique idea is that of the '*k*-plex', proposed by Seidman and Foster (1978). Whereas the concept of the *n*-clique involves increasing the permissible path lengths that define the clique, the concept of the *k*-plex involves

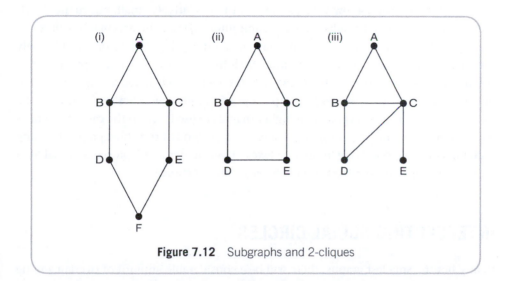

**Figure 7.12**  Subgraphs and 2-cliques

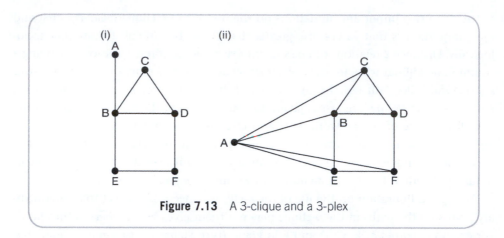

**Figure 7.13**  A 3-clique and a 3-plex

reducing the number of other points to which each point must be connected. Thus, the points in a *k*-plex are connected at distance 1, but not all points will be connected to one another. A *k*-plex is a set of points in which each point is adjacent to all except *k* of the other points.[24] Thus, if *k* = 1, a 1-plex is equivalent to a 1-clique, and so it is a maximal complete subgraph. Each member of the 1-plex is connected to *n* – 1 other points. When *k* is equal to 2, all members in the 2-plex are connected to at least *n* – 2 of the other members, but the 2-plex may not be a 2-clique. In Figure 7.13, graph (i) is a 3-clique, as all pairs of points are connected at distance 3 or less. It is not, however, a 3-plex, as A, C, E and F are each connected to fewer than three other members. Graph (ii) is both a 3-clique and a 3-plex.[25]

An important consideration in the analysis of *k*-plexes is that of the minimum size that the researcher will regard as acceptable for a plex. In particular, higher values of *k* ought to involve the choice of a higher cut-off threshold for the size of acceptable *k*-plexes. When *k* takes a low value, *k*-plexes can be relatively small, but higher levels of *k* will produce trivial results unless the minimum size of the acceptable *k*-plexes is increased. The reason for this is that small subgraphs at high levels of *k* will be only minimally cohesive. As a rule of thumb, the minimum size for an acceptable *k*-plex should be *k* + 2. Nevertheless, the concept of the *k*-plex, considered as a generalisation of the basic clique idea, seems to grasp more of the idea of cohesion than does the *n*-clique, especially when values of *n* higher than 2 are used.[26] As in the case of *n*-cliques and components, the basic idea of a *k*-plex can be extended to valued graphs by using a slicing criterion to analyse 'nested *k*-plexes'. Basic analysis of *k*-plexes is available in UCINET through the NETWORK > SUBGROUPS > K-PLEX menu choice.

## INTERSECTING SOCIAL CIRCLES

In any but the smallest graphs, there will be a considerable amount of overlap among the various *n*-cliques and *k*-plexes of which the graph is composed. Clique analyses (of both $n$-cliques and $k$-plexes) will tend to produce long lists of overlapping cliques, and these results may be difficult to interpret. A relatively dense network will tend to comprise a large number of overlapping cliques, with many points being members of numerous different cliques. A graph with 20 points and a high density, for example, could contain anything up to 2,000 overlapping cliques. In these circumstances, the density of the overlap among cliques may be more significant than the composition of the cliques themselves. Alba (1982) proposed, therefore, that social network analysts should use concepts that explicitly recognise this fact of overlap. Drawing on work undertaken with Kadushin and Moore (Kadushin, 1966, 1968; Alba and Kadushin, 1976; Alba and Moore, 1978), he argued that the concept of the 'social circle' can be used to grasp significant structural features of social networks.

This idea was devised by Kadushin from the initial insights of Simmel (1908), who first outlined the importance of the 'intersection of social circles'. The cohesion of a social circle is not founded on the direct 'face-to-face' contacts of its members, but on the existence of short chains of indirect connections that weld them together. Circles emerge from interaction and may not be visible to their participants, as their boundaries are only loosely defined by the ramification of these indirect connections.

Alba's contribution was to formalise the idea of the circle in sociometric terms by relating it to other graph-theoretical concepts. His basic argument is that overlapping cliques can be aggregated into circles if they have more than a certain proportion of their members in common. Alba suggested that the most appropriate procedure is to use a kind of 'snowballing' method in which cliques are aggregated into progressively larger, and looser, circles. The first step in an analysis of circles is to identify 1-cliques of size 3 (triads) and then to merge into a circle all of those cliques that differ by only one member. Put in a slightly different way, the initial criterion for identifying circles is to merge cliques into a circle if two-thirds of their members are identical. The result might then be one or more circles, together with a number of separate cliques and isolated points. At a second step the remaining cliques might be merged with those circles with which there is a lower level of overlap. Alba suggested that a one-third overlap in membership might be appropriate in this second step. The result of this aggregation will be a large circle or a set of smaller circles surrounded by a periphery of less well-connected cliques and points. Figure 7.14 shows a simplified analysis of social circles. Two circles are identified at step 1, but they are merged into a single circle at step 2. As in so many graph-theoretical procedures, it is important to note that the level of overlap chosen for aggregation is arbitrary. The levels suggested by Alba were chosen on common-sense mathematical grounds, and it will be necessary for researchers to decide whether his suggestions make sense in specific applications.

The measurement of circles, therefore, takes the extent of the overlap between cliques as a measure of the distance between them. The particular way in which the cliques have been identified (as $n$-cliques or $k$-plexes, for example) hardly matters in this procedure, as the subtle differences in the procedures rapidly disappear during the process of aggregation. In practice, the end result of an aggregation into circles is barely affected by the initial clique detection method used.[27]

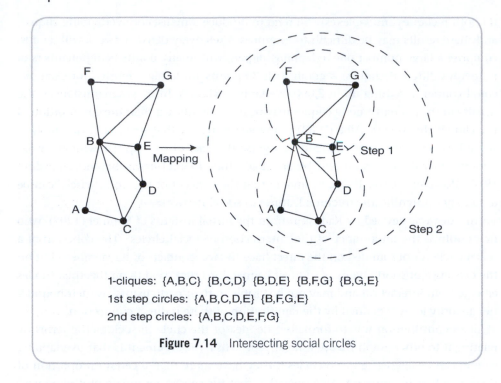

1-cliques: {A,B,C} {B,C,D} {B,D,E} {B,F,G} {B,G,E}
1st step circles: {A,B,C,D,E} {B,F,G,E}
2nd step circles: {A,B,C,D,E,F,G}

**Figure 7.14**   Intersecting social circles

# COMPONENTS AND CITATION CIRCLES

These network decomposition measures can be illustrated from studies in the sociology of science that have used data on communication, co-authorship, and citation. Crane's (1972) study of the 'invisible college' was one of the earliest pieces of research to use the idea of networks of communication among scientists as a way of explaining the growth of scientific knowledge. Her study involved the use of questionnaires to obtain information on patterns of communication and influence among rural sociologists, and she analysed such phenomena as co-publication and the advice given on areas of research specialisation. Her particular concern was to outline the size and significance of the invisible college of collaborators in this research specialism, but she used few sociometric concepts to uncover its internal structure. Mullins (1973) adopted a different strategy, looking at work in theoretical sociology in order to discover its subgroups of specialists. Using material on education and career appointments as well as co-publication, he constructed sociograms to show social relations among those engaged in structural functionalist theory, small-group theory, causal theory and a number of other areas.[28] Unfortunately, the boundaries of the research specialisms were not themselves derived from sociometric analyses, and so Mullins's work was able to give little information on the overall structure of components and cliques in the field of theoretical sociology.

An interesting example that adopted a rigorous sociometric approach to the discovery of network structures in science is that of Gattrell (1984a, 1984b). Gattrell used the techniques of Q-analysis (see footnote 18) to identify the structure of components in research groups. It is unnecessary to discuss the details of this complex procedure, which Gattrell used simply in order to construct a model of nested components, and his ideas can readily be translated into the terminology of this chapter.[29] A set of geographical papers published between 1960 and 1978, taken as the key contributions to the literature on spatial modelling, were used as the population for study, and Gattrell constructed a network of citation relations from their bibliographies and footnotes. A citation of paper A in paper B is treated as a line between the two papers, allowing multiple citations to generate valued data. Gattrell also assigned a direction to the relations, seeing such a citation as a directed line from paper B to paper A and as indicating a published recognition of the influence that the latter was felt to have had on the former. Citations can, therefore, be compiled into a binary matrix of directed lines. Gattrell ordered the rows and columns of the matrix chronologically, by date of publication, and so it was easy for him to perceive any obvious shifts in citation patterns. If, for example, authors cited only relatively recent papers, the '1' entries in the matrix would lie close to the diagonal. The more scattered are the '1' entries, the more widespread in time are the citations. Gattrell interpreted any clustering around the diagonal as evidence for Price's (1965) hypothesis of the 'immediacy effect' in citation, but he found little support for this idea.

The main aim of Gattrell's paper was to examine the component structure of the citation data, and from his initial incidence matrix he produced two analyses. First, he analysed the structure of the adjacency matrix of papers cited (the rows of the original matrix), and second, he analysed the adjacency structure of the citing papers (the columns). Two cited papers are connected to one another if they are each cited in the same source, and a component comprises a set of papers that are connected through a continuous chain of such connections.[30] Where two cited papers have more than one of their citers in common, they are connected at a higher level of multiplicity, and it is possible to investigate the nesting of components at various levels of multiplicity.

Gattrell found that, at the lowest level, 49 of the papers were formed into a single large component. At a multiplicity level of 6, however, this component had reduced to seven members. The seven papers in this component formed the core of the network, a 6m-core in the terminology introduced above. At the heart of this group were two highly cited papers by Hudson (1969) and Pedersen (1970). Hudson's paper received 17 citations and Pedersen's received 15, but only eight of their citations were in the same source papers. Thus, Hudson and Pedersen formed a component of size 2 at multiplicity 8 (calculated from Gattrell, 1984b: 447). Gattrell concludes that:

> The general picture ... is of a small group of highly cited papers, to which other literature is connected at lower ... [multiplicity] levels. A small component of papers concerned with hierarchical diffusion emerges, and other papers are added to this nucleus as a result of their being cited by some of the sources that cite the seminal papers. (Gattrell, 1984b: 448)

The analysis of nested components in citation patterns, then, highlights the 'star' cited papers and the extent to which there is any consensus over their star rating. The analysis of components and their cores allows an investigation of the structure of influence in scientific research and points to the important role played by scientific cliques and circles in the promotion of particular ideas and approaches within a specialism.

While the citation of papers is one form of scientific connectivity and is closely related to influence and impact, relations of co-authorship point to collegial relations in the process of scientific production. There is, however, some relationship between the two: it has been found that papers with two or more authors tend to receive more citations than single-authored papers (Beaver, 2004). In a study by Newman (2001) of biomedicine, physics and computer science it was found that sub-fields in all disciplines showed the existence of a very large component in their networks of co-authorship, the large component typically containing 80–90 per cent of all authors of papers. It was suggested that in the humanities, where lone scholarship is more significant, specialisms would be more fragmented.

Studies of citation and co-authorship can tell us a great deal about the social structure of scientific specialisms. In his review of the area, however, Howard White (2011) shows that they cannot be used to demonstrate the productivity, quality or impact of individuals or departments, and that they are very poor substitutes for peer review (see also Hicks, 2009).

--- EXERCISE ---

Select one issue of a journal in an area of social science familiar to you. (You will probably find this exercise easier if you choose a specialist journal rather than a general one.) Using your preferred software, construct an incidence matrix in which the published papers are the cases (the rows) and the papers and books listed in their bibliographies and footnotes are the affiliations (the columns). The entries in each row of the matrix should show which of the papers and books is cited by the authors of the relevant paper. Your data will be directed data (from rows to columns), but disregard the direction for this exercise.

When you have compiled your data, construct the adjacency matrix for the columns. This will show the relations among the cited articles and books.

- List the papers and books by their degree. This will show the most frequently cited publications. Using your understanding of the topics discussed in Chapter 5, consider what this tells you about citation practices in this area.
- Identify the structure of components within your network. Can you give any intellectual meaning to the publications included in the various components? If your data show a high level of multiplicity in citation patterns, examine the pattern of nested components and see if you can identify a core of highly cited publications.

- Identify the structure of cliques in your network. Does this tell you anything different about citation patterns?
- What implications does date of publication of the cited publications have for the interpretation of your results?

Consider what limitations result from choosing just one issue of a journal. How many issues would you need to select in order to improve your analysis and for what time period should you select them? How would or could you sample the issues of the journal?

## FURTHER READING

Davis, A., Gardner, B.B. and Gardner, M.R. (1941) *Deep South*. Chicago: University of Chicago Press.

This marvellous ethnography contains the original discussion of the data on the cliques formed by women in a southern city. This was first reanalysed using formal matrix methods in:

Homans, G.C. (1951) *The Human Group*. London: Routledge & Kegan Paul.

The website of Howard White (http://www.cis.drexel.edu/faculty/HUD.Web/HDWpubs.html) contains links to many of his studies of citation patterns and the uses of citation evidence.

# EIGHT

## Structural Locations, Classes and Positions

This chapter discusses:

- Structural positions in social networks
- The structural equivalence of points and partitioning a network
- Block modelling to disclose positions or locations within networks
- Studies of corporate interlocks

The network concepts that have been discussed so far have mainly been concerned with the particular patterns of direct and indirect contacts maintained by agents, with their formation of cohesive social groupings, and with their influence on the actions of those particular others to whom they are connected. However, I have, at a number of points, alluded to the analysis of 'positions' rather than individual agents and their connections. Warner and Lunt (1942), for example, attempted an empirical investigation of the formation of positions within a social structure, while Nadel (1957) argued for the structural analysis of social roles. Those who developed these early insights moved away from issues of group formation to the idea of 'structural equivalence'. This involves a focus on the general types of social relations maintained by particular categories of agents. Social positions or locations are occupied by agents who are 'substitutable' one for another with respect to their relational ties (Sailer, 1978; Burt, 1982). They are, in certain important respects, interchangeable with one another. Such positions are manifest only in the particular relations that link specific agents, but they cannot be reduced to these concrete connections.

## THE STRUCTURAL EQUIVALENCE OF POINTS

Two people may have direct connections to totally different individuals, yet the types of relations they have with these others may, nevertheless, be similar. Two fathers, for example, will relate to different sets of children, but they might be expected to behave, in certain respects, in similar 'fatherly' ways towards them. The two men, that is to say, are 'structurally equivalent' to one another: they occupy the same social position – that of 'father' – and so are interchangeable as far as the sociological analysis of fathers is concerned. They are not, of course, interchangeable so far as their children are concerned: they simply play a similar role towards them.

The idea behind structural equivalence, therefore, is that of identifying uniformities of action associated with enduring social locations or positions. Once positions within a network have been identified, the relations among them can be explored. For example, the relations between fathers, mothers, children and siblings may be seen as forming the family relations that constitute a structure of kinship relations. This approach involves a move beyond the principles of graph theory to a consideration of the algebraic models of set theory.

It might seem that the analysis of structural equivalence is simply the analysis of social roles. The clearest cases of structural equivalence are, indeed, those that arise when people occupy institutionalised roles, as in the example of the two fathers. The occupants of clearly specified and institutionalised cultural roles comprise structurally equivalent categories of agents: they do similar things in relation to similar others. However, there are also structured uniformities of action that are neither culturally recognised nor identified in socially defined roles (Scott, 2011b: Ch. 6). Agents may occupy a distinct location relative to others and act in similar ways towards them, even though this is not recognised by the various participants as comprising specific roles. Thus, those who occupy similar locations relative to the distribution of economic resources may be regarded as classes. Those in a particular class location occupy a structurally equivalent position and so have equivalent structurally determined interests and life chances in relation to the members of other classes. Class location may affect their actions without there being any consciousness of class or explicit class imagery. Indeed, this may be one of the ways in which new roles emerge: new forms of action arise and relations between more or less clearly defined categories of agents begin to crystallise long before people come to perceive what is going on and to give a name to it. In this sense, the identification of structurally equivalent categories of agents may be one basis for identifying emergent roles.

The starting point for all formal discussions of structural equivalence has been an influential paper by Lorrain and White (1971), who saw structurally equivalent agents as defined by their interchangeability with respect to activities within the network and as having similar experiences or opportunities (Friedkin, 1984; Burt, 1987; Mizruchi, 1993). Lorrain and White's paper describes some of the limitations of graph theory as a complete model for network structure, and outlines a complementary strategy based on algebraic ideas. Their approach has two major defining features that set it apart from other approaches to social network analysis. First, all points and their connections are handled simultaneously, rather than attention being limited to the lines, paths, and cycles that connect particular points. Second, the approach does not use the adjacency matrix, but involves a combined analysis of both the rows and the columns of the original incidence matrix. The approach, therefore, is a direct analysis of two-mode data. People and the organisations of which they are members, for example, can be analysed together rather than separately.

According to Lorrain and White, the overall pattern of connections in a network can be converted into a system of structurally equivalent positions by aggregating the individual points into larger sets of points. The underlying structure of a system, they argue, is more apparent in the relations that exist between the sets than it is in the more numerous and more concrete relations that exist between the individual agents who make up these sets. Figure 8.1 shows Lorrain and White's view of the 'reduction' of a complex network to its 'block model' or 'image matrix'. The points of the original incidence matrix are rearranged through a method of cluster analysis to form the structurally equivalent sets of the image matrix. In Figure 8.1, for example, the set M1 comprises the row points that are structurally equivalent to one another yet structurally different from the structurally equivalent points that make up set M2. The most fundamental features of a network, argued Lorrain and White, are apparent in the relations among the sets, and the nature of these relations is shown by the values in the cells – the blocks – of the image matrix. The aim of much of White's subsequent work was to suggest how such block models might be produced.[1]

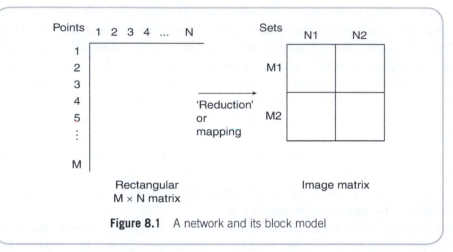

**Figure 8.1** A network and its block model

The concept of structural equivalence holds, in its strongest sense, that the members of a set are identical with one another as regards their relations to other members of the network. It is, however, very unusual to find agents that are perfectly equivalent in this strong sense. Most analysts of structural equivalence have, therefore, argued that the criterion needs to be weakened if it is to be of use in the study of real social networks. Instead of searching for those agents who are identical in their social relations, the aim is to identify those who are sufficiently similar to be regarded as structurally equivalent. Whatever the chosen measure of similarity, the researcher must decide on a cut-off threshold above which agents are to be regarded as being sufficiently similar to be, in effect, 'substitutable' for one another. This view of structural equivalence is likely to be of greater use in real situations, though it involves deciding on a cut-off level for identifying equivalence that can be substantively justified. The major differences among writers on structural equivalence concern the particular measure of 'similarity' to be used, the method of clustering by which points can be grouped into sets, and the methods for identifying the boundaries of sets.

## CLUSTERS AND SIMILARITY

The words 'cluster' and 'clique' have often been used interchangeably, as in the early discussions of sociometric 'cliques' in Old City and in Yankee City. Even some recent methodological commentators have not distinguished between the two ideas (see Lankford, 1974). I showed in the previous chapter, however, that the concept of the clique can be given a strict sociometric definition from which a whole family of related concepts can be derived. The concept of the cluster needs also to be clearly defined as a separate and very distinct idea.

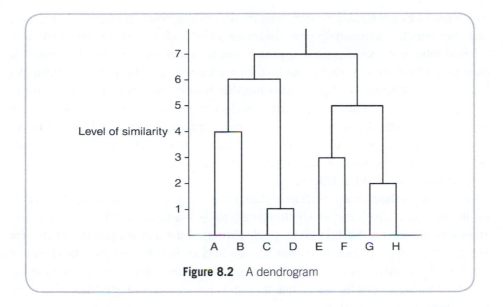

**Figure 8.2** A dendrogram

A cluster, in social network analysis, is a set of points that are judged to be similar with respect to some relational property. 'Similarity' is a relative term, and points can be more or less similar. Points can therefore be grouped into nested sets at varying levels of similarity. This can be illustrated by Figure 8.2, where eight arbitrarily arranged points, A to H, are grouped by their level of similarity. The joining of points at these various levels comprises a 'dendrogram' or tree diagram. This shows that points C and D are linked into a cluster at the first level and so can be seen as the most similar points. Points G and H are linked at the second level, points E and F at the third, and points A and B at the fourth. If the analysis stopped here, four clusters would have been identified. Taking a further step, however, shows that points E, F, G and H can all be identified as members of a single cluster. Similarly, points A, B, C and D are clustered together at a sixth level. Finally, at the seventh level, all points can be aggregated into the same cluster. The number and composition of clusters reported in any investigation will, therefore, depend on the step at which the analysis is stopped.

There are two principal families of cluster analysis methods: 'the agglomerative', in which points are progressively combined; and the 'divisive', in which a large set is progressively divided (Everitt, 1974; Bailey, 1976). Each method is hierarchical, in that small clusters can be nested within larger clusters, but the principles used in constructing the hierarchy of clusters vary between the two cases. The discussion above was couched in terms of an agglomerative model in which individual points are gradually aggregated into larger and larger sets. Points are compared in terms of their structural similarity to each other, and they are grouped together with those to which they are most similar. Agglomerative methods can be of the 'single-linkage' or the 'complete-linkage' type (Johnson, 1967). In a single-linkage method, points are fused into a cluster with those to which they are most similar. Initially, the two most similar points are fused into a cluster, and later steps fuse successively more dissimilar points and clusters. A complete-linkage method follows the same general approach, but measures the similarity between two clusters not by their most similar but by their least similar members.[2] While the single-linkage method tends to 'chain' points together into existing clusters, the complete-linkage method is more likely to initiate new clusters at early stages in the analysis. The single-linkage method, therefore, is less likely to identify the compact and homogeneous clusters of the kind found through complete linkage. In emphasising the connections between clusters, the single-linkage method can mask the existence of important divisions in the network (Alba, 1982: 55–6).

With both methods of agglomerative cluster analysis, it is left to the analyst to decide on the level of similarity at which clusters are to be identified. In a connected graph, all points will, eventually, fuse into a single cluster, so the number and size of clusters identified will depend upon the cut-off threshold chosen. It follows that the choice of a cut-off threshold, as in so many areas of social network analysis, is a matter for the informed judgement of the researcher, though some measures of goodness of fit have been suggested as aids in this task.

A divisive or partitioning approach to clustering starts from the graph as a whole, regarded as a single cluster, and splits off subsets at reducing levels of similarity. There are two approaches to divisive clustering, the 'single-attribute' and the 'all-attribute' methods. Single-attribute methods begin by differentiating those points that possess a particular indicator or value from those that do not, and the initial cluster is split into two on the basis of the presence or absence of this indicator. The same procedure is followed within each cluster at subsequent steps in order to subdivide them further.[3] The single-attribute procedure, therefore, consists of a series of binary splits aimed at producing mutually exclusive sets of points. In an all-attribute method, on the other hand, the first and subsequent splits are based on the average similarity of a set of points to all other points in the graph.

The clusters identified in a particular graph will depend upon both the choice of method and, crucially, the choice of a measure of similarity. The choice of a measure of similarity is fundamental to any attempt to measure structural equivalence. The implications of this can be pursued by considering a particular approach that builds on the work of Lorrain and White (1971).

## DIVIDE AND CONCOR

The earliest workable algorithm for investigating structural equivalence along the lines suggested by Lorrain and White was that formulated by Breiger and Schwartz, two of White's students, who independently rediscovered a matrix clustering method first proposed by McQuitty (1968).[4] Their algorithm is called CONCOR, standing for

'CONvergence of iterated CORrelations', and uses correlation coefficients as measures of similarity. This involves a rather complex and cumbersome procedure, although its general principles are fairly straightforward and it is readily available in UCINET. The CONCOR algorithm operates on sociometric incidence matrices of cases and affiliations, and can be applied to the rows, to the columns, or simultaneously to both the rows and the columns of the incidence matrix. Its general logic can best be understood by following through the steps involved in an analysis of the rows aimed at investigating structural equivalences among the cases.

The first step in the analysis is a calculation of the Pearson correlation coefficients between all pairs of cases in the matrix. Two cases with exactly the same pattern of affiliations would show a correlation of +1, a pair with completely different affiliations would be uncorrelated (with a value of 0), and a pair with completely opposite patterns of affiliation would have a negative correlation of –1. These correlations form a square case-by-case correlation matrix, which can be seen as a type of adjacency matrix. In the second step a clustering procedure groups the cases into structurally equivalent sets, according to their measured correlation. If rows are either perfectly correlated or completely uncorrelated, a strong criterion of structural equivalence could be used to divide the matrix into two sets. The matrix would fall into two sets that are completely connected internally but have no connections with each other. Such a clustering would be possible for the data shown in Figure 2.6. As this kind of patterning is not normally the case with real data, a clustering method that works on a wider range of correlation values must be used as the basis for identifying 'fuzzy' sets of equivalent points.

CONCOR achieves this fuzzy clustering by transforming the raw correlations through calculating, for each pair of cases, the correlation between their scores in the correlation matrix. That is, the correlations among the correlations scores are calculated and are entered into a new correlation matrix. This process is repeated over and over again for each successive matrix: correlating the correlations of the correlations, and so on. Repeated correlations of this kind have been found to eventually produce a matrix in which all cells contain values of either +1 or –1. The iterated, repeated correlations therefore converge to a simple pattern and the rows can be partitioned into two clusters in much the same way as if a strong criterion of structural equivalence had been used. Each resulting cluster constitutes a set of structurally equivalent cases.

Each of the two clusters can then be divided into its constituent elements by precisely the same method. To achieve this, the algorithm returns to the original matrix of raw values and divides this into two separate matrices, one for each of the clusters that have been identified. As in the first round of iterations, the raw group memberships within one of the clusters are converted into correlations, the correlations are correlated, and so on, until a pattern of +1 and –1 entries emerges within the cluster. At this point the cluster can be partitioned once more and the whole process repeated. Division and subdivision of clusters in this way can proceed for as long as the researcher wishes, though the larger the number of clusters, the more difficult it may be to interpret the final results.[5]

While the researcher must make an arbitrary decision about when to stop the process of division and subdivision within clusters, the emergence of a pattern of +1 and −1 values at each step does mean that there is a relatively unambiguous approximation to a strong criterion for identifying structural equivalence. The partitioning of the cases depends simply on the actual values produced in the final matrix.[6] Unfortunately, the reason why such a pattern should emerge is far from clear. This means that an unspecified and partly obscure clustering principle is at work in the CONCOR algorithm. It is the algorithm itself that produces the conversion of the raw data into structural equivalence categories. This makes it difficult for social investigators to judge whether the assumptions of the method are appropriate for particular kinds of data. The method seems to work and to produce useful data, despite the fact that the reasons for this are unknown.

This process of partitioning into clusters can be repeated for the columns of the original incidence matrix, so as to produce a separate grouping of the affiliations. If the cases are individuals and the affiliations are the organisations of which they are members, a partitioning of the organisations would cluster them according to similarities in their patterns of recruitment. For both the rows and the columns of the original incidence matrix, then, CONCOR can produce a hierarchical partitioning into 'discrete mutually exclusive and exhaustive' structurally equivalent clusters (Knoke and Kuklinski, 1982: 73).

The clusters identified in these ways can be constructed into rearranged image matrices of the type illustrated in Figure 8.1. It is possible to produce a square image matrix for the adjacency matrix of the cases or for the adjacency matrix of the affiliations. Each of the cells in the image matrix – they are termed the 'blocks' – contains a measure of the density of the connections between pairs of sets. If all density values were either 1 or 0, the pattern of relations would be clear. The '0-blocks' (the cells with density 0) would represent 'holes' in the network, the complete absence of connections; and the distribution of cells with density 1 would show the basic structure of the network. Such density patterns rarely occur in real data, and so a block modelling has to convert the actual range of density values into two categories of 'high' and 'low' values as approximations to the 1-blocks and 0-blocks. In the image matrix, the high values – those which are above a specified threshold value – are represented by 1, while low values are represented by 0. The most commonly used method for defining blocks with a high density is to take the average density of the whole matrix as a cut-off point: values at or above the mean are regarded as 'high', while those below it are 'low'. This procedure of block modelling, like so many in network analysis, involves a discretionary choice on the part of the researcher, and the choice must be grounded in theoretical or empirical considerations. It cannot be justified on any purely formal, mathematical principles alone. Friedkin (1998: 8) has also criticised the reliance on density as the sole measure of block formation.

Exactly the same procedures can be used to produce a combined analysis of the rows and columns. CONCOR will produce a clustering of the rows and a clustering of

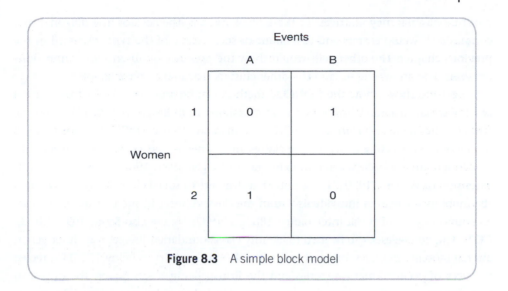

**Figure 8.3**   A simple block model

the columns and will then combine these into a single image matrix of the original rectangular incidence matrix.

Once an image graph containing only 1s and 0s in its cells has been produced, the researcher must attempt to interpret it. Interpretations of block models produced from rectangular incidence matrices are extremely difficult to make, and Breiger and his associates, the originators of block modelling, have published no detailed analyses of such models. In the earliest analysis of an incidence matrix, Breiger et al. (1975) reanalysed the Deep South data collected by Davis et al. (1941) concerning the participation of 18 women in 14 social events.[7] To analyse these data, they computed separate row and column solutions and combined them into the block model shown in Figure 8.3.

It can be seen that women in cluster 1 tend to meet in the events of cluster B and that women in cluster 2 tend to meet at the events of cluster A. The two clusters of women correspond closely to the two 'cliques' identified by Homans (1951) in his commentary on the original data, but Breiger et al. did not go beyond this observation. Although they discuss the composition of the clusters, they give no attention to the pattern of block densities in the image matrix. In the same paper, they also reanalysed Levine's (1972) rectangular matrix of banks and corporations, but they again simply compare the separate row and column analyses with Levine's own analysis.

This failure on the part of the inventors of block modelling to analyse an incidence matrix in any detail suggests the existence of a fundamental difficulty in achieving the concurrent treatment of both rows and columns that was anticipated by Lorrain and White. A rectangular image matrix, if it is fairly simple, may give an initial and schematic overview of the network, but more detailed analyses can only be pursued by analysing the rows and the columns separately. An incidence matrix, then, must be analysed principally through the construction of separate block models for each of its constituent adjacency matrices. In these block models, the cells on the diagonal that contain a '1' would correspond to a clique or social circle of the type discussed in the previous chapter. The other cells would show the presence or absence of connections between the various cliques and the other clusters that make up the graph.[8]

Breiger has shown how the CONCOR method can be applied in one of the central areas of social analysis. Using data on social mobility from Britain (Glass, 1954) and the United States (Blau and Duncan, 1967; Featherman and Hauser, 1978), he constructed a model of class structure in which the classes are defined as sets of occupations identifiable in a matrix of occupational mobility rates (Breiger, 1981, 1982). He sees this as an extension of Weber's (1920–21) claim that 'a structure of social classes exists only when the mobility chances of individuals within the classes cluster in such a way as to create a common nexus of social interchange' (Breiger, 1982: 18; see also Scott, 1996: Ch. 2). CONCOR, he suggests, can be used to identify class boundaries. Breiger used inter-generational mobility matrices for adult males, the American matrices being $17 \times 17$ directed matrices of occupational categories and the British being $8 \times 8$ directed matrices. In each matrix, the cells contained the numbers of individuals moving from one category to another, with the rows showing the 'origins' and the columns showing the 'destinations'. For the USA, Breiger (1981) concluded that there was a stable structure of eight classes over the period 1962–73, while for Britain he concluded that the earlier data (they related to 1949) could best be seen as reflecting a three-class structure. The central class boundaries in Britain separated manual from non-manual and the salaried 'middle class' from lower-level clerical and administrative jobs.

By far the easiest of matrices to analyse through block modelling are adjacency matrices with directed data: matrices where, for example, the rows represent relations 'sent' and the columns represent relations 'received'. A useful aid to the interpretation of this kind of data is the construction of arrow diagrams that show the relations among the clusters. This can be illustrated with the matrices in Figure 8.4, which show some hypothetical data on power relations.[9] In these matrices, the power relations are directed from rows to columns. The row entries in the original matrix, for example, would show over which other agents a particular agent exercises power. Conversely, the column entries would show to which other agents a particular agent is subordinate in a power relation. In the block models, agents are clustered according to both their exercise of power and their subordination to power, and the 1 and 0 entries in the image matrices show the densities of the power relations among the clusters.

In model (i) of Figure 8.4, members of cluster 1 exercise power over one another and also over members of cluster 2. This is shown by the entries of '1' in the relevant blocks. Members of cluster 2, however, exercise no power whatsoever, being completely subordinate to the power of those in cluster 1. This structure is summarised in the corresponding arrow diagram. In model (ii), on the other hand, there are two separate and self-regulating categories (clusters 1 and 3), and members of these clusters jointly exercise power over the members of cluster 2. Finally, in model (iii), cluster 1 dominates both cluster 2 and cluster 3, but there is little mutual exercise of power

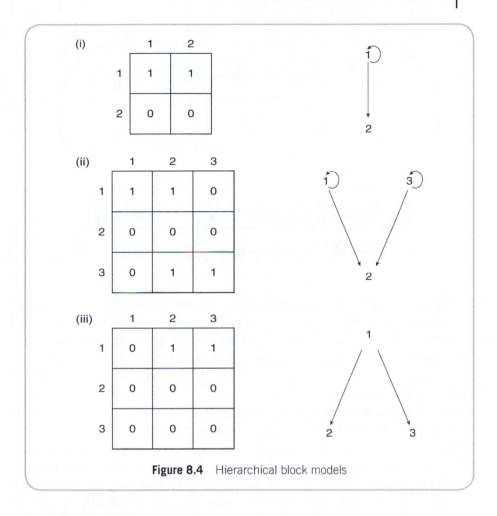

**Figure 8.4** Hierarchical block models

among the members of cluster 1 itself – the individual members of cluster 1 are each relatively autonomous agents.

Undirected matrices are, except in the simplest cases, rather more difficult to interpret, as the lack of any direction to the relations means that it is not possible to construct arrow diagrams to show their structures. Few such analyses have been published, and the application of block modelling to real and complex data sets of various kinds is essential if the value of the procedure is to be demonstrated.[10]

A fundamental problem with the CONCOR algorithm, as I have already suggested, is that it is not known exactly why it produces its solutions. The mathematical reasons for the convergence to a distribution of 1 and 0 entries are uncertain, and so an assessment of the validity of the results is difficult to make. This might seem to be a fairly damning criticism, but the fact that it does work and that it does seem to produce plausible models of small social networks helps to offset this criticism somewhat. There is, however, another difficulty, which suggests a further limitation on its applicability:

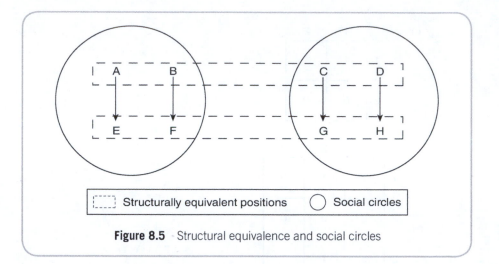

**Figure 8.5** · Structural equivalence and social circles

CONCOR can identify structurally equivalent positions only within the components and subgroups of a graph. If, for example, power relations are divided into distinct components within the network, CONCOR will not group together those dominant in the separate components as a single cluster of 'dominant' agents. Their equivalence as occupants of a position of dominance is masked, so far as CONCOR is concerned, by their sociometric division into separate components. Similarly, when a component is internally divided into relatively distinct cliques and circles, CONCOR will tend to identify only the dominant members within each of the subgroups.

This can be illustrated through Figure 8.5, which shows a network in which A, B, C and D are structurally equivalent as dominant agents, and E, F, G and H are structurally equivalent as subordinate agents. An adequate clustering of the network into structurally equivalent positions should identify two clusters {ABCD} and {EFGH}. If, however, the agents are divided into two distinct social circles, as shown, CONCOR will tend to identify four clusters instead: {AB}, {CD}, {EF} and {GH}. The conclusion that must be drawn is that the CONCOR algorithm combines structural equivalence with conventional sociometric measures of connection and so fails to produce a thoroughgoing analysis of structural equivalence.

## DIVISIONS AND EQUIVALENCE

These limitations of the CONCOR procedure led Ronald Burt to advocate a different approach to structural equivalence that aims to avoid CONCOR's reliance on uncertain mathematical procedures. His approach differs from that of CONCOR both in the measure of similarity used and in the method of clustering. Having examined CONCOR in some detail, it will be fairly easy to understand how Burt's procedure operates and in what respects it is an improvement on CONCOR.[11]

Burt's method uses a similarity measure based on path distances between pairs of points. Where CONCOR looked only at similarity in terms of direct contacts, Burt's method takes account also of indirect connections through paths of distance 2 or more in order to arrive at calculations of the minimum path distances between all pairs of points. The Burt measure of path distance also assumes that the strength of a relation declines with both the path distance and the significance of the path for the agent's overall pattern of contacts. This measure is based on the assumption that agents with large numbers of contacts are able to give less attention to their more distant ones.[12] Thus, the similarity measure used by Burt is a weighted distance measure.[13]

Structurally equivalent points, in the strong sense, are those separated by zero distance. They are perfectly similar and substitutable. Burt has recognised that this strong criterion cannot be applied to most real data, and so has argued for the identification of weak structural equivalence through the use of a cut-off threshold of distance below which points would be regarded as structurally equivalent (Burt, 1980: 101ff.). Burt's method performs a hierarchical clustering of the distance matrix, using Johnson's (1967) aggregative single-linkage method, and the researcher can read off the clusters found, if any, at the chosen cut-off level of distance. While CONCOR's arbitrariness derives from an obscure mathematical procedure, Burt's arbitrariness has the virtue of being grounded in the informed judgement of the specialist researcher.

Once a clustering has been produced through Burt's procedure, a block model can be constructed. An image matrix that shows the density of connections among the clusters is a simplified mapping, a 'homomorphic reduction' of the concrete pattern of relations between agents – and Burt terms this a 'social topology'. If the densities in the image matrix are replaced by entries of 1 or 0, using the density of the whole network as a cut-off threshold, the resulting block model can be analysed in the same way as those resulting from a CONCOR analysis.

Burt argues that the departure from a strict measure of strong structural equivalence means that any analysis must be treated simply as a hypothetical model. Without some kind of statistical test of significance, he argues, researchers are free to choose whichever cut-off threshold produces results that correspond most closely to their preconceptions. A significance test helps to introduce a degree of impartiality and objectivity to the assessment of block models. Burt's recommended test involves an examination of each cluster in order to measure how closely associated each of its members is with the other occupants of the cluster. The best solution, he argues, is that which optimises this measure of association.[14]

While CONCOR takes account only of path distances of length 1, Sailer (1978) proposed a procedure in which the researcher can choose a path length to use and the similarity of connections between pairs of points is calculated at that chosen level. Sailer's measure, which he terms simply 'substitutability', is then based on the neighbourhood of points. The degree of similarity between two points is measured in proportional rather than absolute terms, the number of contacts that they have in common at the specified path length being standardised by each point's adjacency. That is, the overlap between contacts is measured by the number of common connections expressed as a proportion of each point's total number of connections at that distance. Each point, therefore, can be given a standardised measure of its similarity to each of the other points. A complete overlap in contacts produces a standardised score of 1, while complete absence of overlap gives a score of 0.[15] As in the CONCOR procedure, Sailer sees this as simply a first step in an iterative process. The matrix of similarities is treated as an initial estimate of the 'substitutability' of points, and the continued repetition of the method on each new set of estimates results in a convergence to a solution in which all values are either '1' or '0'. In this way, then, a block model can be produced for analysis. Sailer's procedure, however, fails to overcome the principal limitation of the CONCOR method, which is that it cannot adequately handle networks that are divided into components or tight subgroups of the kind illustrated in Figure 8.5 (see also Carrington and Heil, 1981; Wu, 1984).

The CONCOR procedure is probably the most widely used method for identifying structural equivalence, but a number of alternatives have been suggested. These methods of structural equivalence and block modelling are readily available techniques in UCINET and can be computed with rather more difficulty in Pajek (see De Nooy et al., 2005: 39ff.). They have, however, rarely been applied to real data, and their long-term value has yet to be assessed.

# REGULAR EQUIVALENCE IN ROLES AND FUNCTIONS

CONCOR, as I have shown, faces difficulty in handling data that fall sociometrically into distinct components. An interesting attempt to overcome this sociometric limitation is REGE, an algorithm that is intended to detect 'regular' structural equivalence. This is defined as those equivalences that are regular across all the various subgraphs of a network (White and Reitz, 1983; Winship and Mandel, 1984; Reitz and White, 1989). The concept of regular equivalence is closer to the idea of the substitutability of agents by role or by function within a social system. Where CONCOR sees points as structurally equivalent when they have identical links to all the other points in a graph, REGE sees points as equivalent if they have similar links to points that are themselves structurally equivalent. Two points are regularly equivalent in relation to another set of points if the relation of one point to the points in that set is similar to the relation between the other point and the set. Each point has an identical relation with a counterpart in the same set, though this relation need not be with the same point or points. This can be illustrated by the obvious fact that all fathers are related to children, but they are not all related to the same children. White and Reitz argue, therefore, that the block models produced by REGE are homomorphic reductions, but not necessarily isomorphic reductions of their corresponding graphs.

The way in which REGE works can best be understood through a directed matrix, although it is very difficult to understand the details of the procedure. The algorithm uses a partitioning method that looks at direct connections and also at the contacts of points adjacent to each pair. It begins by making estimates of the equivalence values between all pairs of connected points. These estimates are all initially set at 1, and they are revised with each round of calculation, which involves computing revised estimates of equivalences from the smallest in- and outdegrees for each pair of points. At the end of each round, therefore, there is a new matrix of estimated equivalences between pairs of points. The procedure is, ideally, continued until the revised estimates of equivalence no longer alter; that is, the computations no longer result in any greater precision for the estimates. In practice, the researcher can choose to stop when it appears that further calculations will make little difference to the estimates. It has been suggested that the version of REGE implemented in UCINET produces optimum estimates after three rounds of calculation (see also Borgatti and Everett, 1989; Borgatti et al., 1989).

This approach can be used only on directed data, though Doreian (1987) suggested an adaptation that allows undirected data to be analysed. With a symmetric matrix, as Doreian shows, the initial estimates are not altered by the calculation: the algorithm simply identifies all connected points as regularly equivalent. Such matrices can be analysed only if they are divided into two asymmetric matrices, which can then be jointly analysed by REGE. Doreian suggested using centrality scores to make this division, though Everett and Borgatti (1990) suggested that any graph-theoretical attribute could be used. If centrality is used, for example, one matrix would consist of the relations directed from more to less central points, while the other matrix contains the relations directed from less to more central points.

Despite its limitations, REGE is the first structural equivalence procedure to offer a true approximation to the kind of structural equivalence described by Lorrain and White (1971). The substantive assumptions that it makes about the data are, however, obscured by complex mathematics, and it is difficult for a non-mathematician to assess whether these assumptions are valid and realistic. As with CONCOR, the fact that it does appear to work as expected on small-scale data is a powerful argument in its favour, but researchers must be aware that they are taking a certain amount on trust.

The aspiration of writers such as Nadel, it will be recalled, was to build a framework of sociological analysis in which positional analysis would complement more traditional sociometric concerns with cliques and components. The approaches to structural equivalence that have culminated in REGE have eschewed graph theory and so remain at one remove from these sociometric concerns. The approach of 'graph role analysis', on the other hand, tries to use the structural position of points as measured in graph theory as a basis for a measure of structural similarity (Zegers and ten Berghe, 1985). The procedure uses local dependency or geodesic matrices to calculate correlations between pairs of actors.[16] Structural equivalence is assessed in terms of how similar these measures are for the various points. A pair of points with, for example, similarly high betweenness scores might be recognised as being structurally equivalent in certain important respects. In order to avoid the obvious problem of regarding points as structurally equivalent only if they lie between the same points, the algorithm can compute whether they lie between points that are themselves similar in their betweenness scores. The particularly interesting feature of this procedure is that it begins to build a bridge between the relatively well-understood concepts of graph theory and the rather less well-understood measures of structural equivalence. Instead of conflating the approaches, as in CONCOR, it aims to theorise and to articulate their interdependence.[17]

These approaches to block modelling have all been inductive in character, aiming to derive a model from observed data. Doreian et al. (1994, 2005) have produced a highly generalised approach to block modelling that follows a distinctive strategy, hypothesising a particular block model and then testing its adequacy of fit to the observed data. This approach offers the possibility of a more theoretically informed research process and a move from descriptive models to more thoroughly explanatory ones. Their approach is implemented in Pajek.

## CORPORATE INTERLOCKS AND PARTICIPATIONS

It is in the analysis of corporate connections that the most interesting applications of block modelling have been produced. Burt has pursued a long-standing interest in the question of interlocking directorships in the business world, but has eschewed conventional clique-based approaches to their investigation. His earliest paper on this question (Burt, 1979) set out an aspiration to discover the linkages between profitability and the structural location of enterprises in the corporate system, and his development of the idea of structural equivalence was specifically geared towards this issue of structural location.

His starting point was the hypothesis that many interlocks can be understood as 'co-optive mechanisms' through which enterprises absorb into their own leadership those people from other enterprises who might threaten their continued operations. Thus, the suppliers who create market 'uncertainty' are objects of 'co-optive interlocks' by those to whom they supply goods or capital. Financial institutions, for this reason, are of particular importance in corporate interlocking: 'the use of money as a general resource makes the actions of financial corporations a source of significant uncertainty, so that firms would be expected to establish co-optive interlocks that allow them to secure access to money when it is needed' (Burt, 1979: 416).

Drawing on his earlier discussions of 'positional' concepts (Burt, 1976, 1977a, 1977b), Burt saw the firms that operate in each sector of the economy as structurally equivalent to one another: the economic sectors comprise positions in a social topology. Using input–output data at the sectoral level for the USA in 1967, Burt showed which of the inter-sector exchanges involved a degree of uncertainty that made co-optive interlocking a rational strategy. That is to say, he was interested in seeing whether the structure of constraining economic transactions was reflected in a parallel structure of interlocks. The idea of 'constraint' between sectors was operationalised in terms of competitive pressures: enterprises are more constrained by their transactions with oligopolistic sectors than they are by those with competitive sectors. Market constraint reduces the structural autonomy of enterprises, and interlocking reduces the effects of this constraint and so transforms the economic environment in which enterprises operate. Burt holds that 'structure in the two networks is a symbiotic phenomena [sic]: market structure patterning interlock structure and interlock structure repatterning market structure' (Burt, 1979: 433; see also Burt et al., 1980; Burt, 1982: Chs 4 and 8).

Burt's data comprised two parallel directed adjacency matrices, in which the rows and columns corresponded to economic sectors. One matrix contained information on the economic transactions between sectors, while the other showed their patterns of interlocking. The results of a block modelling of these data have not been directly reported, but Burt concluded that the two networks did mirror one another and that it was possible to identify a 'directorate tie market': a structure of interlocks that provides a 'non-market' context for regulating commercial transactions (Burt, 1983b, 1983c).[18]

Both the power and the limitations of the CONCOR procedure are apparent in an investigation of corporate shareholding which I undertook (Scott, 1986). The 250 largest British companies in 1976 were selected for study, and their largest shareholders were identified from their share registers. This allowed the construction of a $250 \times 250$ incidence matrix of cross-shareholdings among the companies. In this matrix, the rows showed the companies as shareholders and the columns showed them as the targets of shareholding relations: shareholdings were directed from rows to columns. It was found that only 69 of the companies held controlling blocks of shares in other large companies, and that only 140 of them were targets of shareholdings by these 69. Thus, the effective data set was a $69 \times 140$ matrix. Centrality analysis showed that Prudential Assurance was the most central shareholding participant, having shareholdings in 88 of the 140 target enterprises. Similarly, Boots was found to be the most 'blue chip' of the targets: 18 of its 20 largest shareholders were among the 69 leading companies.

The main purpose of the analysis was to uncover some of the global features of the intercorporate network, using the CONCOR algorithm. The controlling companies were regarded as the major agents in the economy, and the research aimed to uncover whether they formed a unified group or were divided into rival and solidaristic coalitions. Analysis of components gave little indication that the enterprises were organised into coalitions, and the initial conclusion was drawn that the network was not fragmented into distinct corporate groupings. Use of CONCOR, however, disclosed the existence of a number of structural positions in the network, and it was possible to identify hierarchical relations among these positions. A joint row and column analysis suggested the existence of five sets of enterprises, shown in the arrow diagram of Figure 8.6.[19]

The arrows in Figure 8.6 indicate the direction of the shareholding links between the various sets that comprise the positions in the network. Sets 1, 2 and 4 together comprise the 'hegemonic controllers' of the economy, with set 1 being the dominant

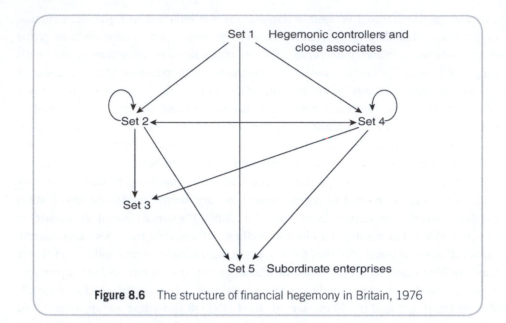

**Figure 8.6** The structure of financial hegemony in Britain, 1976

element in this grouping. Set 1 contains 20 enterprises, including large public sector corporations and merchant banks, and its members were the major shareholding participants in three of the other sets. It owes its position at the top of the corporate hierarchy to the fact that its members were controlled by wealthy families and by the state rather than by other companies. Set 2 contains 11 enterprises involved in one another's capital (indicated by the self-referencing arrow) and that were important participants in controlling sets 3, 4 and 5. Set 4 is rather similar to set 2 (comprising clearing banks, insurance companies and large private sector industrials), but it is distinguished by the fact that its members were less likely to be involved in joint control of the companies and consortiums that made up set 3. Set 5, containing 91 enterprises, comprises subordinate enterprises with virtually no role in the control of other enterprises.

As the British network was not internally fragmented, CONCOR was very effective in disclosing the structurally equivalent positions occupied by corporate enterprises. Using similar data for Japan, however, it was found to be less useful. The Japanese economy was strongly divided into discrete components, each of which operated as cohesive business groupings. These are the familiar *kigyoshudan* of the Japanese business system (Scott, 1991, 1997). Although there are structurally equivalent categories of dominant and subordinate enterprises, CONCOR divided these along the lines of the business groups (Scott, 1986: 186ff.). No single set of structurally equivalent hegemonic controllers was identified by CONCOR. Seven sets were identified in the network, three of them corresponding to the well-known Sumitomo, Mitsui and Mitsubishi business groups, and within each set could be seen a hierarchical division into hegemonic and subordinate enterprises. Thus, the Japanese economy looked very much like Figure 8.5, with the structurally equivalent positions being cross-cut by social circles representing the major business groupings.

---
## EXERCISE
---

Load one of the example data sets into your preferred software program. Derive an incidence matrix, if necessary, and use the CONCOR procedure to produce a block model of the network.

- How many distinct blocks are there in the network?
- How would you interpret the relations among these blocks?
- Are there any sociometric features of the network that limit the conclusions that can be drawn from your analysis of structural equivalence?
- Use the same data set to produce a block model of regular equivalence. How different are the results from that produced by CONCOR?

---
## FURTHER READING
---

Light, J.M. and Mullins, N.C. (1979) 'A Primer on Blockmodelling Procedures', in P. Holland and S. Leinhardt (eds) *Perspectives on Social Networks*. New York: Academic Press.

An overview of block modelling procedures that sets the scene for later work.

Burt, R.S. (1982) *Towards a Structural Theory of Action*. New York: Academic Press.

A key source on structural approaches in network analysis that is well worth reading.

Burt, R.S. (1983) *Corporate Profits and Cooptation*. New York: Academic Press.

An application of Burt's ideas in an empirical study.

# NINE

## Social Change and Development

This chapter outlines recent work on:

- Statistical approaches to social change
- Testing of explanatory hypotheses
- 'Small-world' networks
- Exponential random graph methods

The approaches to social network analysis that I have so far considered have been largely static. They have focused on describing the structural features of a network at a particular period, and for a long time this was all that many people believed social network analysis to be concerned with. However, it actually reflected limitations in the computational possibilities open to social network analysts. Changes in network structure over time could be considered only through using cross-sectional data, presenting successive static descriptions of network structure. This procedure did not provide a moving picture but a series of fixed snapshots. This did not allow researchers to track actual changes in any detail, nor did it provide any way of exploring how local-level decisions might produce large-scale structural changes. Recent advances have made it possible to move beyond this descriptive focus and to develop models of the internal dynamics of networks and of the ways in which these endogenous processes can produce long-term structural transformations. Models have now been developed that allow properly longitudinal studies to be undertaken.

These novel approaches have used statistical techniques rather than graph theory as their basis and see change as a 'stochastic' process. This allows a direct connection to wider uses of statistics in hypothesis testing and to ways of assessing the significance of modelled processes of change. Static descriptions of network structure have frequently been met by the critical comment of 'so what?'. These critics have suggested that analysts need to demonstrate that the structures described do actually have some constraining effect on the actions of individuals and organisations. Use of the new statistical methods now makes it possible to answer this question in convincing ways.

In this chapter I look at these processual models and their approach to longitudinal investigation and I relate this to recent work on the complexity and 'small-world' issues recently raised by scientists working in physics. I finally consider the new statistical approaches to significance testing.

## STRUCTURAL CHANGE AND UNINTENDED CONSEQUENCES

Uses of social network analysis in sociology and anthropology have most commonly originated as attempts to model kinship and community structures and so have tended to emulate the rather static approach that has typically been employed in these fields. The structural-functional theories that informed many of these arguments were, nevertheless, grounded in a theory of action that is able to show how structures emerge and are transformed as the unintended consequences of purposive action. However, these arguments were not translated directly into network analyses because the kinds of graph-theoretical methods then available did not encourage this. Theories of action do now, however, provide a way of integrating established methods of social network analysis with newly emerging methods concerned with network dynamics.

The sociological model of the unintended consequences of action originated in the classical political economy of Adam Smith (1766) and the tradition of economic theory that this inspired. Further developed in the marginalist economics of Menger (1871) and Marshall (1890), this was worked up into a systematic theory of action by von Mises (1949) and von Hayek (1967). It had its greatest influence within sociology in the general form in which it was cast by Merton (1936).

The theory sees human action as purposive, but as carried out under conditions that set both opportunities for and restrictions on the achievement of these purposes. Agents choose goals for themselves and follow norms or rules of action that they feel to be appropriate for them. They assess the conditions that they face and modify their actions according to the perceived opportunities open to them with the intention of facilitating the attainment of their goals. When building social relations, the pattern of their immediate social relations – their egonet – may therefore reflect their intentions and the imperfect state of their knowledge of the conditions under which they act. The larger structures in which they are enmeshed, however, are concatenations of egonets and are likely to have properties that are unintended by any of the participants. A social group has, therefore, a structure that may be largely unknown to any of its individual members. For any one individual, this structure is the pre-existing set of conditions under which they must act. Agents rarely have the capacity to foresee the full consequences of their actions and so they are unable to plan for all contingencies, especially where they act in large groups. The future conditions under which they must act are, therefore, not those they intended to face, and they may still have a very imperfect appreciation of these structural conditions. Actions are, therefore, inevitably undertaken with imperfect knowledge of the conditions that may facilitate or limit the achievement of their intentions. As all member actors are similarly placed within their social network, the outcome of the multiplicity of actions taking place in any period is unlikely to be that intended by any of the participants. Social structures, therefore, develop 'behind the backs' of the agents who produce them and may move in directions unintended by any of the participants yet being highly salient for their future actions. Structural change is therefore the unintended and unanticipated consequence of the intentional acts of a multiplicity of agents.

For classical economics and for structural functionalism this view became the basis of models of self-regulation in systems of action. Competitive markets, for example, were seen as ensuring a match between the supply and demand for goods and services and as ensuring, at a macro level, that employment and investment balance each other, perhaps generating a cyclical pattern of growth and recession. However, the outcomes of action may actually be far more complex than this stable and self-equilibrating stasis. Markets can generate high levels of unemployment or price inflation rather than a perfect balance of supply against demand. Similarly, there may be ongoing structural transformation – morphogenesis – rather than the maintenance of a given structure. Thus, competitive structures of small enterprises may, over time, develop into non-competitive oligopolies. The important point to note is that quite variable macro-level structures and processes may be generated, unintentionally, by the purposive actions of individual agents.

# SMALL-WORLD NETWORKS

The incorporation of these ideas about agency and structure into social network analysis has been made possible by the work of a number of physicists who have begun to make important methodological contributions to network analysis. These physicists began their analyses from a consideration of the 'small-world' issues that I briefly introduced in Chapter 2. The most important of these analysts is Watts (1999), who argued that social networks are typically clustered into zones of relatively high density and show a differentiation between close or strong ties and distant or weak ties. This is why, he argues, egonets are likely to give a misleading view of the overall properties of a social network. The key characteristic of the typical social network is that it has small-world properties. Watts showed that this relative closeness of individuals in social networks is a feature of the relatively high level of redundancy in their social relations: there are multiple paths of connection between any two individuals. Small-world networks, therefore, have numerous 'shortcuts' – relations that form 'wormholes' that reduce the space between two otherwise distant individuals. Very dense networks have few shortcuts, as all individuals tend to be connected to all others. It is the networks that are moderately dense that have these small-world properties. The small-world properties of networks – which underpin many of the measures used in social network analysis – occur only at a specific range in a continuum from completely ordered to completely random graphs. This range lies between certain thresholds that depend upon the average degree of the points in a graph and its total number of points, taking account only of points connected into a single component. Thus, it is components rather than whole networks that have small-world properties. There are upper and lower threshold limits at which a change in the nature of a network in or out of the small-world state occurs. The upper threshold is that at which a graph becomes globally sparse but remains locally dense. The lower threshold is that at which each is connected to a number of other points, but none of the points in its neighbourhood are connected to each other. Beyond these threshold levels, graphs are either too heavily connected (virtually all the points are directly connected to all others) or too randomly and sparsely connected.

Networks with small-world properties are those in which a large number of shortcuts exist. These shortcuts are lines connecting points that would otherwise be widely separated. Such graphs have moderate densities relative to their size. In a small-world network, the distribution of the degrees of the points forms a 'power-law' or 'scale-free' distribution, often referred to as a Pareto distribution. This is a highly skewed distribution in which a few points have a relatively high degree while most points have a very low or zero degree. Though presented as a novel discovery by Barabási (2002), this had been a commonplace empirical discovery from numerous empirical studies by sociologists. The real significance of the arguments of physicists such as Barabási and Watts, however, was to recognise this as a necessary and defining feature of small-world networks.

Watts has used the analysis of small-world properties to highlight dynamic features of networks. In particular, he looks at whether the relatively small changes in connectivity that take a network across one of the threshold levels can result in large changes in network structure. Such 'jump processes' in a network may involve more or less radical changes in network structure. Watts concludes that the rate of diffusion of ideas across a whole network, the possibility of communication among agents, or the prospects of coalition formation may all be significantly affected by relatively small local-level changes that have these macro-level effects.

Typically, change may be gradual, with significant change resulting only from the accumulation of a large number of small changes. At other times, however, there may be a sudden change from one state to a radically different one. The latter changes are non-linear alterations that have been described as 'catastrophe points' (Thom, 1972) or areas of 'phase transition'. These small changes – often referred to as 'random rewirings' – are purely local-level changes that are not made with respect to their effects on the overall structure of the network. These are not, of course, 'random' in the sense of occurring purely by chance, they are simply intentional acts undertaken without full knowledge of their actual consequences. In the case of social networks, then, they are purposive acts based on a definition of the situation and immediate interests but that have unanticipated, and so unintended, consequences that stretch beyond the agent's immediate situation.

# MODELLING SOCIAL CHANGE

The modelling of these action processes has been developed most recently in so-called actor-based computational models, and it is in this form that the argument has been taken up in social network analysis. Agent-based computational models see agents as following simple rules that specify how they are to act within their given immediate circumstances. These can be investigated in simulation models, using hypothesised rules of action, to generate predicted patterns of network evolution. Comparing the outcome of the model with actually observed patterns is the basis for testing the adequacy of the hypothesised rules. If the predictions of the model are seriously discrepant with the observations, then the hypothesis is falsified. If the rules in the model can be altered to produce a pattern that better corresponds with an observed structure, then the simulation can be held to have become more successful.

Tom Snijders (1996; Snijders and van Duijn, 1997; Snijders et al., 2010) has been the leading figure using actor-based models for longitudinal network analysis. In his basic model, agents are seen as choosing to make or break social relations according to specified rules and subject to an optimising strategy. Random factors can be included, making the model a stochastic one, and using the stochastic simulations leads Snijders to show that the assumptions of his model not merely are more realistic than other simulation models, but also allow the construction of a battery of statistical inference measures of goodness of fit and significance.

In Snijders's model, agents' choices to make or break relations generate a directed data set in which each agent is seen as controlling his or her own outgoing choices. Changes in outgoing relations are seen as oriented towards gaining an immediate or deferred advantage (or avoiding a disadvantage). Thus, each agent acts under the constraints of his or her immediate relational environment, and this environment is itself the shifting outcome of the choices made by all other agents. In the model, the successive states of the network are formed into a Markov chain that is seen as a sequence of 'holding times', in which some relations persist and others have altered, punctuated by the jump processes at which system states change. As jump processes involve agents acting under the constraints of the current holding state, the structure of the holding state at any one time determines the probability of any further development of the network at later states.

Snijders's longitudinal model of change has been implemented in his SIENA program.[1] This allows the analyst to hypothesise various sets of rules that are believed to be followed by agents and to simulate their consequences. It is important to note that this procedure does not require the adoption of pure rational choice assumptions. It is possible to specify any rules of action, including altruistic rules and other departures from narrow instrumentality. By comparing alternative outcomes with the actually observed state of the network, a best-fit solution can be identified. This procedure helps the analyst to conclude that the specified rules may be a reasonable approximation to those actually followed by agents in the real situations studied.

## TESTING EXPLANATIONS

The move from static network analysis to dynamic, longitudinal approaches allows a corresponding move to be made from purely descriptive to explanatory concerns. Network analysts can hypothesise a pattern of network change and, if this corresponds to an observed pattern of change, then the assumptions of the underlying model can be taken to provide a best-fit explanation for the observed pattern.

However, a mere correspondence between observed and hypothesised patterns is not sufficient to draw such firm conclusions. If the model is to be claimed as an explanation, then it must be shown that the correspondence could not have occurred simply by chance. It must be shown that the correspondence is a highly probable consequence of the particular model employed and is unlikely to have occurred for any other reason.

This is a general problem in scientific hypothesis testing, where it must be shown that a model generates statistically significant results. This is typically achieved through the use of tests of statistical significance, but conventional significance tests assume attribute data that are normally distributed. As I have shown, this is not usually the case for relational data, which more typically follow a scale-free distribution: a small proportion of the points accounts for a large proportion of the connections. For this reason, novel techniques for significance testing have had to be developed.

In statistical terms, significance tests measure the variance that can be explained by a model. One approach to this issue is the QAP or 'quadratic assignment procedure' in which a correlation coefficient is calculated for two networks and the result is compared with the correlation coefficient calculated for one of the networks and a randomly rearranged version of the other network. Continued repetition with different permutations of the original networks makes it possible to calculate the proportion of times that the results from the randomised network differ from the actually observed network. This proportion is treated as a significance measure and if it is lower than, say, 0.05, then the result can be regarded as statistically significant. This measure can be computed in UCINET through the TOOLS > TESTING HYPOTHESES menu option.

An alternative method, based on the coefficient of determination ($R^2$) in a linear regression analysis, has been developed by Wasserman, Snijders, Pattison and colleagues (Wasserman and Pattison, 1996; Wasserman and Robins, 2005; Snijders et al., 2006; Robins et al., 2007). This approach involves the use of exponential random graph models and has been termed the ERGM or $p*$ approach. The method developed has been extended from undirected to directed and valued relational data and so provides a powerful suite of measures for use in all areas of social network analysis. Calculation of the significance of the results from a longitudinal analysis is possible from within the SIENA program, and this makes it possible to assess statistical significance as a normal part of any such analysis.

The method operates by examining various local features of a network, such as densities, reciprocities, and egocentric stars. The latter are particularly important degree-based measures and include 2-stars, 3-stars, and 4-stars. The $p*$ coefficient is a measure of the probability for a single observation in a stochastic directed graph, and the model computes the distribution of such probabilities for a number of measures. The observed distribution of these features is compared with those produced from a large number of random simulations from the same data so as to see how likely it is that the observed pattern could have been produced by chance alone. The lower this probability, the greater confidence there can be that the hypothesised explanation is positing a mechanism that actually is responsible for the observed data.

The use of longitudinal data and the ERGM approach can best be illustrated from a small-scale study undertaken by Snijders himself (Snijders, 2001). A total of 32 freshers at a Dutch university were studied at three-week intervals, giving three sets of cross-sectional data. At each data collection point, the students were asked about those others with whom they had formed friendships. The density of the network increased steadily over the period from 0.15 to 0.18 and then 0.22. This reflected 60 changes in relations between the first and second time periods and 51 changes between the second and third time periods. The ERGM analysis calculated parameters and standard errors for a number of measures, including some that related to gender differences. Calculation of $t$-statistics showed which measures were significant at the 5 per cent level. Non-significant effects could be included and other measures introduced to refine the model.

Snijders's conclusion from his analysis was that women are more active than men in forming positive friendship relations, though men are the recipients of more positive choices. Further analysis showed that those who make more out-directed friendship choices are more likely to change their relationships over time and that relations with those of the opposite sex are terminated more quickly than relations with those of the same sex. Friendly relations with those of the opposite sex are less stable than those with the same sex and there is no evidence to suggest that friendship relations are less likely to be initiated with those of the opposite sex than with those of the same sex. In an extension of this analysis, smoking was shown to have a significant effect on friendship choices.

In another small study, Snijders used data from an early investigation by Freeman into the friendship choices of social scientists engaged in electronic communication (Freeman and Freeman, 1980). Studying two time periods, eight months apart, Snijders showed that a preference for friends of the same discipline was far stronger for mathematicians and statisticians than it was for sociologists, anthropologists and psychologists. In all disciplines, however, there was a strong tendency to make friendship choices with those who were already popular members of the network.

ERGM approaches are in their infancy and much remains to be done. The particular results in these brief examples may not be especially surprising, but the important thing to note is that the conclusions are statistically significant and so can be asserted with confidence. This is a striking advance on the purely descriptive approaches adopted so far, where the stated conclusions have always been somewhat tentative and have prompted critics to ask whether the reported patterns mean anything or are simply more or less pretty patterns produced by random processes. The move to dynamic models, longitudinal analysis and significance testing is, perhaps, the most important advance in social network analysis since the Harvard innovations of the 1960s and 1970s.

## EXERCISE

The topics discussed in this chapter may be too complex for any quick revision exercise. You may, however, find it useful to explore the small-world issue. This has been popularised in the 'six degrees of Kevin Bacon' game. This is a game in which participants have to discover the shortest path between a randomly chosen actor and Kevin Bacon through links in a path consisting of films. Thus, A was in film X with B; B was in film Y with C; and C was in film Z with Kevin Bacon. This is a path of length 3 from actor A to Kevin Bacon. The point of the game is that any actor can be connected with Kevin Bacon with a maximum path length of six films. There is nothing special about Kevin Bacon in this respect: the game can be played with any actor because the movie industry is a small world.

- Go to www.oracleofbacon.org and explore connections between actors chosen at random.

------------------------ FURTHER READING ------------------------

Snijders, T.A.B. (2005) 'Models for Longitudinal Network Data' in P.J. Carrington, J. Scott and S. Wasserman (eds) *Models and Methods in Social Network Analysis*. Cambridge: Cambridge University Press.

Wasserman, S. and Robins, G. (2005) 'An Introduction to Random Graphs, Dependence Graphs, and $p^*$', in P.J. Carrington, J. Scott and S. Wasserman (eds) *Models and Methods in Social Network Analysis*. New York: Cambridge University Press.

These two sources cover a range of key issues in this new and demanding area of analysis.

# TEN
## Visualising and Modelling

This chapter explores:

- Methods for constructing and presenting pictorial representations of social networks
- Circle diagrams
- Multi-dimensional scaling and principal component analysis procedures
- Programs for visual model building and computer displays
- Novel techniques to show moving images of network change
- Studies of communities, elites, and business power

One of the earliest aspirations of those involved in social network analysis was to produce pictorial representations of the networks they studied. The drawing of sociograms has remained a crucial means for the development and illustration of social network concepts, and network diagrams have been used extensively throughout this book for just that purpose. The concept of centrality, for example, is readily conveyed by a sociogram in which a central point is made the 'hub' of a series of radiating 'spokes' that connect it to the more peripheral points. However, the conventional sociogram has a number of limitations as a method for representing and displaying relational data. Principal among these limitations is that its use is restricted by the difficulties involved in drawing large graphs on a sheet of paper. When a network contains more than 10 or 20 points the number of cross-cutting connections produces an uninterpretable thicket of lines, even in networks with a relatively low density. At the same time, the arrangement of the points on the page is purely arbitrary, designed – if at all possible – to clarify the pattern of lines rather than to consider the location of points relative to one another. The difficulty of constructing satisfactory sociograms for large networks was one of the inspirations behind the abandonment of visual models in favour of mathematical measures.

## TAKING SPACE SERIOUSLY

The continuing attraction of visual methods led some social network analysts to experiment with simple and summary depictions of networks. Various ad hoc extensions to the idea of the sociogram have been used in attempts to overcome the limitations discussed. Researchers have tried to complement their formal mathematical measures with artistic techniques that convey a more qualitative feel for the shape of the social structures studied. A common technique has been to construct the sociogram around the circumference of a circle, so that the pattern of lines becomes clearer (Grieco, 1987: 30). Figure 10.1 shows one example of this method from a study of Scottish company interlocks (Scott and Hughes, 1980). In this technique, a circle is used simply as an arbitrary visual framework for organising data, and the order in which the points are arranged around the circle is determined only by the attempt to ensure a minimum of overlap among the lines that connect them. The researcher must engage in a trial-and-error process of drafting and redrafting until an aesthetically satisfactory solution is achieved.[1]

These circle diagrams can make the structure of a set of relations clearer, but they involve a rather arbitrary arrangement and embody no specific mathematical properties. The points are arranged in arbitrary positions, and the drawn lengths of the various lines reflect this arbitrary arrangement. In an experimental study, McGrath et al. (1997) showed how sensitive data interpretation is to the particular visual configuration presented. When presented with different spatial arrangements, people could be

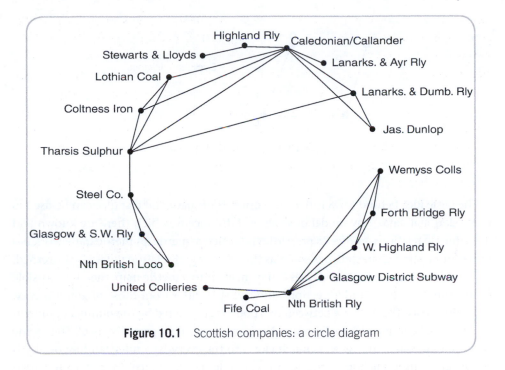

**Figure 10.1** Scottish companies: a circle diagram

led to identify differing numbers of subgroups in the network. This suggests that great care must be taken in choosing both the spatial framework and the criteria by which points are to be located within it.

McGrath et al. concluded that if a researcher wishes to infer something about the actual sociometric properties of a network then the physical distance between points should correspond as closely as possible to the graph-theoretical distances among them. This conclusion reinforces the long-standing desire of social network analysts to move away from metaphorical and illustrative diagrams and to produce more rigorous maps of social structure that, like geographical maps, retain the mathematical properties of the graph and allow new features to be discovered. Such maps would have the further advantage of making the data comprehensible and more meaningful to those who read the research reports.

A mathematical approach termed 'multi-dimensional scaling' (MDS) embodies all the advantages of the conventional sociogram and its artistic extensions, but results in something much closer to a 'map' of the space in which the network is embedded. This is a very important advance, and one that returns to some of the central insights of field theory. Just as a two-dimensional map of the British Isles, for example, may allow its users to make new discoveries about the geography of the country, so long as they are familiar with the principles of map reading, so a sociogram produced through MDS may allow the discovery of new structural knowledge about the network under investigation.

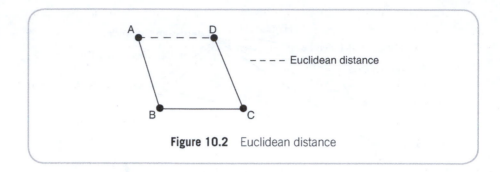

**Figure 10.2** Euclidean distance

The basic idea behind MDS is that the concepts of space and distance can be used to map relational data.[2] Any model of space and distance in which there are known and determinate relations among its properties is termed a 'metric'. A metric framework has rather interesting characteristics so far as the mapping of relational data is concerned. If a configuration of points and lines can be made into a metric map, then it is possible to measure 'distances' and 'directions' in ways that differ from those of graph theory. In graph theory, the distance between two points is measured by the number of lines in the path that connects them. Distance, then, is measured as 'path distance'. The metric concept of distance, however, is much closer to the everyday understanding of physical distance. In a 'Euclidean' metric, for example, the 'distance' from A to B, which is exactly the same as the distance from B to A, is measured by the most direct route that can be taken between them.[3] It is a distance that follows a route 'as the crow flies', which may be across 'open space' and need not – indeed, normally will not – follow a graph-theoretical path. In Figure 10.2, for example, the path distance between A and D is 3 lines, while the Euclidean metric distance is 18 millimetres.

## USING MULTI-DIMENSIONAL SCALING

MDS, at its simplest, is an attempt to convert graph measures such as path distance into metric measures analogous to physical distance.[4] Although the term 'Euclidean' may be unfamiliar and, indeed, rather daunting, it simply describes the most familiar, everyday concepts of distance and space that correspond to the ideas set out in Euclid's geometry. MDS is, therefore, a particularly convenient model to use in social network analysis. A Euclidean map of social relations can be readily understood by analogy with atlases, maps, and other familiar spatial models of everyday life.

MDS takes graph-theoretical measures of the 'closeness' of points and expresses these relations of closeness and distance in metric terms. This involves, more formally, the use of 'proximity data' to construct a metric configuration of points. The first step in such an analysis is to produce a case-by-case proximity matrix from graph-theoretical measures. In this matrix, the values in each cell show how 'similar' or 'different' a pair of points are from one another. Proximity measures for relational data would include such things as the number or frequency of contacts between individuals, the size of shareholding relations between enterprises, the number of members in common between organisations, and so on. The metric properties of many of these values will be obscure, and it may not be known whether a particular measure conforms to the assumptions of a Euclidean metric. For this reason, they are often converted into correlation coefficients, which are known to conform to a Euclidean metric. Two points with identical patterns of connection in a graph, for example, will be perfectly correlated, and so the proximity measure for this pair will be 1. This measure is termed a similarity measure because high values on the proximity measure indicate 'closeness' and the proximity matrix is said to contain data on 'similarities'. The other principal type of proximity measure is 'dissimilarity', in which low values indicate closeness. It is vitally important for researchers to be clear about whether they are using 'similarities' or 'dissimilarities', as the operation of particular MDS procedures may differ in each case.[5] Whichever type of data is used, the aim is to produce a metric configuration in which the pattern of metric distances corresponds to the pattern of proximities.

The use of MDS can most easily be illustrated by considering the mapping of a network of towns onto the two-dimensional page of an atlas. A matrix of road mileages between towns contains proximity (dissimilarity) measures of mileage that can easily be converted into centimetre distances between points on the page of an atlas. This 'scaling' gives a two-dimensional configuration in which distances are located along the conventional East–West and North–South dimensions. Such a map might not, however, correspond perfectly with the actual arrangement of towns in the country as roads meander around physical obstacles and boundaries and so rarely follow the shortest and straightest routes between towns. For this reason, the road mileages will not be true Euclidean distances. Similarly, the map would take no account of the third dimension of height: the actual roads go up hill and down dale rather than running across perfectly flat plains. The atlas map, nevertheless, gives a reasonable and useful approximation, and its 'lack of fit' with any better solution can be assessed.

The case of a simple physical map, then, gives a good insight into the multi-dimensional scaling of relational data. The ways in which MDS works on relational data can also be understood by examining the geometrical principles used in map construction. These geometrical principles can be seen in the very simple case of drawing a map to show the correct spatial arrangement and locations of three towns from a knowledge only of the distances between them. This task corresponds, in fact, to a classic problem in old-fashioned school geometry, which was to draw a triangle when only the lengths of the three sides are known.

The solution to this geometrical problem is to see the corners of the triangle as the centres of circles whose radii correspond to the distances between the corners. Consider, for example, the case of a triangle with sides AB (length 3 cm), BC (length 4 cm) and AC (length 5 cm). The first step in constructing this triangle would be to draw any one of the lines, say AB. This line can be drawn at any position on the paper. Since it is known that AC measures 5 cm, it can be inferred that C must lie somewhere on the circumference of a circle centred on A and with a radius of 5 cm. It is also known that C must lie on the circumference of a circle centred on B and with a radius of 4 cm. The second step in constructing the triangle, therefore, is to draw these two circles and to identify the place at which they intersect. C can be positioned at the point of intersection, because it is only at this point that all three known distances will be correct.

Figure 10.3 shows that there are, in fact, two points of intersection and so there are two possible locations for point C. For the moment it is sufficient simply to choose one of the two intersection points to represent the location of C. It does not matter which of these points is chosen, as the triangle ABC' is simply a mirror reflection of the triangle ABC. Here, then, is the solution to the problem of mapping three towns. If A, B and C represent the towns, and the given lengths of the lines AB, BC and AC represent the scaled mileages between them, then the triangle ABC is a simple two-dimensional map of the locations of the towns.

But what would have happened if C' had been chosen instead of C as the location for the third town? Would ABC' have been equally acceptable as a map? The triangle ABC' is simply an 'upside-down' version of the original map, and so there is no need to choose between ABC and ABC' as maps of the three towns. The choice does not matter in the slightest when one configuration is simply a perfect reflection of the other. Which configuration is taken as being the most useful will depend only upon the convenience of the user of the map. A physical map and its mirror image contain exactly the same information.

The same geometrical procedure can be used for four or more points. If it is known that a point D lies 3 cm from B, 6 cm from A, and 5 cm from C, its position can be plotted by drawing three additional circles centred on A, B and C. Once the initial choice of location has been made for point C, the position of D is uniquely determined by a single point of intersection for all these circles (see Figure 10.3). As a general principle, then, there is a unique configuration for a two-dimensional map once the positions of its first three points have been fixed.[6]

This piece of school geometry can be seen as giving a two-dimensional solution for the location of a set of points in a metric space. From the distance matrix shown in Figure 10.3, the two-dimensional configuration can be constructed. The two dimensions are the conventional horizontal (left–right) and vertical (up–down) dimensions of a flat piece of paper. In producing a map for an atlas, the configuration of points would normally be moved to a position in which the most northerly point is towards the top of the page and the most westerly point is towards the left of the page. In this way, the vertical and horizontal dimensions represent the known North–South and East–West dimensions. In MDS, this movement of the configuration is termed a 'rotation'. Only in the case of conventional mapping, however, does rotation generally involve aligning the configuration to known dimensions. More typically with the results of MDS, rotation is aimed at the discovery of meaningful dimensions. I shall return to this question of rotation later in the chapter.

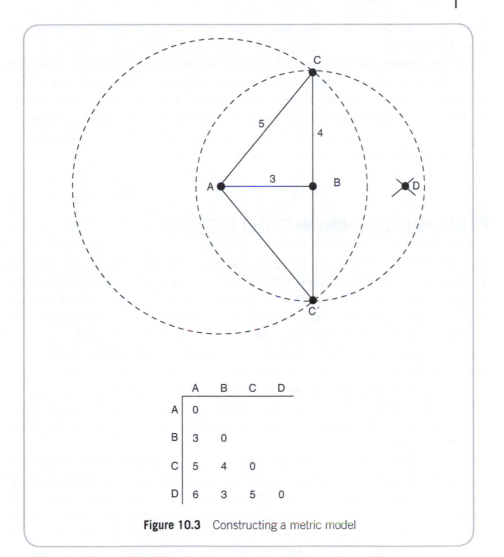

**Figure 10.3** Constructing a metric model

MDS operates, in effect, in a very similar way to the method described in this simple geometrical case. Although computer programs for MDS do not normally use such an inefficient method as the construction of circles, the end result is the same. The earliest forms of MDS were developed from Torgerson's (1952) pioneering work on psychometric scaling. In metric MDS, as I have shown, proximity data are used as if they correspond to Euclidean distances. If dissimilarity measures are used, as in the case of the road mileage example, principles similar to the geometrical ones that I have described could be used to produce a metric map of the data. The raw data are treated as distance measures and they are plotted, to scale, on the final map. Algorithms for MDS use geometrical principles to ensure a 'fit' between the given proximity data and the final configuration of points in the map. The various approaches to metric MDS differ mainly in the details of their methods for generalising the procedure to three or more dimensions.

The Pajek drawing program includes a facility for the rapid construction of an MDS configuration, using a technique known as spring embedding. The procedures used to produce the configuration are completely invisible to the user, who is able to specify the number of dimensions to use in mapping the data and can visualise and rotate the configuration on screen. Three-dimensional visualisations offer especially powerful ways of inspecting configurations from various points of view.[7]

# PRINCIPAL COMPONENTS AND FACTORS

An approach that conforms closely to this metric method of multi-dimensional scaling is principal components analysis (PCA). This is, in some texts, called 'factor analysis', though there are important differences between PCA and classical factor analysis. For present purposes, however, this distinction is not especially important, and the availability of PCA as part of the factor analysis routine in SPSS has made it a widely used method of data analysis (Daultrey, 1976; Goddard and Kirby, 1976; Kim and Mueller, 1978; Kline, 1994).[8] More recently, the technique of multiple correspondence analysis has been used, and this works on similar principles (Le Roux and Rouanet, 2010). Correspondence analysis has been widely used on attribute data, most notably by Bourdieu (1979), but it has also increasingly been used with relational data (Denord et al., 2011).

PCA developed from early attitude and intelligence scaling methods, where researchers sought some underlying factor common to a number of specific measures of attainment or attitude. 'General intelligence', for example, was seen as a 'factor' underlying performance on a number of specific tests of logical reasoning. By extension, there may be two or more distinct 'factors' underlying any given set of data. PCA developed as a way of analysing a case-by-variable attribute matrix to discover one or more factors or components common to the variables. It is an attempt to use raw data to discover a set of coordinates or axes (the factors or dimensions) that can be used to plot a scatter diagram of the data. When relational data in a case-by-affiliation matrix are used, the scatter map is such that the spatial distance and compass direction from one point to another convey some real information about their relative positions.

PCA can most easily be understood through its use on a case-by-variable matrix of attribute data. A simple PCA algorithm would first convert the case-by-variable matrix into a variable-by-variable matrix showing the correlations among the variables (the columns of the original matrix). Thus, the new matrix shows how well, or how badly, the variables are associated with one another. The next step is to search the matrix for those variables that are highly correlated with one another and to replace them with a constructed, artificial variable that measures their correlation with one another.

Thus, a set of variables that are all mutually correlated at or above a specified level would be replaced by the constructed variable. This constructed variable is termed the first principal component. The next step is to look for another set of variables that are correlated highly with one another, but that are not correlated with the first set. The constructed variable that replaces this set is the second principal component. By continuing in this way, principal components analysis can identify a set of uncorrelated principal components that, taken together, account for all the variation found in the data. Such a complete analysis continues until all possible components have been identified. Through this procedure, the original variable-by-variable correlation matrix is, in effect, converted into a variable-by-component correlation matrix.

The first principal component stands for the most highly correlated set of variables. The second principal component is, by definition, uncorrelated with the first: it is 'orthogonal' to it. This independence means that the two components can be drawn at right-angles to one another as the axes of a two-dimensional scatter diagram. The same general principle holds for larger numbers of components, each dimension being orthogonal to, or uncorrelated with, any of the others. It is, of course, more difficult to draw or to visualise three-dimensional scatter diagrams, and diagrams with more than three dimensions simply cannot be drawn. Nevertheless, the logic of the approach is the same, regardless of how many principal components are identified. It is normal in PCA to search for the smallest number of principal components able to explain a high proportion of the variance in the data. In practice, any stopping point that falls short of a complete account of the variance is arbitrary, and it is normal for a researcher to stop when any additional principal component adds little more to the variance than has already been explained.

The starting point for PCA, therefore, is a variable-by-variable correlation matrix, constructed from the original case-by-variable matrix. From this matrix a variable-by-component matrix is constructed in which the cell entries show the 'loadings' computed for each variable against each component. The principal components are used as axes for a scatter diagram and the loadings are used to plot the position of each variable within these axes. In an extension of multiple correspondence analysis, the scattered points are described as forming 'clouds' with an internal geometry or structure.

A complication arises from the possibility of 'rotation', which was touched on in the simple geometrical example discussed earlier. The purpose of rotating a configuration is to give a clearer picture of its structure. If the scatter of points seems to spread in a particular direction across the space, for example, it would make sense to rotate the configuration until the greatest spread in the points is aligned with the first component. In Figure 10.4, for example, diagram (ii) shows a rotation of the configuration to give a better alignment with the axes than in the unrotated diagram (i). More generally, rotation procedures aim to produce a positioning of the configuration that gives the best possible alignment with the main axes. The outcome of a rotation is a new variable-by-component matrix that contains a revised set of loadings for each variable.[9]

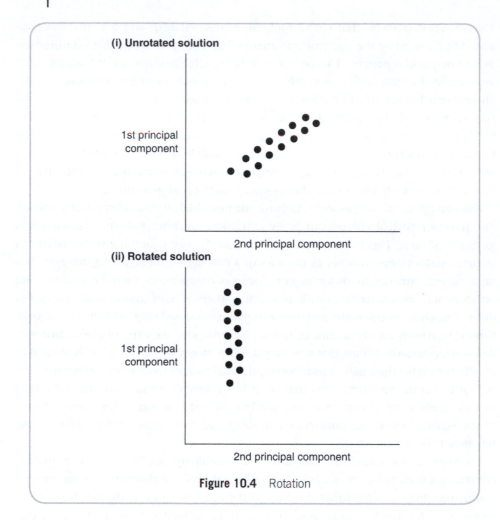

**(i) Unrotated solution**

1st principal
component

2nd principal component

**(ii) Rotated solution**

1st principal
component

2nd principal component

**Figure 10.4** Rotation

In a direct analysis of an incidence matrix of people and organisations, a PCA algorithm investigates the organisations in order to find those that are most similar in terms of their membership. As with CONCOR, the correlation coefficient is used as a measure of proximity. The sets of similar organisations discovered are replaced by principal components, and the various organisations can be plotted as points in a space defined by the axes that correspond to the components. The Euclidean distance between the points in this scatter diagram is a measure of the closeness of the organisations. A transposition of the original incidence matrix would allow an analysis of the cases to be made. As was seen with CONCOR and the other block modelling procedures discussed in the previous chapter, a 'column solution' and a 'row solution' produced from the same input data would be the 'dual' of each other. They are different but complementary representations of the same data.

It is possible to analyse an adjacency matrix using PCA, though with the symmetric data matrix for undirected relations the row and column solutions would be identical with one another. In the case of a directed adjacency matrix, however, the two solutions would differ; one of them would correspond to the network created by the 'sending' of relations and the other to the network involving the 'receiving' of relations.[10]

# NON-METRIC METHODS

There are a number of limitations to both metric MDS and PCA in investigations of relational data. Many relational data sets are binary in form, indicating simply the presence or absence of a relation, and this type of data cannot be directly used to measure proximity. As I have shown, binary data must first be converted into measures, such as correlation coefficients, which do have metric properties. But this data conversion procedure may lead researchers to make unwarranted assumptions about their relational data. Even when the raw input data are valued, metric assumptions may not be appropriate. In particular, the use of ratio or interval measurement may not be appropriate. Two companies with four directors in common, for example, may not be twice as close to one another as companies that have just two directors in common. While it may be realistic to consider the former as being 'closer' than the latter, it is difficult to be certain about how much closer they might be. Fortunately, some powerful MDS techniques have been developed that do not require the direct input of metric data, and these methods can be used in a much wider range of circumstances than their metric counterparts.[11]

These techniques of non-metric MDS, often called 'smallest-space analysis', have become more widely available in standard computer packages. The Pajek drawing techniques, for example, are based on non-metric MDS. Non-metric MDS procedures work on a symmetric adjacency matrix in which the cells show the similarities or dissimilarities among cases, using either correlation coefficients or actual valued data. The procedure does not convert these values directly into Euclidean distances, but takes account only of their rank order. That is to say, the data are treated as measures at the ordinal level. The non-metric procedures seek a solution in which the rank ordering of the distances is the same as the rank ordering of the original values.

This procedure can be illustrated with the data in Figure 10.5. The first step is to sort the cell values of the original matrix into descending order (from high to low). A new matrix is then constructed in which the original cell values are replaced by their ranks in the sorted distribution of values. In Figure 10.5, for example, the dissimilarity between A and B is the highest value in the original matrix and so is replaced by a value of 1 in the ordinal data matrix. The dissimilarity between A and C is the lowest of the six values, and so this is replaced by a value of 6 in the ordinal data matrix. It is then necessary to construct a matrix of Euclidean distances that have the same rank ordering as the original cell values.

These Euclidean distances can be used to draw a metric scatter plot similar to those produced by PCA. In this case, the rank order of the distances is the same as the rank order of the proximities, but no assumptions are made about the nature of the proximity data themselves. If the proximity measures did have metric properties, the procedure

**(i) Original matrix (dissimilarities)**

|   | A  | B  | C  | D |
|---|----|----|----|---|
| A | 0  |    |    |   |
| B | 60 | 0  |    |   |
| C | 10 | 40 | 0  |   |
| D | 30 | 50 | 20 | 0 |

**(ii) Matrix with ordinal data**

|   | A | B | C | D |
|---|---|---|---|---|
| A | – |   |   |   |
| B | 1 | – |   |   |
| C | 6 | 3 | – |   |
| D | 4 | 2 | 5 | – |

**(iii) Loadings: two-dimensional solution**

|   | Dim. 1 | Dim. 2 |
|---|--------|--------|
| A | 0.575  | 0.404  |
| C | −0.993 | 0.114  |
| B | 0.195  | 0.177  |
| D | 0.222  | −0.695 |

**Figure 10.5**   Data for non-metric multi-dimensional scaling

would, of course, produce a final matrix in which the values exactly matched those of the original matrix, allowing only for the scaling down of all values by the same amount. This is not the case in Figure 10.5, as the original data are not metric. While a variant of the simple geometrical method cannot be applied to the original data, it can be used on the values in the final matrix. The final matrix shows the 'best fit' metric distances for the non-metric data, and Figure 10.5(iii) shows the loadings of the four points against the two dimensions of a two-dimensional solution.

How, then, can the matrix of Euclidean distances be calculated? The usual algorithm begins by computing a 'guess' of what these distances might be. This guess forms the initial or trial configuration, and the rank order of its distances is compared with that of the proximities. Successive trial-and-error refinements of the initial estimates lead to progressively better trial configurations. A configuration is accepted as an improvement over its predecessor if there is a better match between the distance and the proximity rank orderings. Eventually, one of the trial configurations will be found to have the best achievable fit with the original data.

In order to begin, therefore, a suitable trial configuration must be produced. The initial configuration itself can be randomly generated or, if something of the structure of the network is already known, estimated distances can be supplied by the researcher. The choice of method is immaterial, as the initial configuration is simply a starting point for the analysis and its accuracy, or inaccuracy, has no bearing upon the rest of the analysis. The only disadvantage in using a randomly chosen starting point is that the analysis may take slightly longer to complete, as a larger number of steps may be necessary before the final configuration is discovered. In fact, the widely used MINISSA algorithm normally produces an initial configuration from a principal components analysis.[12]

How is it known when a satisfactory final configuration has been produced? The rank ordering of the distances in the initial configuration must be compared with that for the original proximity data in order to see the disparity in ranking for each pair of points. This comparison shows in which direction, and by how much, the various points must be moved relative to one another in order to reduce the disparities. Where there is a large positive disparity in rank, for example, the points must be moved closer together than in the trial configuration. This comparison of disparities takes place with each successive configuration. The results of each step can be plotted on a diagram such as Figure 10.6(i).

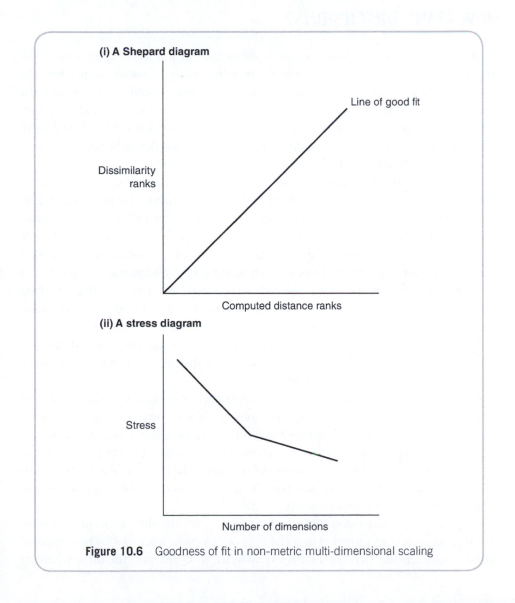

**Figure 10.6** Goodness of fit in non-metric multi-dimensional scaling

In this diagram, termed a Shepard diagram after its inventor, the rank order of distances in a trial configuration is plotted against the rank order of dissimilarities in the original data. If the points are scattered widely about the diagram, there is a bad fit; but if they are clustered close to the 45° line, then the fit is better. A perfect fit is achieved when the points follow exactly the 45° line.[13] Gradually, by constant adjustment to reduce the disparities, a configuration is produced in which no changes can be made that do not worsen the fit. When this point has been reached, perhaps after quite a large number of steps, the best possible fit with the original data has been achieved.

## HOW MANY DIMENSIONS?

I have so far written as if the number of dimensions is unproblematic. Indeed, the simple illustration in Figure 10.5 assumed a two-dimensional solution. In practice, the researcher must decide on the number of dimensions that should be used to plot the data. A Shepard diagram can be drawn for each dimensional solution, and a 'best-fit' configuration can be discovered. There will, for example, be a best fit in two dimensions and another best fit in three dimensions. The Shepard diagrams give no indication of which solution is to be preferred.

A non-metric MDS procedure does not, itself, determine the appropriate number of dimensions. The researcher must undertake a number of analyses for varying numbers of dimensions and then try to discover which of various dimensional solutions gives the best overall fit with the original data. This can be achieved by calculating a statistic called the 'stress'. This measures the average spread of points around the line of good fit in the Shepard diagram. By plotting the stress value for each dimensional solution, a diagram similar to that in Figure 10.6(ii) will be produced. It can be seen that the stress initially decreases as the number of dimensions is increased, but that an 'elbow' point is eventually arrived at, and further increases in the number of dimensions produce no significant reductions in stress. When this plateau level has been reached, the best possible dimensional solution has been achieved. Further dimensions may reduce the stress, but not to any appreciable extent.

In addition to this comparison of stress values, it is also necessary to take account of the absolute level of stress in the preferred solution. If no solution is able to bring the stress below about 10 per cent, argues Kruskal (1964a), then the results should not be regarded as giving an adequate fit to the original data. Kruskal suggests that 5 per cent or lower indicates a good fit, while 10 per cent could still be regarded as a 'fair' fit. Stress values approaching 20 per cent are 'poor'. The stress value for the two-dimensional solution of the data in Figure 10.5 is 0.

The idea of the 'dimensions' of a metric space is not the only concept of dimensionality that has been proposed in social network analysis. Atkin (1974) has proposed an idea of dimensionality based on his Q-analysis. In Q-analysis, the dimensionality of a point is one less than its row or column total in the incidence matrix. According to Atkin, this figure gives the number of dimensions needed to represent the point adequately. Thus, a director who sits on the boards of four companies, for example, must be represented in three dimensions. From this point of view, however, each case in a network will have its own dimensionality, and these may differ from the dimensionality of the whole network.

While this approach has the virtue of being rooted in ideas close to those of graph theory, its value in relation to more familiar ideas is uncertain. Freeman (1983), therefore, rejected the Q-analytic idea of the dimensionality of a graph and proposed, instead, to combine graph theory with the geometrical dimensions discovered through MDS. The dimensionality of a graph, he argues, is the minimum number of dimensions necessary to embed the graph in a space with a good fit. His criterion of good fit is, however, stronger than that of Kruskal, and requires a stress value of 0.

The two-dimensional scatter plot drawn on a flat sheet of paper is familiar and comprehensible, but the number of dimensions that gives the best fit, at an adequate absolute level, will often be more than two. In these cases, it is not possible to draw the final configuration on a flat sheet of paper. Perspective drawing or cartographical techniques may be used to indicate a third dimension, but such representations can rarely be more than illustrative (see the work of Levine, 1972, discussed below). A substantial improvement over pencil-and-paper methods is to use computer graphics to display a three-dimensional configuration, but this procedure runs into similar problems if more than three dimensions have to be used. The most common solution for results with larger numbers of dimensions has been to display on paper successive two-dimensional 'slices' through the configuration. In a three-dimensional solution, for example, the configuration can be represented on paper as three separate two-dimensional views of the overall configuration: dimension 1 with dimension 2, dimension 2 with dimension 3, and dimension 1 with dimension 3. Computer-based visualisation techniques, discussed in the next section, offer a significant advance and allow three-dimensional solutions to be displayed and rotated on screen.

Using the output from an MDS program, a configuration of points can be plotted within a space defined by the number of dimensions discovered. It is then that the process of interpretation can begin. There are two issues for interpretation: the meaning of the dimensions and the significance of the spatial arrangement of the points. In an atlas map, for example, the dimensions can, in general, be treated unambiguously as the East–West and North–South dimensions of ordinary geographical space. With models of social networks, however, the initial task of the analyst will be to arrive at a sociological interpretation of the dimensions. It may be decided, for example, that one dimension reflects the economic resources of individuals, while another reflects their political affiliations. Rotation of the configuration may often help in interpreting the dimensions. It is also necessary to give some meaning to the spatial arrangement of the points themselves. A common procedure is to group the points together, using the output from a cluster analysis of the original data. Points within

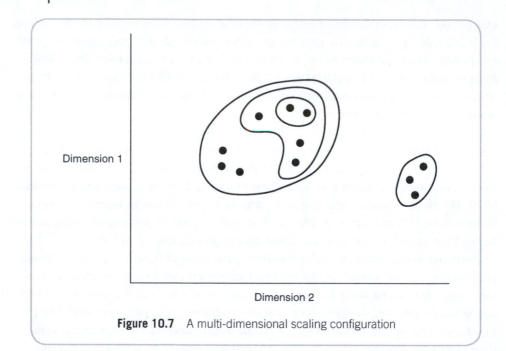

**Figure 10.7** A multi-dimensional scaling configuration

clusters are encircled by contour lines, and a hierarchical clustering approach allows the construction of a contour map of the points. A cluster analysis of Euclidean distances of the kind proposed by Burt, for example, could be used to plot the clusters on a Euclidean MDS solution. Alternatively, the results of multiplicity- and degree-based analyses of graph components and their cores can be mapped onto an MDS solution. Whereas the 'contour maps' of nested components discussed in Chapter 7 were drawn in arbitrary positions on the page, those associated with an MDS solution may represent a more 'natural' arrangement of the data. Figure 10.7 shows a simple example of this procedure (and see Knoke and Yang, 2008: 90–92).

Having produced a diagram such as that shown in Figure 10.7, a researcher can search for some characteristic common to the points in the cluster, as these are the distinct neighbourhoods of the space. Thus, a full interpretation involves identifying the clusters and then using the dimensions to give some meaning to their position in relation to one another. It should be noted that this process of interpretation is a creative and imaginative act on the part of the researcher. It is not something that can be produced by a computer alone. The researcher remains in control of the process and is responsible for arriving at any interpretations placed upon the results. Indeed, there is no guarantee that the dimensions will be capable of substantive interpretation: they may be mere artefacts of the methods of sampling or analysis. There has been much debate in psychology, for example, over the question of whether IQ testing indicates a real factor of general intelligence or simply reproduces features of the process of testing.

# WORTH A THOUSAND WORDS?

MDS and associated technologies have done much to integrate the concepts of graph theory with spatial ideas. However, the results of these analyses – particularly for large social networks – can often show simply a dense thicket of points and lines that cannot easily be visually inspected. For this reason, a number of social network analysts have explored the possibilities of marrying MDS with powerful techniques of structural modelling that can help to visualise and explore network structure in more intuitive ways.[14]

Freeman (1996a) has tried to develop some general principles for network visualisation, and he has devised and adapted a number of physical science methods for use in the analysis of social networks. He holds that, at the very least, points and lines should be colour-coded or otherwise distinguished in order to bring out their relational properties, that the layout should be organised around the most important structural features of the data, and that time-dependent aspects of a network should be brought out by animation procedures.

Freeman's particular interest is in using molecular modelling techniques from chemistry on social network data. In these techniques, points and lines are represented by three-dimensional balls and sticks, and a number of programs are available that allow this to be undertaken by computer rather than as a physical model. One of the earliest attempts to do this was that of Klovdahl (1981, 1986, 1989), whose VIEWNET program drew on molecular modelling methods and used simple three-dimensional ball and stick representations of points and lines.

Freeman has made a great deal of use of MOVIEMOL, an animation program that shows dynamic changes in structures (chemical or social) over time. This program, however, limits the placement of points, as it assumes that the laws of chemistry should govern where points are located. At present, it is difficult to modify it for social network data, though Freeman (1996b) has found it to be useful in analysing changes in small networks.

A more flexible modelling program is MAGE.[15] This allows for greater flexibility in the placing of points (for example, by taking an MDS output file) and can plot lines by their intensity or multiplicity. By using the program in conjunction with web-based VRML viewers (integral to or easily added to web browsers such as Internet Explorer), it is possible to rotate a network model around its various dimensions and to zoom in and out to explore it in greater detail. MAGE is also able to show some changes over time, though it does this as a sequence of stills rather than as a continuous flow. It is possible that further developments could involve morphing procedures to produce something approaching a true animation. The SONIA program, discussed in Chapter 9, provides various techniques for both longitudinal analysis and visualisation (Bender de Mol and McFarland, 2006; Bender de Mol et al., 2008).

Many of these techniques involve the same limitations as paper-and-pencil methods when handling large data sets. The Pajek program, however, was specifically designed for large networks and its on-screen methods allow an easier construction and inspection of such networks, though moving images are not yet supported. Pajek does, however, allow an easy transition from its in-built MDS solutions to two- and three-dimensional visualisations that can be rotated for inspection.

Novel approaches to large data sets have introduced various forms of data reduction that collapse points into larger structures in order to analyse the relations among these structures. Krempel (1994, 2005) has developed methods for simplifying large and complex structures and to highlight their essential features. His method involves the use of a simple – and arbitrarily chosen – geometric shape as a framework or 'backbone' for organising the features of a network. The circle diagram illustrated in Figure 10.1 is, of course, a simple example of this kind of procedure, and Krempel uses the circle as the basis of his own work. He generalises this approach by devising an algorithm that uses graph-theoretical measures to produce a best fit for the relational data to the circle shape, much as a regression line gives the best linear fit for a scatter of points. Thus, measures of distance or centrality can be used in place of aesthetic criteria to determine the location of points around a circle. Where the data consist of more or less distinct subgraphs, these can each be analysed as separate circles within a larger circle. The known shape of the circle gives the mind a familiar structure for interpreting the overall features of the actual network. Krempel sees this procedure as producing an 'underlying structure' for a particular configuration of relations.

This procedure offers great possibilities for large-scale data sets. It is possible to compress the lower-level circles of an analysis into macro-points that represent a whole subgraph. A sociogram of the macro-points can then be produced, giving a simplified and clearer model. A researcher can choose any particular part of this sociogram for fuller investigation and can decompress a macro-point in order to examine its internal structure. A Krempel diagram, then, is a hierarchy of nested circles, with the amount of detail shown depending on which of the circles are compressed and which are decompressed.

# ELITES, COMMUNITIES AND INFLUENCE

One of the earliest uses of multi-dimensional scaling in sociology was a community study carried out in 1960 by Edward Laumann (1966). This study was subsequently enlarged and extended through a series of related investigations into community power and elite structure. The research originated in Laumann's Harvard doctoral thesis, produced under the supervision of Homans and showing the influence of both Parsons and Harrison White. The research brought together the advanced sociometric concerns of the Harvard researchers with the general theoretical framework of Parsonian system theory, directing these methods and theories to the investigation of community structure. The particular direction taken in data analysis, however, derived from the work of Louis Guttman, whom Laumann met at Michigan. It was through the influence of Guttman that Laumann decided to use the techniques of non-metric MDS to analyse his relational data.

Laumann's starting point was Bogardus's notion of 'social distance', developed in various papers from the 1920s onwards (see the summary in Bogardus, 1959). Laumann interprets the idea of social distance as referring to the patterns of differential association found among the occupants of occupational positions. It is an 'objective' measure of how much, or how little, the occupants of various social positions associate with one another in community life. Laumann contrasts this 'objective' concept of social distance with the 'subjective' feelings of social distance that agents may experience and that are expressed in their adoption of positive or negative attitudes towards one another. Thus, Laumann's work is firmly within the tradition of thought that moved sociometric concerns from the psychological, or 'subjective' level to the sociological level of relational association. His aim was to arrive at an operational measure of 'objective' social distance and then to use MDS to convert this into a metric map of the social structure.

Laumann drew a sample of white male residents in two urban areas in Boston, Massachusetts, aiming to achieve a high degree of occupational diversity in his sample. His concern was to undertake a positional study of the kind discussed in the last chapter, as his units of analysis were to be the occupational positions rather than the individuals themselves. The responses of occupants of each occupational position to his questions on such matters as friendship choices, kinship and neighbouring were aggregated to produce summary measures for each position.

The initial analysis involved the use of five occupational categories: top professional and business, semi-professional and middle business, clerical and small business, skilled manual, and semi-skilled and unskilled manual. These five social positions were used in the construction of a number of position-by-attribute incidence matrices containing frequency data, and these data matrices were analysed as conventional contingency tables. This statistical analysis showed that friendship choices were largely confined to occupational equals, while other social relations were more likely to involve people in different occupational positions.

The truly innovatory part of Laumann's work, however, was his use of MDS to discover whether there was a hierarchy inherent in patterns of differential association (Laumann, 1966: Ch. 6). Conventional studies of the occupational hierarchy were based on 'prestige' rankings, where popular assessments of the standing of particular occupations are used as measures of their status. Laumann rejected such approaches for their reliance on 'subjective' appraisals, and used actual patterns of association – of social distance – to construct a hierarchy. Fifty-five occupational positions taken from the Duncan (1961) index were used and were constructed into a 55 × 55 incidence or 'joint occurrence' matrix for each of seven social relations. The separate matrices were summed into a single incidence matrix of differential association, and the standardised frequency values in the matrix were treated as similarity measures. The greater the frequency with which members of one occupational position interacted with members of another, the 'closer' they were to one another in social space.[16]

The results from Laumann's analysis suggested that a three-dimensional solution gave the best fit with the original data. The 55 occupational positions were plotted in a three-dimensional space, and contour lines were drawn around those close to one another on the Duncan prestige index (Laumann, 1966: Figure 6.3, which gives a fold-out picture of the configuration). Little in the way of detailed information is given about this rather arbitrary clustering, which seems to build in the very 'prestige' assumptions that Laumann was seeking to escape. Nevertheless, his interpretation of the model is informative. He sees the first, and most important, dimension as one of prestige. Scores on this dimension correlated at 0.824 with the Duncan index. It seems that patterns of differential association did, indeed, follow the pattern described in earlier studies of prestige. But the pattern could not be understood in simple one-dimensional terms. The other two dimensions were, however, less easy to interpret, and Laumann failed to produce any satisfactory interpretation for his second dimension. The third dimension he tentatively saw as contrasting entrepreneurial occupations with salaried and bureaucratic occupations.

This approach to community structure was extended in Laumann's later study of Detroit, undertaken in 1966 (Laumann, 1973). Laumann aimed to explore the friendship relations that existed between various social positions, using a sample of 1,013 white males. This work continued the positional focus of the earlier research, but extended it from occupational positions to other social positions. This style of research had much in common with Warner's pioneering positional studies, but Parsons (1951) was the specific theoretical point of reference.

The main analyses were those of the ethno-religious and occupational networks of friendship. Laumann initially analysed ethnicity and religion separately, but discovered that a better MDS solution was achieved if they were combined into a single relation. Twenty-two ethnic groups and 15 religious groups were combined into 27 ethno-religious groups, for which dissimilarity measures were calculated from the friendship choices of their members. His three-dimensional solution (Laumann, 1973: Figure 3.3) showed a strong first dimension, separating out the Protestants, the Catholics and the Jews. The second dimension seemed to measure economic standing and correlated well with family income, while the third dimension measured frequency of church attendance. Thus, the ethno-religious groups were structured by the three dimensions of religion, income, and church attendance. Catholics, for example, were differentiated into high- and low-income groups and were, independently, differentiated by the frequency of their church attendance. The identifiable clusters of positions in the social space frequently had an ethnic basis to them.

The occupational analysis in Laumann's study involved 16 occupational groups, and a two-dimensional solution was found to give the best fit. His discussion of these data largely confirms the results of the earlier study. The first dimension, he again concluded, was status or prestige (it correlated with income and educational attainment), and a second dimension divided the entrepreneurial from the bureaucratic.

Working with Pappi, Laumann further extended his analysis of community structure to the level of the 'elite', drawing on the work of Hunter (1953) and Dahl (1961) and their investigations of community power (Laumann and Pappi, 1973, 1976). They studied the small town of Jülich in Germany, to which they gave the pseudonym 'Altneustadt'. This was a rapidly expanding town during the 1950s and 1960s, and communal divisions had emerged between established and newcomer groups, divisions that had their political foci in, respectively, the Christian Democratic Union and the Social Democratic Party. The study was, again, positional in approach. Although individual occupants of positions were sampled, it was the relations between the positions that were important. The social positions on which they focused were the 'highest positions of authority' in each of the Parsonian A, G, I and L institutional subsystems. Forty-six occupants of these positions were interviewed, each being asked to name which of the other 45 they considered to be most influential in the town. There was a high degree of consensus over this: 'Herr K' received 46 votes as the most influential person and, as he had also nominated himself for this position, the researchers clearly had to take the diagonal of the data matrix seriously. Laumann and Pappi looked at interactions among the 46 people in three kinds of social relationship: business and professional relations; 'social, expressive' relations (e.g., those rooted in education, religion and residence); and community affairs relations (political coalitions and alignments).

Sociometric choices were plotted for each of these relations, but, as the researchers were interested in the presence or absence of a relation rather than in its direction, these were converted into symmetric matrices. The geodesic matrices were used for non-metric MDS, and two-dimensional solutions were produced for each type of relation. The interpretation placed upon the resulting structures was that location towards the centre of the configuration of points could be taken as an indicator of 'integrative centrality' in the community structure. The 'community affairs' network, which showed the political structure of the community, had a central zone that comprised an 'inner circle' of influentials. Figure 10.8 shows a simplified version of the Laumann and Pappi map of the community power structure in Jülich. Points are seen as arranged in zones of decreasing centrality, and lines of political division could be drawn that separated those groups with opposed views on each of five key community issues. This combination of centrality with issue division resulted in the identification of a number of distinct segments in the community power structure.

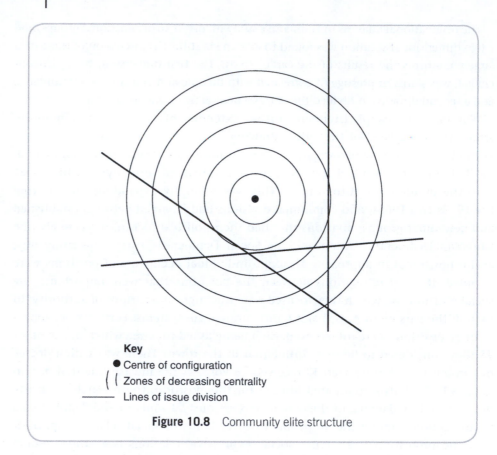

**Key**
● Centre of configuration
( ( Zones of decreasing centrality
—— Lines of issue division

**Figure 10.8**   Community elite structure

# BUSINESS ELITES AND BANK POWER

MDS has proved a useful technique for furthering certain types of investigations of community power and highlighting the existence of local elites. It has also been used most impressively in an investigation of national-level elites. Where Laumann and Pappi used a reputational method for discovering local elites, Levine (1972) has used interlocking directorships in business to identify a national economic elite (see Scott, 2012a).

Levine was one of the original network investigators in the new wave of Harvard researchers and he pioneered the use of MDS rather than graph theory as a technique for social network analysis. Using data from the 1966 Patman enquiry into bank operations in the United States, he investigated the top 100 industrial corporations and their connections with 14 banks in three cities. Seventy of these industrials had bank interlocks, and so Levine constructed a 70 × 14 incidence matrix to show the number of directors in common between each pair of enterprises. The number of directors in common was taken as a measure of 'preference', or similarity, between the enterprises. The incidence matrix was analysed in order to produce a joint space in which both the banks and the industrials could be located.

The results from Levine's analysis showed that a three-dimensional solution gave the best fit with the original data, and Levine was able to give a sociological interpretation to two of these dimensions. The first and most important dimension appeared to reflect a regional structuring of the data, separating out the New York, Pittsburgh and Chicago enterprises. No interpretation could be given to the second dimension, but Levine held that the third dimension separated the banks from the industrials. His results are summarised in Figure 10.9.

Levine's view was that the structure could be seen as forming a sphere around the centre of the joint space. The structure of the sphere comprises an onion-like arrangement of layers or concentric shells. Looking along the third dimension, industrial enterprises are located on various inner shells of this sphere while banks are located on outer shells in the same dimension. This pattern is shown in diagram (i) of Figure 10.9. The exact location of the enterprises on the shells was described by the first and second dimensions, showing that both banks and industrials were regionally differentiated around their respective shells.

The centre of this spherical configuration, argued Levine, is the position that would be occupied by isolated enterprises: those without any interlocks. These enterprises were excluded from his data set and so, in the final configuration, the centre was empty.[17] Those clusters of industrial enterprises that were interlocked with particular banks – the groups that Marxist writers have described as financial interest groups – can be seen as sectors or 'wedges' in the sphere, as shown in diagram (ii) of Figure 10.9. If a line is drawn from each bank to the centre of the sphere, each line, or vector,[18] is the central axis of that bank's sector of the sphere. The distance in space that an industrial enterprise lies from the bank, measured along this vector, is an indication of its closeness to the bank, and the angle between this vector and that which connects the industrial company to the centre of the sphere is a measure of how peripheral the industrial company is within its wedge.

Although describing the overall configuration of bank-industry interlocks as a sphere, Levine also described the wedges associated with each bank as their 'spheres of influence'. The rationale for this terminology was that the two terms relate to differing viewpoints on the same structure. Viewed from the standpoint of each bank, there are spheres of connection around them. Looking at its interlocked enterprises from the standpoint of the apex of the conical wedge that it forms (see Figure 10.9), a bank would see these enterprises as arrayed in a circular pattern around it. But these bank spheres of influence intersect with one another in such a way as to produce the overall spherical configuration of the joint space. Looking at the overall structure, the bank spheres appear as conical wedges of the larger sphere of intercorporate relations. Levine equates this difference in viewpoint with the difference between a geocentric and a heliocentric view of the stellar universe. Instead of remaining at the level of the egonet spheres of particular banks, Levine proposes a shift of viewpoint to see the overall features of the whole network itself.

The final question considered by Levine was that of how best to represent his three-dimensional configuration on a flat two-dimensional sheet of paper. Figure 10.9

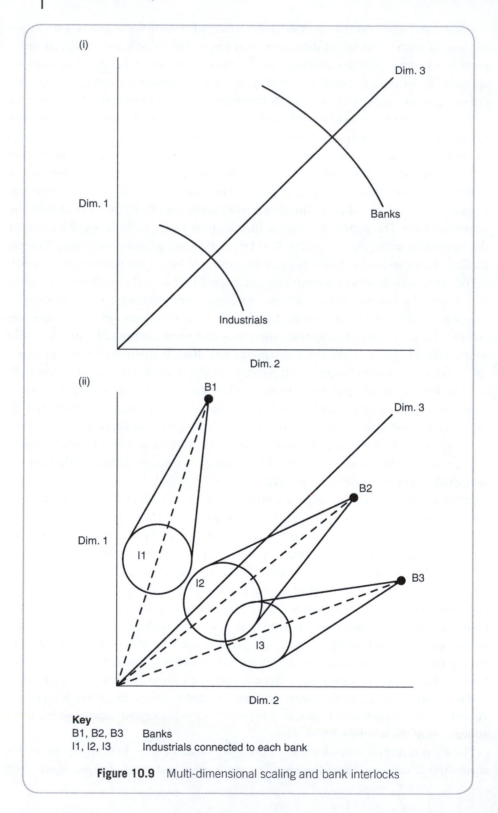

(i)

Dim. 3

Dim. 1

Banks

Industrials

Dim. 2

(ii)

B1

Dim. 3

B2

Dim. 1

I1

I2

B3

I3

Dim. 2

**Key**
B1, B2, B3     Banks
I1, I2, I3       Industrials connected to each bank

**Figure 10.9**   Multi-dimensional scaling and bank interlocks

used the trick of perspective drawing to achieve this, but the limitations of this method have already been indicated. To improve his presentation, Levine turned to the cartographic projection methods used by geographers to map the three-dimensional structure of the earth onto a flat surface. He rejected the idea of using any of the two-dimensional views produced by the MDS procedure itself, as these are based on a 'parallel projection' – a view from infinity – that is rarely used by cartographers because of the distortions that it involves. This is shown in Figure 10.10, where the peak and base of a mountain appear as separate points in a parallel projection. In a parallel projection the vertical separation of the peak and the base produces a horizontal and lateral separation of them in the resulting map.

To solve this problem, Levine proposed a form of 'point projection' from the centre itself. In cartography, this is termed a gnomonic projection. In this projection, all points on the same radius are mapped to the same position on the page. Thus, as shown in Figure 10.10, the peak and base of a mountain appear as a single point. An adequate representation of Levine's data would show clearly the association between particular banks and their linked industrials: they should appear as clear clusters on the page. A gnomonic projection, argues Levine, satisfies this requirement. Each bank appears at the dead centre of its cluster, and the industrials on the inner shells of the sphere are brought closer to those banks on the outer shells to which they are connected. In this way, the separate 'bank spheres of influence' are retained in the map of the overall structure. The gnomonic projection of the configuration is shown in Levine (1972: Figure 10).

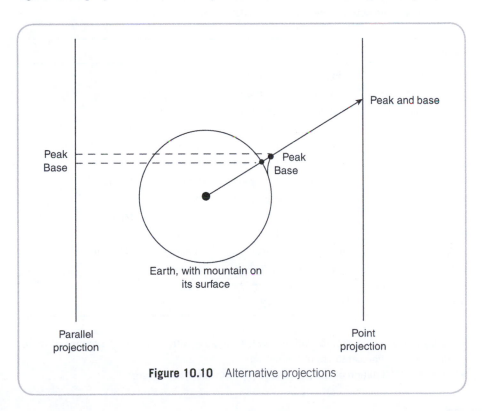

**Figure 10.10** Alternative projections

Levine's work serves as an important indicator of both the promise and the achievement of the methods of social network analysis. It was one of the pioneering studies, carried out by one of the first generation of the new group of Harvard network analysts, yet it remains one of the most advanced examples of how social network analysis can proceed in a substantive application. In Levine's work, egonets and overall network concerns are integrated into a coherent model of the embeddedness of networks in a multi-dimensional space. This pointed the way forward in offering a framework in which the principal concepts of graph theory – density, centrality and social circles of all kinds – can be allied with positional concepts describing regional and industrial sectors and can be displayed in sophisticated and easily comprehended diagrams. Computer-based techniques of visualisation, available only since Levine wrote, offer further advances for this kind of analysis. My aim in this book has been to offer some clarification of the leading theoretical ideas that must figure in such work of methodological and theoretical synthesis.

## EXERCISE

The adjacency matrix below lists actors who may have, but probably did not, work as co-stars in Hollywood films. Enter the data into your preferred social network analysis program and save it as a data file. I suggest that you use alphabetical letters as the column identifiers for each actor and the actual names as the row identifiers.

| Actor | Co-stars | | | | |
|---|---|---|---|---|---|
| Astaire (Fred) | Bogart | Carroll | Farrow | | |
| Bogart (Humphrey) | Astaire | Dietrich | Hudson | | |
| Carroll (Dihann) | Astaire | Dietrich | Eastwood | | |
| Dietrich (Marlene) | Bogart | Carroll | Garbo | Irving | |
| Eastwood (Clint) | Carroll | Farrow | Garbo | | |
| Farrow (Mia) | Astaire | Eastwood | Hudson | | |
| Garbo (Greta) | Dietrich | Eastwood | Hudson | Monroe | |
| Hudson (Rock) | Bogart | Eastwood | Farrow | | |
| Irving (George) | Dietrich | Jolson | Kelly | Monroe | Newman |
| Jolson (Al) | Irving | Kelly | Lamarr | | |
| Kelly (Grace) | Irving | Jolson | Lamarr | Newman | |
| Lamarr (Hedy) | Jolson | Kelly | Monroe | | |
| Monroe (Marilyn) | Garbo | Irving | Lamarr | | |
| Newman (Paul) | Irving | Kelly | | | |

- Using the drawing facility within Pajek (available within UCINET) produce a three-dimensional representation of the network.
- Does a 180° rotation of the network help you to see its structure?

- From visual inspection, which point looks like the most central point?
- Compute the global centralities for the network and compare the scores for each point with their position in the sociogram.
- Compute the *n*-cliques present in the matrix and locate each clique in the sociogram.
- Does your program provide any method of colouring or labelling to represent centrality and/or clique membership? If it does, see if this helps to provide a better visual presentation of the data.
- Do not try to identify any films in which these actors may have co-starred, but perhaps imagine the kinds of film that might have been produced with Al Jolson and Marilyn Monroe as co-stars!

## FURTHER READING

Krempel, L. (2011) 'Network Visualisation', in J. Scott and P.J. Carrington (eds) *The Sage Handbook of Social Network Analysis*. London: Sage Publications.

An excellent overview of visualisation methods in network analysis. You might like to consult also Krempel's website (http://www.mpifg.de/people/lk/index_en.asp) for some fascinating examples.

The website of Lin Freeman (http://moreno.ss.uci.edu/pubs.html) has links to many of his papers that discuss network visualisation.

# Notes

## CHAPTER 1: WHAT IS SOCIAL NETWORK ANALYSIS?

1  A gentle and non-mathematical introduction to social network analysis can be found in my book *What is Social Network Analysis?* (Scott, 2012b).
2  This distinction draws on the earlier arguments of Wellman (1980) and Berkowitz and Heil (1980).
3  But see also the interesting attempts of Abell (1986) to apply the techniques of graph theory to the analysis of sequential patterns of action, and Franzosi (2004, 2010) to generate numerical representations of discourse structure. While these are not, in themselves, examples of social network analysis, graph theory is fundamental to the analysis of social networks.
4  The choice of four friends to name, though common, is quite arbitrary. The general point applies no matter how many friends may be specified in the question. Issues of question wording are considered more fully in Chapter 3.

## CHAPTER 2: THE HISTORY OF SOCIAL NETWORK ANALYSIS

1  The history of social network analysis has been fully and comprehensively discussed in Freeman (2004).
2  Moreno first presented a sociogram at a conference in 1933. Its use was reported in the *New York Times* on 3 April 1933.
3  Balance theory rests on the assumption that individuals will find a state of imbalance uncomfortable and so will act to establish or re-establish some kind of mental balance. This psychological assumption is, of course, contestable. Graph theory itself is a purely mathematical framework and its application does not depend on this psychological assumption.
4  The position outlined in Cartwright and Harary (1956) is more complex than this, as they define balance not simply in terms of triads, but in terms of any 'cycle' of lines. The notion of a cycle is explored further in Chapter 7. The later work of Davis (1967) showed, in fact, that balance could be assessed by taking account only of triads, which, he argued, have a structural significance of the kind recognised by Simmel.

5   This might be taken to support the idea that all cohesive groups define their identities by contrasting themselves with an out-group of aliens or outsiders, whether real or imaginary. See Erikson (1966).

6   Davis misleadingly talks of these subgroups as 'cliques' and 'clusters', but they are neither cliques nor clusters in the sense that it has become customary to define these terms. For this reason, I have used the general term 'subgroup' to outline his position. The terms 'clique' and 'cluster' will be defined in Chapters 7 and 8.

7   Mayo's own wider-reaching accounts of the work can be found in Mayo (1933, 1945).

8   As will be apparent from my discussion in Chapter 7, the substantive concept of 'clique' used by the Hawthorne researchers is different from, and far looser than, those concepts defined in purely sociometric terms.

9   A study by Arensberg and Kimball (1940) of rural Ireland had also been supervised by Warner at Harvard and was closely connected with the Yankee City study.

10  As remarked in note 6 above, this idea does not correspond to the sociometric concept of the clique. Warner's sociological idea might as appropriately have been termed a social 'set' or a 'crowd'.

11  This is not a purely circular process, as it is possible to have individuals from each of the six classes who were, for example, members of a clique with predominantly class 1 membership.

12  From this positional analysis of stacked tables (matrices), they went on to construct image graphs – again, a pioneering and undeveloped attempt at techniques that would not become commonplace for another 30 years. Developments of this approach are discussed in Chapter 8.

13  Homans used the word 'order' instead of the more meaningful term 'direction'.

14  The analysis of 18 women is, in fact, merely an illustrative selection from their data on over 60 cliques in Old City.

15  Homans's presence at Harvard, where many of the original researchers still worked, means that some credence must be given to this statement. It is contradicted, however, by the actual report of Roethlisberger and Dickson (1939).

16  Despite his opposition to Parsons's theoretical position, the distinction between the 'internal' and the 'external' is very similar to that employed by Parsons and that became the basis of a distinction between the external 'A' and 'G' functions and the internal 'I' and 'L' functions. As I note below, Parsons drew his concepts from reflections on the small-group research of Robert Bales (1950).

17  Homans built further on this model by introducing hypotheses about norms, status and leadership. Some of this is illustrated through case studies, but none is specifically sociometric.

18  Bott was not a member of the Department, but was a close associate of its leading members.

19  'Interpersonal order' is probably a better term, as the phrase 'personal network' can easily be confused with that of the egocentric network. The latter idea is discussed below and in Chapter 5.

20  This is the same distinction as found in Parsons and in much sociology of the 1950s and 1960s. See the related view in Lockwood's (1956) discussion of Parsons. It was also related to Homans's distinction between the internal and external systems. The distinction was rediscovered by Habermas (1968).

21  This view of multiplexity and the 'stacking' or combining of relational data has been central to Mitchell's mathematical concerns.

22  Mitchell also gave a brief mention to the 'frequency' of a relation, but this is best seen as a measure of activation rather than of the relations themselves.

23  This model of attenuation is based on the well-known observation that a whispered message passed along a line of people will gradually become distorted. In Granovetter's model, the amount of information that flows is reduced with each step in the chain, so those who are far removed from the source are unlikely to receive much accurate information about the job opportunity.

# CHAPTER 3: DATA COLLECTION FOR SOCIAL NETWORK ANALYSIS

1  These terms have been widely used in discussions of elites (Scott, 1999). It was Laumann et al. (1983) who recently showed their more general relevance for the issue of sampling.
2  See the systematic comparisons made on this basis in Stokman et al. (1985).
3  When a positional approach is used and all cases above a cut-off threshold are selected for study, we are not dealing with a sample in the strict sense. Taking all cases that qualify might be termed 'quasi-enumeration'. It is not a complete enumeration, as links to those outside the selection are ignored. For a proposal on data selection in large-scale corporate networks which avoids this problem, see Berkowitz et al. (1979).
4  The directors do not constitute an independently drawn sample, and this circularity precludes the use of many conventional statistical tests, which assume, for example, the probability sampling of cases.
5  Density, which will be discussed more fully in Chapter 5, can be calculated from the mean number of connections held by agents in a network.
6  The question of popularity in sociometric studies is one form of the measurement of 'centrality' in network analysis. This measure will be discussed in Chapter 6.
7  The initial choice of respondents is, of course, important in a snowball sample if bias is to be avoided.

# CHAPTER 4: ORGANISING AND ANALYSING NETWORK DATA

1  Most word processors save their documents in a proprietary format, and it will be necessary to save the file in raw text format as a txt file. Such a file contains nothing but the codes corresponding to letters and numbers. See Roistacher (1979).
2  The numbers and letters that are used to refer to the cells of the spreadsheet need not be used as data labels, especially if the data are separately labelled and annotated. The numbers and letters are there simply so that there is an unambiguous way to refer to any cell in the spreadsheet. Unfortunately the convention on spreadsheets is the opposite of that for matrices: in referring to the cells of a spreadsheet, columns come before rows. Such is life!
3  Some tasks can be undertaken with a database program such as Access, though these are not especially suitable for social network analysis purposes. It is important to note that the relational database is not, as it might appear, a database for relational data. The word 'relational' is used in two distinct senses. Some of the principles of database construction are well covered in Brent (1985).

4 UCINET requires a header line that describes the format of the data. This line is added above the data, before exporting it, to give information about the number of rows and columns and the type of data.

5 Even if it is physically 'square', having the same number of rows and columns, it is logically rectangular.

6 There can, of course, be three-mode or, more generally, *n*-mode data, depending on the number of separate sets of points that there are. There are, however, no readily available and tested methods for handling these more complicated forms of data.

7 The incidence matrix is, in effect, a one-column vector.

8 Computational procedures that operate directly on an incidence matrix are an exception to this argument. Some of these procedures analyse the rows and some the columns of the matrix, while others analyse both the rows and the columns simultaneously. In such cases, it is necessary to make sure that the appropriate set of agents is made the target of the analysis. If the particular procedure analyses only the columns (as is often the case), the matrix may need to be transposed in order to analyse the agents which have been designated as 'cases' in the original matrix. Certain other exceptions to this claim that the distinction between cases and affiliations is arbitrary will be noted in later chapters.

9 The 'binary' data referred to here and throughout the book involve the use of binary digits to indicate the presence or absence of a relation. This does not involve any attempt to represent the strength of a relation as a binary value. Thus, a relation that has a value of 3 (there are three common affiliations between the two cases) is represented in binary form simply as '1' (a relation is present) and not as the binary numeral 11. This should not normally cause any confusion, and so I follow the normal practice of referring simply to the distinction between binary and valued data.

10 If complex data have been reduced to simpler data, it is possible to return to the original data and to transform them into a different form of simpler data. However, it is not possible to convert raw undirected data, for example, into valued or directed data without drawing on information about values or direction which was not coded into the original, undirected matrix.

11 UCINET Version 6.0 (dated 2007). Available from Analytical Technologies, PO Box 910359, Lexington, KY 40513, USA. Price $250 ($40 to students). The UCINET website is at https:// sites.google.com/site/ucinetsoftware/home. A book on social network analysis written by some of the UCINET development team serves as a partial manual (Borgatti et al., 2013).

12 Pajek can be downloaded free from http://download.cnet.com/Pajek/3000-2076_4-10662544. html. Brief manuals can also be downloaded and a full introductory text and manual can be found in de Nooy et al. (2005: Appendix 1).

13 One that is growing in interest and application is based on the statistical programming language R. Information on this method can be found at https://sna.stanford.edu/rlabs.php.html.

14 INSNA is an international group for the exchange of information and mutual intellectual support. It publishes a newsletter, *Connections*, and was involved in the foundation of the journal *Social Networks*. The INSNA home page is at http://www.insna.org/. This site holds an archive of the newsletter and links to other social network sites. To subscribe to the SOCNET service, send an email to listserv@lists.ufl.edu. The body of the message should say simply 'SUBSCRIBE SOCNET Your Name', replacing 'Your Name' with your own name.

# CHAPTER 5: TERMINOLOGY FOR NETWORK ANALYSIS

1 Points are sometimes referred to as 'vertices' or 'nodes', and lines are sometimes termed 'edges'. There is no real advantage in using these alternative words, and so I have retained the simplest usage.

2 'Graph diagram' is the general term for a definition of a network. 'Sociogram' is the term used for a graph diagram of a social network as opposed to that drawn, for example, for an electrical wiring network. As this book is concerned with the sociological applications of graph theory, I shall sometimes use the two terms interchangeably.

3 A valued graph is sometimes, rather misleadingly, called a 'network'. This terminology is best avoided, as all graphs should be seen as models of networks. Some writers distinguish 'signed graphs', where the relations are characterised as positive or negative, as was seen in the discussion of balance theory in Chapter 2. It seems more appropriate, however, to see the signed graph as a kind of valued graph in which the values are positive or negative binary digits. Alternatively, it could be seen as the compound graph constructed from two simple graphs, one with positive values and one with negative values.

4 In a square matrix, the row sum and the column sum for a particular point will be the same. If only the lower half of the matrix is available, the row and column sums cannot be calculated unless the remaining values are included. Those social network programs which accept data as a lower half matrix will perform these adjustments automatically.

5 At school, teachers often urged us to remember that all measurements must have a unit attached to them. In graph theory, the 'line' is generally the unit. That is, we could say that the distance between two points is '3 lines'. This unit is not, however, normally given in statements of graph theory.

6 Note, however, that points C and A are directly connected by a line.

7 To complete the interrelated formulae, the actual number of lines is equal to half the sum of the degrees, and so density can also be expressed as $\sum d_i/n(n-1)$, where $d_i$ is the degree of point $i$.

8 Inclusiveness, the proportion of points that are actually connected, can sometimes be more meaningfully expressed as a percentage, but this is not appropriate for small numbers.

9 See the discussions of this question in Sharkey (1989, 1990), Timms (1990) and Knoke and Yang (2008).

10 More general arguments on the significance of size can be found in Blau (1977a, 1977b), Rytinä (1982) and Rytinä and Morgan (1982).

11 Morgan and Rytinä (1977) outline some problems and limitations with this approach. Their arguments have been answered by Granovetter (1977).

12 In two dimensions, it could be said that its area would be $c(1.5)2/3$, or $0.75c$.

13 The ratio of the circumference to the diameter of a circle is a constant, $\pi$. The ratio of the circumference to the diameter in a graph, as those concepts have been defined here, does not appear to be a constant. I have glossed over the issue of the units in which the volume of a graph is to be measured. As all distances in graph theory are measured in 'lines', this should be the basis of the measure. Volume would, then, be measured in 'cubic lines'.

14 Wellman gives his calculations as percentage figures, and I have converted them to the base defined earlier in this chapter.

15 Wellman assumed that all relations were symmetrical: if a respondent said that intimate A was close to intimate B, then it was assumed also that intimate B was close to intimate A. Note that this analysis deals only with relations as perceived by respondents, and not, necessarily, with the actual links among intimate associates. The work, therefore, is directly in line with some of the phenomenological assumptions of the earliest studies of balance theory.

16 A British study which looks at reciprocity in support through kinship networks is Werbner (1990).

17 For a general overview of social network analytic techniques in the study of kinship and community, see D. White (2011).

# CHAPTER 6: POPULARITY, MEDIATION AND EXCLUSION

1 This relative measure is calculated by the formula degree/$(n - 1)$, as every point can be connected to a maximum of $n - 1$ other points.

2 See also Marsden (1982). Burt (1982) has developed Simmel's idea of the intermediary as the *tertius gaudens*, the third party that benefits from the conflict or separation of two others. Anthonisse (1971) has proposed a measure called the 'rush', which is closely related to Freeman's notion of betweenness. The rush measure is implemented only in the GRADAP program.

3 As a proportion, this varies from 0 to 1, with a score of 1 showing that the pair of points are completely dependent on Y for their connections.

4 The measurement of centrality, then, depends upon the solution of a set of simultaneous equations. This measure was originally applied in Bearden et al. (1975), where $r_{ij}$ was measured by the number of interlocks between two companies. This research is discussed later in this chapter.

5 $\beta$ is a weighting attached to the raw measured centrality score, it is not a multiplier.

6 But see the application of the idea in Stokman et al. (1985).

7 It is possible that the 'positional' approaches discussed in Chapter 8 could be allied with the Stokman and Snijders approach to produce more reliable discriminations.

8 Their term is 'core' rather than 'centre' but, for reasons that will become apparent in Chapter 7, I do not follow this terminology.

9 In a directed graph the 'in-distance' and 'out-distance' will differ and so the maximum column entry will be the 'in-separation' and the maximum row entry will be the 'out-separation'.

10 Note that, in this case, point B is also equidistant from all other points. This will not be the case in all graphs.

11 Note that, while it may not be possible to identify a unique absolute centre, all the actual or imaginary centres identified through Christofides's procedure will have the same mathematical properties. It is, therefore, possible to use the idea of the absolute centre in calculating other measures.

12 If a graph has a unique actual point of minimum eccentricity, then this will be its absolute centre. If there are two such points with equal eccentricity, as in sociogram (iv) of Figure 5.6, then there will be a unique absolute centre located mid-way between them. If there are more than two points with minimum eccentricity, then there may be no unique absolute centre to the graph. Unfortunately, the Christofides algorithm is not available in any of the standard social network analysis packages.

13  The distinction between strong and weak ties in corporate networks was later systematised in the work of Stokman et al. (1985) as that between 'primary' and 'loose' interlocks.

14  It is arguable that, in this second case, the weighting should also have been based on the size of the recipient board, as the weighting is an attempt to measure the salience of the interlock for the board to which the directors are sent. Further considerations of the Bonacich measure can be found in Mizruchi and Bunting (1981) and in Mariolis and Jones (1982).

15  This idea of a cluster will be examined in Chapter 8.

16  The idea of a 'component' as a connected part of a graph will be more formally defined in the next chapter. For the purposes of the present discussion, its general meaning should be clear.

17  A comparative survey of this and related work can be found in Scott (1997). Useful theoretical discussions are Brass and Burckhardt (1992) and Mizruchi and Galaskiewicz (1994). Mizruchi (1992) provides a related extension of this work into corporate political donations.

# CHAPTER 7: GROUPS, FACTIONS AND SOCIAL DIVISIONS

1  This is one of the implications of the so-called 'small-world' phenomenon. See Milgram (1967), Erickson (1978), Lin et al. (1978) and Kilworth and Bernard (1979).

2  This idea of the 'block' is based on earlier usage in graph theory but is incompatible with more recent usages.

3  Where a knot consists simply of two points connected by a line, the line is termed a 'bridge' between the other knots of which its points are members. This notion of a bridge is very different from that of Everett and from the idea introduced by Schwartz and his colleagues and discussed in the previous chapter. It is an unfortunate fact in social network analysis that words are so often used in contradictory ways to describe very different concepts.

4  Everett (1982) suggests that his approach to 'blocking' is similar to that used in analyses of structural equivalence. In fact, the procedures are radically different and must be distinguished. Structural equivalence is discussed in the next chapter.

5  As with the identification of paths, there may be a number of identical cycles, depending on which point is made the starting point for naming the cycle. In counting the number of cycles in a graph, this double counting must be reckoned with. In what follows, I shall not normally distinguish the identical cycles and will name them simply by an arbitrarily chosen starting point. Sociogram (i) of Figure 6.2, for example, has only three distinct cycles: ABCDA, ABDA and BCDB.

6  Everett claims that his concept of a bridge is similar to that used by Granovetter (1973) to describe the 'weak' ties which connect 'strongly' tied subgroups.

7  It should be noted that all pairs of points in a cyclic component will be connected through a cycle, though many of these may be longer than the cycle length used to define the cyclic component. The cyclic component {E, F, G, H, I, J} in Figure 7.3 is built from 4-cycles, but points E and J, for example, are connected only through a cycle of length 6.

8  This is important, as a cycle in an undirected graph must connect at least three points. Thus, a dyad can never be a cyclic component.

9  In case the analysis still results in the identification of a single large component, Everett argues for the use of a further ad hoc procedure for fragmenting the structure of the graph. He argues that it is possible, for example, to take account only of reciprocated directed lines,

where A directs a line to B and B directs a line to A. These are the strongest lines in the graph, and an analysis which takes account of these alone should, he argues, identify the strongest structural features of the graph. This procedure is implemented in UCINET by reading a directed (asymmetric) matrix as if it were undirected. The program then disregards all unreciprocated lines.

10 The term 'nested components' was first introduced by the GRADAP team in Groningen for a particular procedure, but it has a far wider application.

11 The term 'slicing' is the most descriptive of the procedure involved, though 'dichotomising' is the term used in UCINET. Everett refers to the procedure as 'compression'.

12 In the terminology set out in the following paragraphs, these would be $k$-cyclic $m$-cores, where $k$ is the cycle length and $m$ is the multiplicity.

13 I am here generalising Seidman's (1983) concept of the core in such a way that the general concept is no longer defined by Seidman's $k$ parameter. This is elaborated in the following discussion.

14 It is important to note that the degree in this procedure is measured only in relation to the other members of the core, not in the graph as a whole.

15 I shall examine the cohesive subgroups themselves in the next section. Seidman specifically points to the parallels between his conceptualisation of $k$-cores and Granovetter's (1973) work on weak ties.

16 Note that while the minimum degree ($k$) is calculated only for points within the core, the proportion of points disappearing is based on the total number of points in the graph as a whole. This ensures that the vector is, to a certain extent, standardised for the size of the graph.

17 I have invented the term '$m$-core' to parallel Seidman's notion of the $k$-core. This terminology also has the advantage of keeping clear the distinction between the component itself and the cores of which it is composed. These $m$-cores were applied, without using the name, in Scott and Hughes (1980) and Scott (1986), which referred to them in the context of a network of plural lines.

18 What I have termed $m$-cores are the basis of Atkin's method of Q-analysis, developed as an alternative to graph theory. In Q-analysis, it is possible to construct a matrix of Q-nearness, in which the Q-nearness of two points is, confusingly, one less than the multiplicity of the line connecting them. Thus, a component of points which are all 2-near to one another would correspond to a $3m$-core (see Atkin, 1974, 1977, 1981; Doreian, 1980, 1981, 1983; Beaumont and Gattrell, 1982). The application of Q-analysis is discussed in the Appendix of Scott (1986).

19 A pair of connected points is a clique in only a trivial sense, and clique analysis should normally be concerned only with cliques of size 3 or greater.

20 The formula linking the number of points to the number of lines is that which is used to identify the total possible number of lines in calculating density. It is $n(n-1)/2$, where $n$ is the number of points. This defines the sequence of so-called 'triangular numbers'.

21 In practice, a number of clique detection programs simply will not work on directed graphs. The terminology of strong and weak cliques is an innovation of my own, designed to parallel the distinction between strong and weak components.

22 A further reason for relaxing the strict idea of clique membership was that, during the 1940s and 1950s, it proved difficult to discover algorithms that could identify them in an efficient way. Greater mathematical knowledge and improvements in computing have now removed this obstacle.

23  A technique for the identification of *n*-clans is available in UCINET. Mokken (1974) also introduced the concept of the '*n*-club', a component with maximum diameter *n*. This can usefully be seen as a further extension of the idea of the simple component, though little analysis in this direction has been attempted. Note that a weak component is both an *n*-clan and an *n*-club in which the value of *n* is just large enough to connect the maximum number of points.

24  The concept of the *k*-plex is constructed along similar lines to that of the *k*-core, also developed by Seidman, with both concepts being degree-based. Unfortunately, the letter *k* does not mean the same thing in the two concepts. In a *k*-core it is the minimum degree of points in the core; in a *k*-plex it is the number of points to which a point need not be connected.

25  In fact, graph (ii) is a 2-clique rather than merely a 3-clique.

26  Seidman and Foster develop a further concept, following Mokken's suggestion of limiting the diameters of subgraphs. They extend the *k*-plex idea and identify what they call a 'diameter-*n* *k*-plex'. This is defined as a group in which each point is connected to at least $k - 1$ of the other points at a distance of *n* or less. The concept of a diameter-2 *k*-plex, in particular, seems a very fruitful extension to the clique idea. Unfortunately, the *k* measure is, again, used in a different sense, and so comparisons must be made with care (see Seidman and Foster, 1978: 69–70).

27  The identification of circles might be seen, in a general sense, as a particular kind of clustering method. But in this book I have restricted the idea of the cluster to those subgraphs found through specific hierarchical methods. Circles, cliques and plexes group points on the basis of the degree of their mutual connections, while hierarchical clustering methods take account of their whole pattern of connections to the rest of the network. In this sense, hierarchical clustering is closely linked to the identification of structural equivalence, which is reviewed in the next chapter.

28  Chapter 10 in Mullins (1973) is a study of social network analysts. It includes a data matrix but no sociogram.

29  In fact, Gattrell goes beyond this, but I do not intend to pursue these issues here. The interested reader can consult Beaumont and Gattrell (1982) and then read Gattrell's studies.

30  It is important to note that Gattrell does not carry out a clique analysis and so this does not mean that every paper is directly connected to every other in the component. The data simply show the existence of a chain of connections.

# CHAPTER 8: STRUCTURAL LOCATIONS, CLASSES AND POSITIONS

1  As in so many areas of social network analysis, there are confusing problems of terminology here. Researchers following Lorrain and White have used the word 'block' to refer both to the sets or clusters of points and to the cells of the image matrix. Further confusion arises from the fact, pointed out in Chapter 6, that graph theorists have used the word 'block' to refer to a number of totally different and unrelated ideas. Having eschewed the word 'block' in that chapter, I limit its use in this chapter to describe the cells of image matrices. The sets of points, for reasons set out in the next section, I refer to as 'clusters'.

2 There are other forms of agglomerative cluster analysis, but these are the most common. An intermediate approach is the median distance method used in the UCLUS algorithm. This takes neither the smallest nor the greatest distance between clusters as a measure of similarity. Instead it takes the median distance. Anderberg (1973) has provided an intermediate 'average-linkage' method. See also Allen (1980).

3 Some writers suggest using $\chi^2$ to select the criterion at each step.

4 The most elaborated account of this method can be found in Breiger et al. (1975), Boorman and White (1976) and White et al. (1976). The original method was discussed in McQuitty (1968) and McQuitty and Clark (1968).

5 It has also been suggested that it is unfruitful to divide the matrix into sets that contain fewer than three points, as, in most matrices, a set of size 2 will be only a trivial case of structural equivalence.

6 In practice, it has been found that the process can be halted before all values converge to +1 or −1. It has been suggested that little is gained from the extra computing time in setting the convergence criterion higher than +0.9 and −0.9. The version of CONCOR implemented in UCINET allows the investigator to make this choice of convergence criterion. When such a decision is made, however, an arbitrary element is of course introduced into the procedure.

7 The Breiger et al. (1975) analysis relates not to the original Davis et al. (1941) data, but to the reanalysis of the original data given in Homans (1951).

8 When the actual density of a block is 1.0, the block will be a 1-clique. When it is less than this, however, the block will not form a 1-clique, and it may not even form an *n*-clique. This is hardly surprising, as CONCOR is specifically presented as an alternative to clique detection methods. If CONCOR simply identified cliques, its cumbersome procedures would hardly be worthwhile.

9 More complex, but comparable, real data sets are discussed in Breiger (1979).

10 Further sources on CONCOR and block models can be found in Schwartz (1977), Arabie et al. (1978) and Light and Mullins (1979). CONCOR is extended in Bonacich and McConaghy (1979). See also Carrington et al. (1980).

11 This discussion draws on Burt (1980, 1982) and Burt and Schott (1990). White's later work (1992a) moved in a similar conceptual direction to Burt.

12 Burt terms this the 'frequency decay' assumption.

13 Burt's method calculates 'Euclidean' distances, which I shall discuss in Chapter 9.

14 The actual test recommended by Burt involves performing a principal components analysis on the 'co-variance matrix' of each cluster. The loading of a point on the first component is taken as a measure of its association with the other members of the cluster. This test may seem a little obscure unless the methods of principal components analysis are understood. They are discussed in Chapter 9, and readers may prefer to return to this section after reading the relevant part of that chapter. Burt's approach is criticised in Faust and Romney (1985).

15 As each point has a different number of contacts, the matrix of similarities will not be symmetric.

16 The correlation calculated is not a normal Pearson correlation coefficient, but one that incorporates some of the Euclidean assumptions of Burt's method.

17 For an attempt to specify the relations between structural equivalence and conventional graph-theoretical concerns, see Everett et al. (1990).

18 Burt (1988; see also Burt and Carlton, 1989) has combined structural equivalence with multi-dimensional scaling (MDS) to produce a topology of US markets. MDS is discussed in Chapter 9.

19 A small sixth set with very weak links to the rest of the network is excluded.

# CHAPTER 9: SOCIAL CHANGE AND DEVELOPMENT

1  Details of the SIENA program and a facility to download it can be found at http://www.stats. ox.ac.uk/~snijders/siena/. The program is also available within the StOCNET package: http:// www.gmw.rug.nl/~stocnet/StOCNET.htm

# CHAPTER 10: VISUALISING AND MODELLING

1  KRACKPLOT has a procedure for constructing these circle diagrams, though the order in which the points are arranged still has to be determined by the researcher. The Pajek program constructs circle diagrams and uses a trial-and-error method to find a best fit of the data that minimises cross-overs of lines.

2  Multi-dimensional scaling can also be used to disclose features of attribute data, but this is beyond the scope of this book.

3  Euclidean metrics have additional properties that need not detain us here. Basically, a Euclidean metric allows the use of all the familiar additive arithmetic operations (addition, subtraction, multiplication and division) and conforms to the principles of conventional school geometry (e.g., Pythagoras's theorem). Metric models other than the Euclidean have been proposed, but they have not been especially important in social network analysis. One such model is the curved-space 'Riemannian' metric, in which Pythagoras's and other familiar theorems do not apply.

4  This characterises metric multi-dimensional scaling. The slightly different non-metric approach to multi-dimensional scaling is discussed later in this chapter. A procedure that, for most practical purposes, seems to produce similar results to multi-dimensional scaling is spring embedding (Kamada and Kawai, 1989). Although this is used in the Pajek program, its basis has not yet been worked through in the secondary literature.

5  'Dissimilarities' are sometimes termed 'differences'.

6  There is an exactly similar problem of reflection with respect to the position of A. If the original line had been drawn as BA rather than AB (i.e., running in the opposite direction), ABC would be reflected around the line BC. The curious reader may experiment for her- or himself.

7  Pajek employs non-metric MDS, discussed later in this chapter.

8  It is important not to confuse the concept of 'component' used in principal components analysis with the graph-theoretical idea of a 'component'. In graph theory a component is a particular kind of segment in a graph; in principal components analysis a component is a 'dimension' or 'factor'.

9  The procedure described results in a scattering of the variables. A similar method can give a scattering of the cases. In some texts, this case-by-case analysis is termed 'Q-mode' principal components analysis in order to distinguish it from the usual, variable-by-variable 'R-mode' analysis. This distinction between Q-mode and R-mode analyses is mainly relevant when handling attribute data. The important point to bear in mind is that PCA in its normal 'R-mode' operates on the columns of the original matrix. Thus, an investigation of a sociometric case-by-affiliation incidence matrix would result in an analysis of the affiliations. If the researcher wished to investigate the structure of relations among the cases, it would be necessary to transpose the matrix, so making the cases into the columns of the matrix, as in a Q-mode PCA. It is important not to confuse Q-mode analysis with the Q-analysis of Atkin which was touched on in Chapter 6 and to which I refer later in this chapter.

10 With a non-symmetric adjacency matrix it is often possible to produce a combined row and column solution that shows the joint space occupied by the cases.

11 See Kruskal and Wish (1978) and Coxon (1982). The original sources on non-metric multi-dimensional scaling include Shepard (1962), Kruskal (1964a, 1964b), Guttman (1968) and Lingoes and Roskam (1973).

12 As an initial configuration is simply generated for testing, its source does not matter. Thus, a metric procedure can be used to generate this initial configuration.

13 Strictly speaking, this is an over-simplification, but it corresponds to the general principles used in testing goodness of fit. The most general principle is that the relation between the data ranks and the distance ranks be 'monotonic', that is, the line moves up and to the right in a constant way, though not necessarily at 45° to the axes.

14 See the useful overview in Krempel (2011).

15 UCINET comes with conversion procedures for transforming its own output data files into the format required by MAGE and by many other molecular modelling programs.

16 Although square, the matrix was asymmetric, as the columns were the occupations of respondents and the rows were the occupations of those with whom they claimed to interact. The data were, in this sense, directed from columns to rows. Laumann, therefore, used the asymmetric variant of the Guttman–Lingoes program, the version normally used for rectangular incidence matrices.

17 Note that it is fundamentally incorrect to try to equate 'centrality' in the sphere with any of the ideas of network centrality discussed in Chapter 6. In fact, the 'centre' in Levine's analysis is exactly the opposite of that discussed in relation to the work of Laumann and Pappi. The reason for this is that Levine used similarity data, while Laumann and Pappi used dissimilarities. In Levine's analysis, the centre is the zero point of least similarity. Paradoxically, Levine's 'centre' contains the most 'peripheral' points, and the position of the banks towards the outer layers of the sphere supports the Bearden et al. (1975) view of bank centrality.

18 A vector, in this context, is simply a line drawn through the configuration.

# References

Abell, P. (1986) *The Syntax of Social Life*. Oxford: Oxford University Press.

Alba, R.D. (1973) 'A Graph Theoretic Definition of a Sociometric Clique', *Journal of Mathematical Sociology*, 3.

Alba, R.D. (1982) 'Taking Stock of Network Analysis: A Decade's Results', *Research in the Sociology of Organizations*, 1.

Alba, R.D. and Kadushin, C. (1976) 'The Intersection of Social Circles: A New Measure of Social Proximity in Networks', *Sociological Methods and Research*, 5.

Alba, R.D. and Moore, G. (1978) 'Elite Social Circles', *Sociological Methods and Research*, 7.

Allen, M.P. (1980) 'Cliques versus Clusters in Corporate Networks'. Paper presented to the Pacific Sociological Association, San Francisco.

Anderberg, M.R. (1973) *Cluster Analysis for Applications*. New York: Academic Press.

Ansell, C. (2001) *Schism and Solidarity in Social Movements*. New York: Cambridge University Press.

Antal, T., Krapivsky, P.L. and Redner, S. (2006) 'Social Balance on Networks: The Dynamics of Friendship and Enmity', *Physica D*, 224.

Anthonisse, J. (1971) *The Rush in a Directed Graph*. Amsterdam: University of Amsterdam Mathematical Centre.

Arabie, P., Boorman, S.A. and Levitt, P.R. (1978) 'Constructing Blockmodels: How and Why', *Journal of Mathematical Psychology*, 17.

Arensberg, C.M. and Kimball, S.T. (1940) *Family and Community in Ireland*. London: Peter Smith.

Aron, R. (1964) *German Sociology*. Glencoe, IL: Free Press.

Atkin, R. (1974) *Mathematical Structure in Human Affairs*. London: Heinemann.

Atkin, R. (1977) *Combinatorial Connectivities in Social Systems*. Basle: Birkhäuser.

Atkin, R. (1981) *Multidimensional Man*. Harmondsworth: Penguin.

Bailey, F.G. (1969) *Stratagems and Spoils*. Oxford: Basil Blackwell.

Bailey, K.D. (1976) 'Cluster Analysis', in D.R. Heise (ed.) *Sociological Methodology, 1975*. San Francisco: Jossey-Bass.

Bales, R.F. (1950) *Interaction Process Analysis*. Reading, MA: Addison-Wesley.

Banck, G.A. (1973) 'Network Analysis and Social Theory', in J. Boissevain and J.D. Mitchell (eds) *Network Analysis*. The Hague: Mouton.

Barabási, A.-L. (2002) *Linked: The New Science of Networks*. Cambridge, MA: Perseus.

Barnes, J.A. (1954) 'Class and Committee in a Norwegian Island Parish', *Human Relations*, 1.

Barnes, J.A. (1969) 'Graph Theory and Social Networks', *Sociology*, 3.

Barnes, J.A. (1974) *Social Networks*. Module in Anthropology, No. 26. Reading, MA: Addison-Wesley.

Barnes, J.A. and Harary, F. (1983) 'Graph Theory in Network Analysis', *Social Networks*, 5.

Bauman, Z. (1998) *Globalization*. Cambridge: Polity Press.

Bavelas, A. (1948) 'A Mathematical Model for Group Structure', *Applied Anthropology*, 7.

Bavelas, A. (1950) 'Communication Patterns in Task-Oriented Groups', *Journal of the Acoustical Society of America*, 22.

Bearden, J., Atwood, W., Freitag, P., Hendricks, C., Mintz, B. and Schwartz, M. (1975) 'The Nature and Extent of Bank Centrality in Corporate Networks'. Paper presented to the American Sociological Association. Reprinted in J. Scott (ed.) (2002) *Social Networks: Critical Concepts in Sociology*, Volume 3. London: Routledge.

Beauchamp, M. (1965) 'An Improved Index of Centrality', *Behavioural Science*, 10.

Beaumont, J.C. and Gattrell, A.C. (1982) *An Introduction to Q-Analysis*. Norwich: Geo Publications.

Beaver, D. (2004) 'Does Collaborative Research Have Greater Epistemic Authority?', *Scientometrics*, 60.

Bender de Mol, S. and McFarland, D.A. (2006) 'The Art and Science of Dynamic Network Visualisation', *Journal of Social Structure*, 7.

Bender de Mol, S., Morris, M. and Moody, J. (2008) 'Prototype Packages for Managing and Animating Longitudinal Network Data: Dynamic Networks and RSonia', *Journal of Statistical Software*, 24.

Berkowitz, S.D. (1982) *An Introduction to Structural Analysis*. Toronto: Butterworths.

Berkowitz, S.D., Carrington, P.J., Corman, J.S. and Waverman, L. (1979) 'Flexible Description for a Large Scale Corporate Data Base', *Social Networks*, 2.

Berkowitz, S.D. and Heil, G. (1980) 'Dualities in Methods of Social Network Analysis'. Discussion Paper, University of Toronto Structural Analysis Program.

Blau, P.M. (1977a) *Inequality and Heterogeneity*. New York: Free Press.

Blau, P.M. (1977b) 'A Macrosociological Theory of Social Structure', *American Journal of Sociology*, 83.

Blau, P.M. and Duncan, O.D. (1967) *The American Occupational Structure*. New York: John Wiley & Sons.

Bogardus, E.S. (1959) *Social Distance*. Yellow Springs, OH: Antioch Press.

Boissevain, J. (1974) *Friends of Friends*. Oxford: Basil Blackwell.

Bonacich, P. (1972) 'Technique for Analysing Overlapping Memberships', in H. Costner (ed.) *Sociological Methodology, 1973*. San Francisco: Jossey-Bass.

Bonacich, P. (1987) 'Power and Centrality: A Family of Measures', *American Sociological Review*, 52.

Bonacich, P. and McConaghy, M. (1979) 'The Algebra of Blockmodelling', in K.F. Schuessler (ed.) *Sociological Methodology, 1980*. San Francisco, CA: Jossey-Bass.

Boorman, S.A. and White, H.C. (1976) 'Social Structure from Multiple Networks, II. Role Structures', *American Journal of Sociology*, 81(6): 1384–446.

Borgatti, S., Boyd, J. and Everett, M.G. (1989) 'Iterated Roles: Mathematics and Applications', *Social Networks*, 11.

Borgatti, S. and Everett, M.G. (1989) 'The Class of All Regular Equivalences: Algebraic Structure and Computation', *Social Networks*, 11.

Borgatti, S. and Everett, M.G. (1999) 'Models of Core/Periphery Structure', *Social Networks*, 21.

Borgatti, S. P., Everett, M. G. and Johnson, J. C. (2013). *Analyzing Social Networks*. London: Sage.

Borgatti, S. and Lopez-Kidwell, V. (2011) 'Network Theory', in J. Scott and P. Carrington (eds) *The Sage Handbook of Social Network Analysis*. London: Sage.

Bott, E. (1955) 'Urban Families: Conjugal Roles and Social Networks', *Human Relations*, 8.

Bott, E. (1956) 'Urban Families: The Norms of Conjugal Roles', *Human Relations*, 9.

Bott, E. (1957) *Family and Social Network*. London: Tavistock.

Bott, H. (1928) 'Observation of Play Activities in a Nursery School', *Genetic Psychology Monographs*, 4.

Bourdieu, P. (1979) *Distinction: A Social Critique of the Judgment of Taste*. London: Routledge, 1984.

Boyd, J.P. (1969) 'The Algebra of Group Kinship', *Journal of Mathematical Sociology*, 6.

Brass, D.J. and Burckhardt, M.E. (1992) 'Centrality and Power in Organizations', in N. Nohira and R.G. Eccles (eds) *Networks and Organizations*. Boston: Harvard University Press.

Breiger, R.L. (1979) 'Toward an Operational Theory of Community Elite Structure', *Quality and Quantity*, 13.

Breiger, R.L. (1981) 'The Social Class Structure of Occupational Mobility', *American Journal of Sociology*, 87.

Breiger, R.L. (1982) 'A Structural Analysis of Occupational Mobility', in P.V. Marsden and N. Lin (eds) *Social Structure and Network Analysis*. Beverly Hills, CA: Sage Publications.

Breiger, R.L., Boorman, S.A. and Arabie, P. (1975) 'An Algorithm for Blocking Relational Data, with Applications to Social Network Analysis', *Journal of Mathematical Psychology*, 12.

Brent, E.E. (1985) 'Relational Database Structures and Concept Formation in the Social Sciences', *Computers and the Social Sciences*, 1.

Brint, S. (1992) 'Hidden Meanings: Cultural Content and Context in Harrison White's Structural Sociology', *Sociological Theory*, 10.

Buchanan, M. (2002) *Small World: Uncovering Nature's Hidden Networks*. London: Weidenfeld and Nicolson.

Buckley, W. (1967) *Sociology and Modern Systems Theory*. Englewood Cliffs, NJ: Prentice Hall.

Bulmer, M. (1985) 'The Rejuvenation of Community Studies? Neighbours, Networks, and Policy', *Sociological Review*, 33.

Burt, R.S. (1976) 'Positions in Social Networks', *Social Forces*, 55.

Burt, R.S. (1977a) 'Positions in Multiple Network Systems, Part One', *Social Forces*, 56.

Burt, R.S. (1977b) 'Positions in Multiple Network Systems, Part Two', *Social Forces*, 56.

Burt, R.S. (1979) 'A Structural Theory of Interlocking Corporate Directorates', *Social Networks*, 1.

Burt, R.S. (1980) 'Models of Network Structure', *Annual Review of Sociology*, 6.

Burt, R.S. (1982) *Towards a Structural Theory of Action*. New York: Academic Press.

Burt, R.S. (1983a) 'Studying Status/Role-Sets Using Mass Surveys', in R.S. Burt and M.J. Minor (eds) *Applied Network Analysis*. Beverly Hills, CA: Sage Publications.

Burt, R.S. (1983b) *Corporate Profits and Cooptation*. New York: Academic Press.

Burt, R.S. (1983c) 'Firms, Directors and Time in the Directorate Tie Network', *Social Networks*, 5.

Burt, R.S. (1987) 'Social Contagion and Innovation: Cohesion versus Structural Equivalence', *American Journal of Sociology*, 92.

Burt, R.S. (1988) 'The Stability of American Markets', *American Journal of Sociology*, 94.

Burt, R.S. (1992) *Structural Holes*. New York: Cambridge University Press.

Burt, R.S. (2005) *Brokerage and Closure. An Introduction to the Theory of Social Capital*. Oxford: Oxford University Press.

Burt, R.S. and Carlton, D.S. (1989) 'Another Look at the Network Boundaries of American Markets', *American Journal of Sociology*, 95.

Burt, R.S., Christman, K.P. and Kilburn, H.C. (1980) 'Testing a Structural Theory of Corporate Cooptation: Interlocking Directorate Ties as a Strategy for Avoiding Market Constraints on Profits', *American Sociological Review*, 45.

Burt, R. and Schott, T. (1990) *STRUCTURE 4.1 Reference Manual*. New York: Columbia University Press.

Carrington, P.J. and Heil, G.H. (1981) 'COBLOC: A Hierarchical Method for Blocking Network Data', *Journal of Mathematical Sociology*, 8.

Carrington, P.J., Heil, G.H. and Berkowitz, S.D. (1980) 'A Goodness-of-Fit Index for Blockmodels', *Social Networks*, 2.

Carroll, W.K. (2002) 'Does Disorganised Capitalism Disorganise Corporate Networks?', *Canadian Journal of Sociology*, 27.

Carroll, W.K. (2004) *Corporate Power in a Globalizing World: A Study in Elite Social Organization*. Don Mills, Ontario: Oxford University Press.

Carroll, W.K. and Fennema, M. (2002) 'Is There a Transnational Business Community?', *International Sociology*, 17.

Cartwright, D. and Harary, F. (1956) 'Structural Balance: A Generalisation of Heider's Theory', *Psychological Review*, 63. Reprinted in S. Leinhardt (ed.) (1984) *Sociological Methodology, 1985*. San Francisco: Jossey-Bass.

Cartwright, D. and Zander, A. (eds) (1953) *Group Dynamics*. London: Tavistock.

Castells, M. (2000) *The Rise of the Network Society: The Information Age: Economy, Society and Culture*. Oxford: Blackwell.

Christofides, N. (1975) *Graph Theory: An Algorithmic Approach*. New York: Academic Press.

Coleman, J.S., Katz, E. and Menzel, H. (1966) *Medical Innovation: A Diffusion Study*. Indianapolis: Bobbs-Merrill.

Cook, K.S. (1977) 'Exchange and Power in Networks of Inter-organisational Relations', *Sociological Quarterly*, 18.

Cook, K.S. (1982) 'Network Structure from an Exchange Perspective', in P.V. Marsden and N. Lin (eds) *Social Structure and Network Analysis*. Beverly Hills, CA: Sage Publications.

Cook, K.S. and Whitmeyer, J.M. (1992) 'Two Approaches to Social Structure: Exchange Theory and Network Analysis', *Annual Review of Sociology*, 18.

Coxon, A.P.M. (1982) *The User's Guide to Multidimensional Scaling*. London: Heinemann.

Crane, D. (1972) *Invisible Colleges*. Chicago: University of Chicago Press.

Creswell, J.W. (1994) *Research Design: Qualitative and Quantitative Approaches*. Beverley Hills, CA: Sage Publications.

Creswell, J.W. and Plano, C.V.L. (2007) *Designing and Conducting Mixed Methods Research*. Beverley Hills, CA: Sage Publications.

Crossley, N. (2010) *Towards Relational Sociology*. London: Routledge.

Crossley, N., Bellotti, E., Edwards, G., Everett, M., Koskinen, J. and Tranmer, M. (2015) *Social Network Analysis for Ego-Nets*. London: Sage.

Dahl, R.A. (1961) *Who Governs?* New Haven, CT: Yale University Press.

Daultrey, S. (1976) *Principal Components Analysis*. Norwich: Geo Abstracts.

Davis, A., Gardner, B.B. and Gardner, M.R. (1941) *Deep South*. Chicago: University of Chicago Press.

Davis, J.A. (1967) 'Clustering and Structural Balance in Graphs', *Human Relations*, 20. Reprinted in S. Leinhardt (ed.) (1984) *Sociological Methodology, 1985*. San Francisco: Jossey-Bass.

Davis, J.A. (1968) 'Structural Balance, Mechanical Solidarity, and Interpersonal Relations', *American Journal of Sociology*, 68.

De Nooy, W., Mrvar, A. and Batagelj, V. (2005) *Exploratory Social Network Analysis with Pajek*. New York: Cambridge University Press.

Denord, F., Hjellbrekke, J., Korsnes, O., Lebaron, F. and Le Roux, B. (2011) 'Social Capital in the Field of Power: The Case of Norway', *Sociological Review*, 59.

Doreian, P. (1979) *Mathematics and the Study of Social Relations*. London: Weidenfeld & Nicolson.

Doreian, P. (1980) 'On the Evolution of Group and Network Structure', *Social Networks*, 2.

Doreian, P. (1981) 'Polyhedral Dynamics and Conflict Mobilisation in Social Networks', *Social Networks*, 3.

Doreian, P. (1983) 'Levelling Coalitions in Network Phenomena', *Social Networks*, 4.

Doreian, P. (1987) 'Measuring Regular Equivalence in Symmetrical Structures', *Social Networks*, 9.

Doreian, P., Batagelj, V. and Ferligoj, A. (1994) 'Partitioning Networks on Generalized Concepts of Equivalence', *Mathematical Sociology*, 19(1).

Doreian, P., Batagelj, V. and Ferligoj, A. (2005) *Generalized Blockmodelling*. Cambridge: Cambridge University Press.

Duncan, O.D. (1961) 'A Socio-economic Index for all Occupations', in A.J. Reiss (ed.) *Occupations and Social Status*. New York: Free Press.

Emerson, R.M. (1962) 'Power-Dependence Relations', *American Sociological Review*, 21.

Emerson, R.M. (1964) 'Power-Dependence Relations: Two Experiments', *Sociometry*, 21.

Emirbayer, M. (1997) 'Manifesto for a Relational Sociology', *American Journal of Sociology*, 103.

Emirbayer, M. and Goodwin, J. (1994) 'Network Analysis, Culture, and the Problem of Agency', *American Journal of Sociology*, 99.

Erdős, P. and Rényi, A. (1959) 'On the Evolution of Random Graphs', *Publications of the Mathematical Institute of the Hungarian Academy of Sciences*, 5.

Erickson, B.H. (1978) 'Some Problems of Inference from Chain Data', in K.F. Schuessler (ed.) *Sociological Methodology, 1979*. San Francisco: Jossey-Bass.

Erickson, B.H. and Nosanchuk, T.A. (1983) *Understanding Data*. Toronto: McGraw-Hill.

Erickson, B.H., Nosanchuk, T.A. and Lee, E. (1981) 'Network Sampling in Practice: Some Second Steps', *Social Networks*, 3.

Erikson, K.T. (1966) *Wayward Puritans*. New York: John Wiley & Sons.

Evans, K.M. (1962) *Sociometry and Education*. London: Routledge & Kegan Paul.

Everett, M.G. (1982) 'A Graph Theoretic Blocking Procedure for Social Networks', *Social Networks*, 4.

Everett, M.G. (1983a) 'EBLOC: A Graph Theoretic Blocking Algorithm for Social Networks', *Social Networks*, 5.

Everett, M.G. (1983b) 'An Extension of EBLOC to Valued Graphs', *Social Networks*, 5.

Everett, M.G. (1984) 'An Analysis of Cyclically Dense Data Using EBLOC', *Social Networks*, 6.

Everett, M.G. and Borgatti, S. (1990) 'A Testing Example for Positional Analysis Techniques', *Social Networks*, 12.

Everett, M.G. and Borgatti, S. (1999) 'The Centrality of Groups and Classes', *Journal of Mathematical Sociology*, 23.

Everett, M.G. and Borgatti, S. (2005) 'Extending Centrality', in P.J. Carrington, J. Scott and S. Wasserman (eds) *Models and Methods in Social Network Analysis*. Cambridge: Cambridge University Press.

Everett, M.G., Boyd, J.P. and Borgatti, S. (1990) 'Ego-Centered and Local Roles: A Graph Theoretic Approach', *Journal of Mathematical Sociology*, 15.

Everitt, B. (1974) *Cluster Analysis*. London: Heinemann.

Fararo, T.J. and Sunshine, M.H. (1964) *A Study of a Biased Friendship Net*. Syracuse, NY: Syracuse University Press.

Faust, K. and Romney, A.K. (1985) 'Does "Structure" Find Structure? A Critique of Burt's Use of Distance as a Measure of Structural Equivalence', *Social Networks*, 7.

Featherman, D.L. and Hauser, R.M. (1978) *Opportunity and Change*. New York: Academic Press.

Fennema, M. (1982) *International Networks of Banks and Industry*. Hague: Martinus Nijhoff.

Festinger, L. (1949) 'The Analysis of Sociograms Using Matrix Algebra', *Human Relations*, 2.

Festinger, L. (1957) *A Theory of Cognitive Dissonance*. Evanston, IL: Row Peterson.

Festinger, L., Riecken, H.W. and Schachter, S. (1959) *When Prophecy Fails*. New York: Harper and Row.

Festinger, L., Schachter, S. and Back, K.W. (1950) *Social Pressures in Informal Groups*. New York: Harper Bros.

Fischer, C.S. (1977) *Networks and Places: Social Relations in the Urban Setting*. New York: Free Press.

Fischer, C.S. (1982) *To Dwell among Friends*. Chicago: University of Chicago Press.

Frank, O. (1978a) 'Sampling and Estimation in Large Networks', *Social Networks*, 1.

Frank, O. (1978b) 'Estimation of the Number of Connected Components in a Graph by Using a Sampled Sub-graph', *Scandinavian Journal of Statistics*, 5.

Frank, O. (1979) 'Estimation of Population Totals by Use of Snowball Samples', in P. Holland and S. Leinhardt (eds) *Perspectives on Social Networks*. New York: Academic Press.

Frank, O. (1988) 'Random Sampling and Social Networks: A Survey of Various Approaches', *Mathématiques, Informatique et Sciences Humaines*, 104: 19–33.

Frank, O. (2011) 'Survey Sampling in Networks', in J. Scott and P. Carrington (eds) *The Sage Handbook of Social Network Analysis*. London: Sage.

Frankenberg, R. (1966) *Communities in Britain*. Harmondsworth: Penguin.

Franzosi, R. (2004) *From Words to Numbers: Narrative, Data, and Social Science*. Cambridge: Cambridge University Press.

Franzosi, R. (2010) *Quantitative Narrative Analysis*. London: Sage.

Freeman, L.C. (1979) 'Centrality in Social Networks: I. Conceptual Clarification', *Social Networks*, 1: 215–39.

Freeman, L.C. (1980) 'The Gatekeeper, Pair Dependency and Structural Centrality', *Quality and Quantity*, 14.

Freeman, L.C. (1983) 'Spheres, Cubes, and Boxes: Graph Dimensionality and Network Structure', *Social Networks*, 5.

Freeman, L.C. (1996a) 'Visualizing Social Networks'. <http://carnap.ss.uci.edu/vis.html>

Freeman, L.C. (1996b) 'Using Molecular Modelling Software in Social Network Analysis: A Practicum'. <http://eclectic.ss.uci.edu/-lin/chem.html>

Freeman, L.C. (2004) *The Development of Social Network Analysis: A Study in the Sociology of Science*. Vancouver: Empirical Press.

Freeman, L.C. and Freeman, S.C. (1980) 'A Semi-visible College: Structural Effects of Seven Months of EIES Participation by a Social Networks Community', in M.M. Henderson and M.J. McNaughten (eds) *Electronic Communication: Technology and Impacts*. Washington, DC: American Association for the Advancement of Science.

Freeman, L.C. and Thompson, C.R. (1989) 'Estimating Acquaintanceship Volume', in M. Kochen (ed.) *The Small World*. Norwood, NJ: Ablex.

Friedkin, N.E. (1981) 'The Development of Structure in Random Networks', *Social Networks*, 3.

Friedkin, N. (1984) 'Structural Equivalence and Cohesion Explanations of Social Homogeneity', *Sociological Methods and Research*, 12.

Friedkin, N. (1998) *A Structural Theory of Social Influence*. New York: Cambridge University Press.

Galtung, J. (1967) *Theory and Methods of Social Research*. London: George Allen & Unwin.

Gattrell, A.C. (1984a) 'Describing the Structure of a Research Literature: Spatial Diffusion Modelling in Geography', *Environment and Planning, B*, 11.

Gattrell, A.C. (1984b) 'The Growth of a Research Speciality', *Annals of the Association of American Geographers*, 74.

Glass, D.V. (1954) *Social Mobility in Britain*. London: Routledge & Kegan Paul.

Goddard, J. and Kirby, A. (1976) *An Introduction to Factor Analysis*. Norwich: Geo Abstracts.

Granovetter, M. (1973) 'The Strength of Weak Ties', *American Journal of Sociology*, 78.

Granovetter, M. (1974) *Getting a Job*. Cambridge, MA: Harvard University Press.

Granovetter, M. (1976) 'Network Sampling: Some First Steps', *American Journal of Sociology*, 81.

Granovetter, M. (1977) 'Reply to Morgan and Rytinä', *American Journal of Sociology*, 82.

Granovetter, M. (1979) 'The Theory-Gap in Social Network Analysis', in P. Holland and S. Leinhardt (eds) *Perspectives on Social Networks*. New York: Academic Press.

Granovetter, M. (1982) 'The Strength of Weak Ties: A Network Theory Revisited', in P.V. Marsden and N. Lin (eds) *Social Structure and Network Analysis*. Beverly Hills, CA: Sage Publications.

Grieco, M. (1987) *Keeping It in the Family*. London: Tavistock.

Gruzd, A. and Haythornthwaite, C. (2011) 'Networking Online: Cybercommunities', in J. Scott and P. Carrington (eds) *The Sage Handbook of Social Network Analysis*. London: Sage.

Guttman, L. (1968) 'A General Non-metric Technique for Finding the Smallest Coordinate Space for a Configuration of Points', *Psychometrika*, 33.

Habermas, J. (1968) 'Labour and Interaction: Remarks on Hegel's Jena Philosophy of Mind', in J. Habermas, (1974) *Theory and Practice*. London: Heinemann.

Hage, P. and Harary, F. (1983) *Structural Models in Anthropology*. Cambridge: Cambridge University Press.

Hage, P. and Harary, F. (1991) *Exchange in Oceania: A Graph Theoretic Analysis*. Oxford: Oxford University Press.

Hage, P. and Harary, F. (1998) *Island Networks: Communication, Kinship, and Classification Structures in Oceania*. Cambridge: Cambridge University Press.

Harary, F. (1969) *Graph Theory*. Reading, MA: Addison-Wesley.

Harary, F. and Norman, R.Z. (1953) *Graph Theory as a Mathematical Model in Social Science*. Ann Arbor, MI: Institute for Social Research.

Harary, F., Norman, R.Z. and Cartwright, D. (1965) *Structural Models*. New York: John Wiley & Sons.

Heider, F. (1946) 'Attitudes and Cognitive Orientation', *Journal of Psychology*, 21. Reprinted in S. Leinhardt (ed.) (1977) *Social Networks: A Developing Paradigm*. New York: Academic Press.

Helmers, H.M., Mokken, R.J., Plijter, R.C. and Stokman, F.N. (1975) *Graven naar Macht*. Amsterdam: Van Gennep.

Hicks, D. (2009) 'Evolving Regimes of Multi-University Research Evaluation', *Higher Education*, 57.

Hollstein, B. and Dominguez, S. (eds) (2012) *Mixing Methods in Social Network Research*. New York: Cambridge University Press.

Homans, G.C. (1941) *English Villagers of the Thirteenth Century*. Cambridge, MA: Harvard University Press.

Homans, G.C. (1951) *The Human Group*. London: Routledge & Kegan Paul.

Homans, G.C. (1961) *Social Behaviour*. London: Routledge & Kegan Paul.

Hudson, J.C. (1969) 'Diffusion in a Central Place System', *Geographical Analysis*, 1.

Hunter, F. (1953) *Community Power Structure*. Chapel Hill: University of North Carolina Press.

Ikegami, E. (2005) *Bonds of Civility. Aesthetic Networks and Political Origins of Japanese Culture*. New York: Cambridge University Press.

Jennings, H.H. (1948). *Sociometry in Group Relations*. Washington, DC: American Council on Education.

Johnson, S.C. (1967) 'Hierarchical Clustering Schemes', *Psychometrika*, 32.

Kadushin, C. (1966) 'The Friends and Supporters of Psychotherapy', *American Sociological Review*, 31.

Kadushin, C. (1968) 'Power, Influence and Social Circles: A New Methodology for Studying Opinion Makers', *American Sociological Review*, 33.

Kamada, T. and Kawai, S. (1989) 'An Algorithm for Drawing General Undirected Graphs', *Information Processing Letters*, 31.

Katz, F. (1966) 'Social Participation and Social Structure', *Social Forces*, 45.

Kerr, C. and Fisher, L.H. (1957) 'Plant Sociology: The Elite and the Aborigines', in M. Komarovsky (ed.) *Common Frontiers of the Social Sciences*. Glencoe, IL: Free Press.

Kilworth, P.D. and Bernard, H.R. (1979) 'A Pseudo-model of the Small World Problem', *Social Forces*, 58.

Kim, J. and Mueller, C.W. (1978) *Introduction to Factor Analysis*. Beverly Hills, CA: Sage Publications.

Kline, P. (1994) *An Easy Guide to Factor Analysis*. London: Routledge.

Klovdahl, A.S. (1981) 'A Note on Images of Networks', *Social Networks*, 3.

Klovdahl, A.S. (1986) 'viewnet: A New Tool For Network Analysis', *Social Networks*, 8.

Klovdahl, A.S. (1989) 'Urban Social Networks: Some Methodological Problems and Prospects', in M. Kochen (ed.) *The Small World*. Norwood, NJ: Ablex.

Knoke, D. and Burt, R.S. (1983) 'Prominence', in R.S. Burt and M.J. Minor (eds) *Applied Network Analysis*. Beverly Hills, CA: Sage Publications.

Knoke, D. and Kuklinski, J.H. (1982) *Network Analysis*. Beverly Hills, CA: Sage Publications.

Knoke, D. and Yang, S. (2008) *Network Analysis*, 2nd edition (of Knoke and Kuklinski, 1982). Beverly Hills, CA: Sage Publications.

Köhler, W. (1925) *The Mentality of Apes*. New York: Harcourt, Brace & Co.

König, D. (1936) *Theorie der endlichen und unendlichen Graphen*. New York: Chelsea (1950 edition).

Krempel, L. (1994) 'Simple Representations of Complex Networks: Strategies for Visualizing Network Structure'. <http://www.mpi-fg-koeln.mpg.de/~lk/algo5a/algo5a.html>

Krempel, L. (2005) *Visualisierung komplexer Strukturen*. Frankfurt am Main: Campus.

Krempel, L. (2011) 'Network Visualisation', in J. Scott and P.J. Carrington (eds) *The Sage Handbook of Social Network Analysis*. London: Sage Publications.

Kruskal, J.B. (1964a) 'Multidimensional Scaling by Optimizing Goodness of Fit to a Nonmetric Hypothesis', *Psychometrika*, 29.

Kruskal, J.B. (1964b) 'Nonmetric Multidimensional Scaling: A Numerical Method', *Psychometrika*, 29.

Kruskal, J.B. and Wish, M. (1978) *Multidimensional Scaling*. Beverly Hills, CA: Sage Publications.

Lankford, P.M. (1974) 'Comparative Analysis of Clique Identification Methods', *Sociometry*, 37.

Latour, B. (2005) *Reassembling the Social – An Introduction to Actor-Network-Theory*. Oxford: Oxford University Press.

Laumann, E.O. (1966) *Prestige and Association in an Urban Community*. Indianapolis: Bobbs-Merrill.

Laumann, E.O. (1973) *Bonds of Pluralism*. New York: John Wiley & Sons.

Laumann, E.O., Marsden, P.V. and Prensky, D. (1989) 'The Boundary Specification Problem in Network Analysis', in L.C. Freeman, D.R. White and A.K. Romney (eds) *Research Methods in Social Network Analysis*. New Brunswick, NJ: Transaction Books, (1992 edition).

Laumann, E.O. and Pappi, F.U. (1973) 'New Directions in the Study of Community Elites', *American Sociological Review*, 38. Reprinted in S. Leinhardt (ed.) (1984) *Sociological Methodology, 1985*. San Francisco: Jossey-Bass.

Laumann, E.O. and Pappi, F.U. (1976) *Networks of Collective Action*. New York: Academic Press.

Layder, D. (1992) *New Strategies in Social Research*. Cambridge: Polity Press.

Lee, N.H. (1969) *The Search for an Abortionist*. Chicago: University of Chicago Press.

Le Roux, B. and Rouanet, H. (2010) *Multiple Correspondence Analysis*. Thousand Oaks, CA: Sage.

Levine, J.H. (1972) 'The Sphere of Influence', *American Sociological Review*, 37. Reprinted in J. Scott (ed.) (1990) *The Sociology of Elites*, Vol. 3. Cheltenham: Edward Elgar.

Lewin, K. (1936) *Principles of Topological Psychology*. New York: McGraw-Hill.

Lewin, K. (1951) *Field Theory in the Social Sciences*. New York: Harper.

Light, J.M. and Mullins, N.C. (1979) 'A Primer on Blockmodelling Procedures', in P. Holland and S. Leinhardt (eds) *Perspectives on Social Networks*. New York: Academic Press.

Lin, N. (1982) 'Social Resources and Instrumental Action', in P.V. Marsden and N. Lin (eds) *Social Structure and Network Analysis*. Beverly Hills, CA: Sage Publications.

Lin, N. (2001) *Social Capital. A Theory of Social Structure and Action*. New York: Cambridge University Press.

Lin, N., Dayton, P.N. and Greenwald, P. (1978) 'Analysing the Instrumental Use of Relations in the Context of Social Structure', *Sociological Methods and Research*, 1.

Lin, N. and Erikson, B.H. (2008) *Social Capital: An International Research Program*. Oxford: Oxford University Press.

Lingoes, J.C. and Roskam, E.E. (1973) 'A Mathematical and Empirical Analysis of Two Multidimensional Scaling Algorithms', *Psychometrika*, 38.

Lockwood, D. (1956) 'Some Remarks on "The Social System"', *British Journal of Sociology*, 6.

Lorrain, F. and White, H.C. (1971) 'Structural Equivalence of Individuals in Social Networks', *Journal of Mathematical Sociology*, 1.

Luce, R.D. and Perry, A. (1949) 'A Method of Matrix Analysis of Group Structure', *Psychometrika*, 14.

Lundberg, G. (1936) 'The Sociography of Some Community Relations'. *American Sociological Review*, 1.

Lundberg, G. and Steele, M. (1938) 'Social Attraction-Patterns in a Village'. *Sociometry*, 1.

Maoz, Z. (2011) *Networks of Nations. The Evolution, Structure, and Impact of International Networks, 1816–2001*. Cambridge: Cambridge University Press.

Mariolis, P. (1975) 'Interlocking Directorates and Control of Corporations', *Social Science Quarterly*, 56.

Mariolis, P. and Jones, M.H. (1982) 'Centrality in Corporate Networks: Reliability and Stability', *Administrative Science Quarterly*, 27.

Marsden, P.V. (1982) 'Brokerage Behaviour in Restricted Exchange Networks', in P.V. Marsden and N. Lin (eds) *Social Structure and Network Analysis*. Beverly Hills, CA: Sage Publications.

Marsden, P.V. (2011) 'Survey Methods for Network Data', in J. Scott and P. Carrington (eds) *The Sage Handbook of Social Network Analysis*. London: Sage.

Marshall, A. (1890) *Principles of Economics*. London: Macmillan.

Martin, J.L. (2003) 'What is Field Theory?', *American Journal of Sociology*, 109.

Mayhew, B.H. and Levinger, R. (1976) 'Size and the Density of Interaction in Human Aggregates', *American Journal of Sociology*, 82.

Mayo, E. (1933) *The Human Problems of an Industrial Civilization*. Cambridge, MA: Macmillan.

Mayo, E. (1945) *The Social Problems of an Industrial Civilization*. London: Routledge & Kegan Paul (1946 edition).

McCallister, L. and Fischer, C.S. (1978) 'A Procedure for Surveying Social Networks', *Sociological Methods and Research*, 1.

McGrath, C., Blythe, J. and Krackhardt, D. (1997) 'Seeing Groups in Graph Layouts'. <http://www.andrew.cmu.edu/user/cm3t/groups.html>

McQuitty, L. (1968) 'Multiple Cluster Types and Dimensions for Interactive Columnar Correlation Analysis', *Multivariate Behavioural Research*, 3.

McQuitty, L. and Clark, J.A. (1968) 'Clusters from Interactive Columnar Correlation Analysis', *Educational and Psychological Measurement*, 28.

Meek, R.L. and Bradley, I. (1986) *Matrices and Society*. Harmondsworth: Penguin.

Menger, C. (1871) *Grundsätze der Volkswirtschaftslehre*. Aalen: Scientia Verlag, 1968.

Merton, R.K. (1936) 'The Unanticipated Consequences of Purposive Social Action', *American Sociological Review* 1.

Milgram, S. (1967) 'The Small World Problem', *Psychology Today*, 1.

Mintz, B. and Schwartz, M. (1985) *The Power Structure of American Business*. Chicago: University of Chicago Press.

Mische, A. (2003) 'Cross-Talk in Movements: Reconceiving the Culture-Network Link', in M. Diani and D. McAdam (eds) *Social Movements and Networks*. Oxford: Oxford University Press.

Mische, A. (2011) 'Relational Sociology, Culture and Agency', in J. Scott and P. Carrington (eds) *The Sage Handbook of Social Network Analysis*. London: Sage Publications.

Mitchell, J.C. (1969) 'The Concept and Use of Social Networks', in J.C. Mitchell (ed.) *Social Networks in Urban Situations*. Manchester: Manchester University Press.

Mizruchi, M.S. (1982) *The American Corporate Network, 1904–1974*. Beverly Hills, CA: Sage Publications.

Mizruchi, M.S. (1992) *The Structure of Corporate Political Action: Inter-firm Relationships and their Consequences*. Cambridge, MA: Harvard University Press.

Mizruchi, M.S. (1993) 'Cohesion, Equivalence, and Similarity of Behaviour: A Theoretical and Empirical Assessment', *Social Networks*, 15.

Mizruchi, M.S. (1994) 'Social Network Analysis: Recent Achievements and Current Controversies', *Acta Sociologica*, 37.

Mizruchi, M.S. and Bunting, D. (1981) 'Influence in Corporate Networks: An Examination of Four Measures', *Administrative Science Quarterly*, 26.

Mizruchi, M.S. and Galaskiewicz, J. (1994) 'Networks of Inter-organizational relations', in S. Wasserman and J. Galaskiewicz (eds) *Advances in Social Network Analysis*. Beverley Hills, CA: Sage Publications.

Mizruchi, M. and Schwartz, M. (eds) (1987) *Inter-corporate Relations*. Cambridge: Cambridge University Press.

Mokken, R.J. (1974) 'Cliques, Clubs and Clans', *Quality and Quantity*, 13.

Monge, P.R. and Contractor, N.S. (2003) *Theories of Communication Networks*. Oxford: Oxford University Press.

Moreno, J. (1934) *Who Shall Survive?* New York: Beacon Press.

Moreno, J. and Jennings, H.H. (1938) 'Statistics of Social Configurations', *Sociometry*, 1.

Morgan, D. and Rytinä, S. (1977) 'Comment on "Network Sampling: Some First Steps" by Mark Granovetter', *American Journal of Sociology*, 83.

Mullins, N.C. (1973) *Theories and Theory Groups in Contemporary American Sociology*. New York: Harper and Row.

Nadel, S.F. (1957) *The Theory of Social Structure*. London: Cohen and West.

Newcomb, T. (1953) 'An Approach to the Study of Communicative Acts', *Psychological Review*, 60.

Newman, M.E.J. (2001) 'The Structure of Scientific Collaboration Networks', *Proceedings of the National Academy of Sciences*, 98.

Niemeijer, R. (1973) 'Some Applications of the Notion of Density', in J. Boissevain and J.D. Mitchell (eds) *Network Analysis*. The Hague: Mouton.

Nieminen, V. (1974) 'On Centrality in a Graph', *Scandinavian Journal of Psychology*, 15.

Pahl, R.E. and Winkler, J.T. (1974), 'The Economic Elite: Theory and Practice', in P. Stanworth and A. Giddens (eds) *Elites and Power in British Society*. Cambridge: Cambridge University Press.

Park, R.E., Burgess, E.W. and McKenzie, R.D. (1925) *The City*. Chicago: University of Chicago Press.

Parsons, T. (1951) *The Social System*. Glencoe, IL: Free Press.

Parsons, T., Bales, R.F. and Shils, E. (1953) *Working Papers in the Theory of Action*. Glencoe, IL: Free Press.

Pedersen, P.O. (1970) 'Innovation Diffusion within and between National Urban Systems', *Geographical Analysis*, 2.

Pool, I. de S. (1978) 'Contacts and Influences', *Social Networks*, 1.

Powell, C. and Dépelteau, F. (2013a) *Conceptualizing Relational Sociology: Ontological and Theoretical Issues*. Basingstoke: Palgrave Macmillan.

Powell, C. and Dépelteau, F. (2013b) *Applying Relational Sociology. Relations, Networks, and Society*. Basingstoke: Palgrave Macmillan.

Price, D.J. de S. (1965) 'Networks of Scientific Papers', *Science*, 149.

Putnam, R.D. (2000). *Bowling Alone: The Collapse and Revival of American Community*. New York: Simon and Schuster.

Rapoport, A. (1952) 'Ignition Phenomena in Random Nets', *Bulletin of Mathematical Biophysics*, 14.

Rapoport, A. (1958) 'Nets with Reciprocity Bias', *Bulletin of Mathematical Biophysics*, 20.

Reitz, K.P. and White, D.R. (1989) 'Rethinking the Role Concept: Homomorphisms on Social Networks', in L.C. Freeman, D.R. White and A.K. Romney (eds) *Research Methods in Social Network Analysis*. New Brunswick, NJ: Transaction Books (1992 edition).

Rex, J.A. (1962) *Key Problems of Sociological Theory*. London: Routledge & Kegan Paul.

Robins, G., Snijders, T.A.B., Wang, P., Handcock, M. and Pattison, P. (2007) 'Recent Developments in Exponential Random Graph ($p^*$) Models for Social Networks', *Social Networks*, 29.

Roethlisberger, F.J. and Dickson, W.J. (1939) *Management and the Worker*. Cambridge, MA: Harvard University Press.

Rogers, E. (1962) *Diffusion of Innovations*, 5th edition. New York: Free Press 2003.

Roistacher, R.C. (1979) 'Acquisition and Management of Social Network Data', in P. Holland and S. Leinhardt (eds) *Perspectives on Social Networks*. New York: Academic Press.

Rose, M. (1975) *Industrial Behaviour*. Harmondsworth: Allen Lane.

Rytinä, S. (1982) 'Structural Constraints on Interpersonal Contact', in P.V. Marsden and N. Lin (eds) *Social Structure and Network Analysis*. Beverly Hills, CA: Sage Publications.

Rytinä, S. and Morgan, D. (1982) 'The Arithmetic of Social Relations', *American Journal of Sociology*, 88.

Sabidussi, G. (1966) 'The Centrality Index of a Graph', *Psychometrika*, 31.

Sailer, L. (1978) 'Structural Equivalence: Meaning and Definition', *Social Networks*, 1.

Schwartz, J.E. (1977) 'An Examination of Concor and Related Methods for Blocking Sociometric Data', in D.R. Heise (ed.) *Sociological Methodology, 1978*. San Francisco: Jossey-Bass.

Schweizer, T. and White, D.R. (eds) (1998) *Kinship, Networks, and Exchange*. New York: Cambridge University Press.

Scott, J. (1986) *Capitalist Property and Financial Power*. Brighton: Wheatsheaf.

Scott, J. (1990) *A Matter of Record: Documentary Sources in Social Research*. Cambridge: Polity Press.

Scott, J. (1991) 'Networks of Corporate Power', *Annual Review of Sociology*, 17.

Scott, J. (1996) *Stratification and Power: Structures of Class, Status and Command*. Cambridge: Polity Press.

Scott, J. (1997) *Corporate Business and Capitalist Classes*. Oxford: Oxford University Press.

Scott, J. (1999) 'Studying Power', in K. Nash and A. Scott (eds) *The Blackwell Companion to Political Sociology*. Oxford: Basil Blackwell.

Scott, J. (ed.) (2006) *Documentary Research* (4 volumes). London: Sage Publications.

Scott. J. (2011a) 'Social Physics and Social Networks', in J. Scott and P. Carrington (eds) *The Sage Handbook of Social Network Analysis*. London: Sage Publications.

Scott, J. (2011b) *Conceptualising the Social World. Principles of Sociological Analysis*. Cambridge: Cambridge University Press.

Scott, J. (2012a) 'Studying Power', in K. Nash, A. Scott and E. Amenta, (eds) *The Wiley-Blackwell Companion to Political Sociology*. Oxford: Wiley-Blackwell.

Scott, J. (2012b) *What is Social Network Analysis?* London: Bloomsbury.

Scott, J. and Hughes, M. (1980) *The Anatomy of Scottish Capital*. London: Croom Helm.

Seidman, S.B. (1983) 'Network Structure and Minimum Degree', *Social Networks*, 5.

Seidman, S.B. and Foster, B.L. (1978) 'A Note on the Potential for Genuine Cross-Fertilisation between Anthropology and Mathematics', *Social Networks*, 1.

Sharkey, P. (1989) 'Social Networks and Social Service Workers', *British Journal of Social Work*, 19.

Sharkey, P. (1990) 'Social Networks and Social Service Workers: A Reply to Timms', *British Journal of Social Work*, 20.

Shepard, R.N. (1962) 'The Analysis of Proximities', Parts 1 and 2, *Psychometrika*, 21.

Simmel, G. (1908) *Soziologie*. Berlin: Duncker and Humblot (1968 edition).

Sklair, L. (2001) *The Transnational Capitalist Class*. Oxford: Blackwell.

Smith, A. (1766) *The Wealth of Nations*. London: J.M. Dent, 1910.

Smith, R.M. (1979) 'Kin and Neighbours in a Thirteenth Century Suffolk Community', *Journal of Family History*, 4.

Snijders, T.A.B. (1981) 'The Degree Variance', *Social Networks*, 3.

Snijders, T.A.B. (1996) 'Stochastic Actor-Based Models for Network Change', *Journal of Mathematical Sociology*, 21.

Snijders, T.A.B. (2001) 'The Statistical Evaluation of Social Network Dynamics', in M.E. Sobel and M.P. Becker (eds) *Sociological Methodology, Volume 31*. Oxford: Basil Blackwell.

Snijders, T.A.B. (2005) 'Models for Longitudinal Network Data' in P.J. Carrington, J. Scott and S. Wasserman (eds) (2005) *Models and Methods in Social Network Analysis*. Cambridge: Cambridge University Press.

Snijders, T.A.B., Pattison, P., Robins, G. and Handcock, M.S. (2006) 'New Specifications for Exponential Random Graph Models', in R.M. Stolzenberg (ed.) *Sociological Methodology, Volume 36*. Oxford: Basil Blackwell.

Snijders, T.A.B., Steglich, C.E.G. and Van De Bunt, G.G. (2010) 'Introduction to Actor-Based Models for Network Dynamics', *Social Networks*, 32.

Snijders, T.A.B. and van Duijn, M.A.J. (1997) 'Simulation for Statistical Inference in Dynamic Network Models', in R. Conte, R. Hegselmann and P. Terna (eds) *Simulating Social Phenomena*, Lecture Notes in Economics and Mathematical Systems, 456. Berlin: Springer.

Sonquist, J.A. and Koenig, T. (1975) 'Interlocking Directorships in the Top US Corporations', *Insurgent Sociologist*, 5.

Spencer, L. and Pahl, R.E. (2006) *Rethinking Friendship: Hidden Solidarities Today*. Princeton, NJ: Princeton University Press.

Stacey, M. (1969) 'The Myth of Community Studies', *British Journal of Sociology*, 20.

Stokman, F.N., Ziegler, R. and Scott, J. (1985) *Networks of Corporate Power*. Cambridge: Polity Press.

Tarde, G. (1890) *The Laws of Imitation*. New York: H. Holt and Co., 1903.

Thom, R. (1972) *Structural Stability and Morphogenesis*. London: Benjamin, 1975.

Timms, E. (1990) 'Social Networks and Social Service Workers: A Comment on Sharkey', *British Journal of Social Work*, 20.

Torgerson, W.S. (1952) 'Multidimensional Scaling 1. Theory and Method', *Psychometrika*, 17.

Travers, J. and Milgram, S. (1969) 'An Experimental Study of the Small World Problem'. *Sociometry*, 32.

Useem, M. (1984) *The Inner Circle*. New York: Oxford University Press.

van Poucke, W. (1979) 'Network Constraints on Social Action: Preliminaries for a Network Theory', *Social Networks*, 2.

von Hayek, F. (1967) 'The Results of Human Action But Not of Human Design', in von Hayek, F. (ed.) *Studies in Philosophy, Politics and Economics*. London: Routledge & Kegan Paul.

von Mises, L. (1949) *Human Action*. New Haven, CT: Yale University Press.

Wang, H. and Wellman, B. (2010) 'Social Connectivity in America', *American Behavioral Scientist*, 53.

Warner, W.L. and Lunt, P.S. (1941) *The Social Life of a Modern Community*. New Haven, CT: Yale University Press.

Warner, W.L. and Lunt, P.S. (1942) *The Status System of a Modern Community*. New Haven, CT: Yale University Press.

Wasserman, S. and Pattison, P. (1996) 'Logit Models and Logistic Regression for Social Networks: I. An Introduction to Markov Graphs and $p^*$', *Psychometrika*, 61.

Wasserman, S. and Robins, G. (2005) 'An Introduction to Random Graphs, Dependence Graphs, and $p^*$', in P.J. Carrington, J. Scott and S. Wasserman (eds) *Models and Methods in Social Network Analysis*. New York: Cambridge University Press.

Watts, D.J. (1999) *Small Worlds: The Dynamics of Networks between Order and Randomness*. Princeton, NJ: Princeton University Press.

Watts, D.J. (2003) *Six Degrees. The Science of a Connected Age*. New York: W.W. Norton.

Watts, D.J. and Strogatz, S.H. (1998) 'Collective Dynamics of "Small-World" Networks'. *Nature*, 393.

Weber, M. (1920–21) *Economy and Society*. Berkeley, CA: University of California Press, (1968 edition).

Wellman, B. (1979) 'The Community Question: The Intimate Networks of East Yorkers', *American Journal of Sociology*, 84.

Wellman, B. (1982) 'Studying Personal Communities', in P.V. Marsden and N. Lin (eds) *Social Structure and Network Analysis*. Beverly Hills, CA: Sage Publications.

Wellman, B. (1985) 'Domestic Work, Paid Work and Network', in S. Duck and D. Perlman (eds) *Personal Relationships*, Vol. 1. Beverly Hills, CA: Sage Publications.

Wellman, B. (1980) 'Network Analysis: From Metaphor and Method to Theory and Substance'. Discussion Paper, University of Toronto Structural Analysis Program. Revised version in B. Wellman and S.D. Berkowitz (eds) (1988) *Social Structures*. Cambridge: Cambridge University Press.

Wellman, B. and Berkowitz, S.D. (eds) (1988) *Social Structures*. Cambridge: Cambridge University Press.

Wellman, B., Hogan, B., Berg, K., Boase, J., Carrasco, J.-A., Cote, R., Kayahara, J., Kennedy, T. and Tran, P. (2006) 'Connected Lives: The Project', in P. Purcell (ed.) *Networked Neighborhoods: The Online Community in Context*. New York: Springer.

Werbner, P. (1990) *The Migration Process*. New York: Berg.

White, D. (2011) 'Kinship, Class, and Community', in J. Scott and P. Carrington (eds) *The Sage Handbook of Social Network Analysis*. London: Sage Publications.

White, D. and Reitz, K.P. (1983) 'Group and Semi-group Homomorphisms on Networks of Relations', *Social Networks*, 5.

White. H.C. (1963) *An Anatomy of Kinship*. Englewood Cliffs, NJ: Prentice Hall.

White, H.C. (1970) *Chains of Opportunity*. Cambridge, MA: Harvard University Press.

White, H.C. (1992a) *Identity and Control: A Structural Theory of Social Action*. Princeton, NJ: Princeton University Press.

White, H.C. (1992b) 'Social Grammar for Culture: Reply to Steven Brint', *Sociological Theory*, 10.

White, H.C. (1993) *Careers and Creativity: Social Forces in the Arts*. Boulder, CO: Westview Press.

White, H.C. (2008) *Identity and Control: How Social Formations Emerge*, 2nd edition. Princeton, NJ: Princeton University Press.

White, H.C. (2011) 'Scientific and Scholarly Networks', in J. Scott and P. Carrington (eds) *The Sage Handbook of Social Network Analysis*. London: Sage Publications.

White, H.C., Boorman, S.A. and Breiger, R.L. (1976) 'Social Structure from Multiple Networks, I. Blockmodels of Roles and Positions', *American Journal of Sociology*, 81.

Whitten, N.E. and Wolfe, A.W. (1973) 'Network Analysis', in J.J. Honigmann (ed.) *Handbook of Social and Cultural Anthropology*. Chicago: Rand McNally.

Willer, D. (ed.) (1999) *Network Exchange Theory*. Westport, CT: Praeger.

Willmott, P. (1986) *Social Networks, Informal Care and Public Policy*. London: Policy Studies Institute.

Willmott, P. (1987) *Friendship Networks and Social Support*. London: Policy Studies Institute.

Winship, C. and Mandel, M. (1984) 'Roles and Positions: A Critique and Extension of the Blockmodelling Approach', in S. Leinhardt (ed.) *Sociological Methodology, 1985*. San Francisco: Jossey-Bass.

Wu, L. (1984) 'Local Blockmodel Algebra for Analysing Social Networks', in S. Leinhardt (ed.) *Sociological Methodology, 1985*. San Francisco: Jossey-Bass.

Yablonsky, L. (1962) *The Violent Gang*. Harmondsworth: Penguin.

Zegers, F. and ten Berghe, J. (1985) 'A Family of Association Coefficients for Metric Scales', *Psychometrika*, 50.

# Index